Over&Over Again! 2

Edited by
Ronald Alan Knott

Over&Over Again! 2

150 Adventists Share

Personal Faith Stories

About Stewardship

SEVENTH-DAY
ADVENTIST CHURCH
North American Division

Over and Over Again! Volume Two
  General Editor and Project Coordinator, Ronald Alan Knott
  Line editing by Bill Knott, Ronald Alan Knott
  Copyediting by Eugene Lincoln, Madeline S. Johnston, Esther R. Knott
  Text design by Bill Kirstein
  Cover design by Willie Duke, adapted by Matt Hamel
  Electronic layout by Renee Skeete
  Data entry by Ramnarine Ramharacksingh, Esther R. Knott
  Typeset: 10.5/12.5 Galliard

CONTENTS

PREFACE

GROWING up in Massachusetts, I inherited a time-honored and dubious New England work ethic stated simply as follows: "No matter how big the woodpile is, it's never big enough." So when I actually installed a woodstove in our home two years ago, I knew I was tempting temptation.

Our corner of Michigan enjoys relatively modest electric rates, so we certainly didn't need the stove to balance the family budget. We just wanted to enjoy that extra measure of homey comfort only wood heat can provide; and, encouraged by uncomfortable experience, we wanted a backup for our electric-driven geothermal furnace, should the power go out for a day or two in mid-winter. That, supposedly, was all.

We set the furnace thermostat at a generous baseline of 70 degrees and used the woodstove to keep the furnace off. But as I learned the tricks of managing the stove efficiently, I soon realized that the hobby of staying a degree or two ahead of the furnace thermostat was quickly becoming an obsession. No longer were lower electric bills a pleasant side benefit to the cozy comfort of radiant heat. Lower electric bills were becoming a vital requirement for my mental stability. How easily things get out of joint.

And then some Michigan-winter morning as I gazed out the window, gloating over my impressive woodpile, and rejoicing for the silence of a house where the furnace fan wasn't blowing, the thought occurred to me that I should tithe the woodpile. Initially, I objected, but I was in a mellow, honest mood. Given my recent obsession with the electric bills, I couldn't deny that the wood had economic value. So I figured the value of wood and the next Sabbath at church I turned in a tithe check for $100. Soon enough, of course, the electric bills got even lower, and, by the grace of God, so did the temperature of my acquisitiveness.

That's just one of the little ways this book and its forerunner (the first volume of *Over and Over Again!*) have influenced my life. They have put me on a path of intentionality. That is, they've helped me actually think about the mundane matters of everyday life, and put them more clearly in the context of a Heavenly Father who lovingly presides over everything I do. I am a better steward, and, more importantly, I earnestly want to be a better steward.

This new intentionality is like a benevolent virus that, when given half a chance, gloriously infects other aspects of my life. For example, I decided—not for any legalistic reason, but simply as an expression of thanks to God—that I would give the woodstove and myself a break on Sabbaths. And I decided that I'd be more thoughtful about what I asked the people at FedEx and the post office to do for me during Sabbath hours. That is, I refrain from shipping things on

Fridays if, in my heart, I know I would want them to move on Sabbath to meet my business agenda. Whenever my wife and I must stay in a hotel over Sabbath, we leave a double tip and a note for the housekeeper on Sabbath morning. Our typical note reads:

> Dear Housekeeper:
>
> We invite you to take a break.
>
> You need not clean or make up our room today. As Seventh-day Adventist Christians, we believe that God's word in the Bible calls us to enjoy a blessing of rest from normal work on the seventh-day Sabbath—Saturday. Where possible, as He asks, we try to extend that blessing to others, and are delighted to extend it to you.
>
> God bless you, and Happy Sabbath.

We have found our gesture to be greeted with genuine appreciation, and we can only pray that by God's leading it may have some influence for good.

The simple stories in these books have also inspired me to be intentional about how I take care of my body, and so I am much more thoughtful about diet, rest, and exercise. And of course these testimonies have encouraged me, yet again, to enlarge still further my understanding of how God can use my means to advance His interests through His church and its various ministries. It's my earnest desire that these books will do for every reader what they are doing for me.

Of course, I can't let this go to press without thanking some who have made it possible. Kermit Netteburg, from the North American Division, engineered for the second time the opportunity for me to do this good work. And again, my loving family has contributed enormously. My darling wife Esther has been, in effect, the second editor, gently offering the most helpful counsel, and giving up vacation time and free time for typing, reading, correcting, and more reading and more correcting. Esther's parents, Alice and Ramnarine Ramharacksingh, ran our household for many days while I was preoccupied on this project and Esther was engaged in her full-time ministry as a pastor at Pioneer Memorial Church. And Ram logged scores of hours himself typing stories, managing data, making telephone calls and sending faxes. Our daughter Olivia, a five-year-old, had the grace and understanding to accept that some fun things to do on a sunny spring afternoon would have to be postponed—as she volunteered—"until the book is done."

Finally, we all owe a great debt to the writers of these stories. By the grace of God, they opened their hearts and their schedules to share personal testimonies of faith for the benefit of the larger church family. What richer, greater benefits await that family when each of us fulfills our God-given obligation to do the same.

Ronald Alan Knott
Berrien Springs, Michigan
May 11, 2000

Our confession of His
faithfulness is Heaven's chosen agency
for revealing Christ to the world. . . .
That which will be most effectual
is the testimony of our own experience.
We are witnesses for God
as we reveal in ourselves
the working of a power that is divine.
Every individual has a life
distinct from all others, and an
experience differing essentially from theirs.
God desires that our praise shall ascend to Him,
marked by our own individuality.
These precious acknowledgments
to the praise of the glory of His grace,
when supported by a Christlike life,
have an irresistible power that works
for the salvation of souls.

—Ellen G. White, The Desire of Ages, *p. 347*

The FIRST MEETING

Come and hear, all ye that fear God, and I will declare what he hath done for my soul.

Psalm 66:16

Walter L. Wright

Lori L. Hopkins

Katherine and Reger Smith

Victor Czerkasij

S. L. Bailey

Bryce R. Hickerson

Timothy Atolagbe

Jerry Page

Jeanette Rawson

Stella Bicky Hill Young

THREE INCHES, FIVE GALLONS, AND MORE THAN ENOUGH
By Walter L. Wright

MANY years ago I was one of those pitiful creatures who thought that if I put $3 in the offering plate each Sabbath, I had done my duty. After all, if every member gave as much as I, the church would have a tidy sum to manage. It never occurred to me that I was partly responsible for creating the church operating deficit, which was reported each month by the church treasurer. Apparently everyone was not contributing as much as I.

Our church held a stewardship emphasis weekend, conducted by the conference stewardship director. When my turn came for my personal interview with him, I was horrified and incredulous when he described a formula that showed I should be contributing $45 per month for church operating (this was many years ago, and it did not include my tithe, which I faithfully returned). That amount was nearly four times as much as I was presently doing. I didn't see how such a thing could be possible, but he convinced me to trust God and make Him my partner as I stepped out in faith.

Now I had a place for that $45, and it was not for church expense. It was wintertime in southwestern Ohio. Our heating oil tank was almost empty, and I needed that $45 to buy more oil to keep my little family warm and snug from the blustery weather.

However, from that Friday's paycheck I deducted $45 to place in my offering envelope for Sabbath morning. My wife and I decided that we would trust God, at least a little. If He didn't come through for us before the oil tank ran dry, we could always go to my parents' home for the weekend to keep warm.

That Friday evening we opened the Sabbath in worship, and then I used the dipstick to check the oil tank just outside the kitchen door. The level read three inches—or about five gallons for that size tank. I hoped it would get us through until the morning. The old furnace rumbled and blew all night.

It was a very cold night outside, and on Sabbath morning I noticed that the outside of the windows on our house were covered with ice. Just before leaving for Sabbath school, I checked the oil tank again. It showed three inches—or about five gallons!

"This is strange business," I said to myself. "We sure are lucky." Isn't it amazing how long it sometimes takes us to recognize God's working?

I was nervous all through church that day, especially when I put my envelope in the offering plate. We rushed home, gathered our food, and prepared to hurry to my parents' home for warmth and shelter. The house was still warm as we loaded up the car, so I decided to check the tank one last time to get some idea of when it would finally run out. It showed three inches—or about five gallons.

Even I am not so stupid as to miss completely a miracle of God when it slams me in the face! The furnace grumbled and rumbled all Saturday night. Early Sunday morning I grabbed that dipstick to see what God had done. Yes, indeed—three inches—or about five gallons! By now I was so confident that God was proving Himself that I relaxed and watched a football game on TV. My favorite team, the Cleveland Browns, beat the Chicago Bears, and I was warm and comfortable while they did it!

Monday I received a small check, and it was more than enough to fill the oil tank. When the oilman came after my urgent call for a delivery, I yelled a greeting to him and asked him to hurry with the fill-up. He ran the dipstick into the tank and exclaimed, "What's the hurry? You've still got three inches, or about five gallons!"

Jackie my wife and I have never since doubted the power of God to provide for His children. No, He didn't fill my dangerously low oil tank, but He never let it run out, either. To my way of thinking, that is more than enough.

For the jar of flour was not used up and the jug of oil did not run dry, in keeping with the word of the Lord. 1 Kings 17:16, NIV.

Walter L. Wright is secretary of the Lake Union Conference of Seventh-day Adventists in Berrien Springs, Michigan. He is a member of the Niles Philadelphia Seventh-day Adventist Church in Niles, Michigan.

THE HOUSE AND THE SCHOOL
By Lori L. Hopkins

IN THE WINTER of 1997 my husband Jim decided we must eliminate our debt. We needed to free up money for our three children's education in Adventist schools. In a year and a half our oldest would be at Wisconsin Academy. In our current financial situation we wouldn't be able to afford that.

After much thought and prayer Jim decided we could sell our home and eliminate our mortgage. By doing that we would have most of the money we would need for our tuition bills. At the same time, we would have to build another home, and it would have to be in an area without a building inspector and occupancy permits. This would make it possible to live in an unfinished house and complete it using money we had on hand, eliminating a house payment.

We started the process of selling our home and began searching for property. Our criteria were a conventional percolation soil test, a walkout basement, no building inspector, and woods. We looked at 60 parcels, and none of them met the criteria.

Jim felt impressed one day to go back and look at a piece of property he had seen before. After walking around on it and praying some more, he decided it was a workable 3.3 acres of woods. The next step was to negotiate the price. We decided to offer 30 percent below asking price.

I hadn't been entirely enthusiastic about the whole idea from the beginning. I was sure our offer would never be accepted and that this plan would never work. I started telling God what He should be doing for us. I told Him how to answer our prayer instead of trusting in Him.

About a week after we made our offer, we were told that it had been accepted. Jim was pleased and not at all surprised. I was in shock. I couldn't believe that property was now ours.

It took nine months to sell our home. When we got discouraged, we tried to focus on how God had led us in the past and to trust Him to continue to lead. In His own good time we were finally able to start construction on our new home.

As I write this, our oldest child is now in his second year at Wisconsin Academy, where he is a senior. He was joined this year by a sister, who is a junior. Our youngest son attends our local church school. The bills we face are not small when it comes to our children's education, but with God's help we are able to keep up with them. Being "debt-free" doesn't mean that we always know how those tuition bills are going to get paid, but it has helped. We know that God has asked us to be the best stewards we can with what He has given us. When we do our part, He does His part, and our needs are met.

Trust in the Lord with all your heart, and lean not on your own understanding; in all your ways acknowledge Him, and He shall direct your paths. Proverbs 3:5, 6, NKJV.

Lori L. Hopkins is a homemaker in Green Bay, Wisconsin. She is a member of the Green Bay Seventh-day Adventist Church.

SHE SAID, HE SAID
By Katherine and Reger Smith

*K*ATHERINE: I was a stay-at-home mom for fourteen years. When our fourth child was two years old, it became obvious that I needed to join the work force to help my husband support our family and to provide church-school tuition for our children.

So I went to work and faithfully carried my share of the load until the children were out of college and we were in the "empty-nest" stage. But I was still working. Many enjoyable things at home and in the community I could not do because of my busy work schedule.

By age 62 I found I was working longer hours (as a dormitory dean) and keeping busier than when I was younger. My husband reminded me that I must work until age 65 to receive full Social Security benefits and that we would not be prepared for retirement if I did otherwise.

I felt there was no reprieve. I began to resent being forced into the mold of our being a "two-job family" in order to survive. So by age 64 I rebelled and retired. I felt strongly that our well-being should not be dependent on my employment, that the Lord did not intend for our lives to be so burdened down with "things," and that He would provide for our needs.

Reger: As husband and main financial planner, I panicked. During most of our marriage I had been trying to recover from too much borrowing and supporting four children through their education in Christian schools. Just a few years before Katherine retired, I had begun modest retirement savings.

With her retirement, I envisioned losing one third of our income, with debts yet to be paid off. I matched our monthly obligations against our now reduced income and became angry at my wife for not only giving us "an impossible cash flow" but also reducing our permanent retirement income by about $100 a month. Retirement looked bleak with no money for usual retirement activities. I did some serious worrying.

For some time we had given about seven percent of our income in church offerings in addition to tithe. I was impressed to increase the offerings to ten percent. We both prayed that the Lord would bless us and keep us solvent.

I also have now been retired for more than three years, and God has blessed us "far more abundantly than all that we ask or think" (Ephesians 3:20, RSV).

Reger and Katherine: Here are some of the blessings God sent our way:

Our Social Security income is more than we had expected.

We realized that we had already returned tithe on most of our current Social Security income.

Reger's part-time income has increased to provide more than enough to permit us to visit our children, travel for recreation, and engage in other enjoyable retirement activities.

The Lord has blessed us with unexpected gifts and gratuities.

We have purchased excellent transportation without borrowing.

We enjoy good health.

We are finding great satisfaction in volunteering to develop a new front-line, church-based ministry to help needy families in our congregation and in the community.

Now glory be to God who by his mighty power at work within us is able to do far more than we would ever dare to ask or even dream of—infinitely beyond our highest prayers, desires, thoughts, or hopes. Ephesians 3:20, *The Living Bible*.

Katherine and Reger Smith, in retirement, are volunteer directors of social-work ministries at Pioneer Memorial Church in Berrien Springs, Michigan, where they are members.

THE BEST WAY TO FLY
By Victor Czerkasij

THE BUSINESS world is flooded with books, tapes, and seminars about managing time. When I consider how much I have spent on these materials, I sometimes wish I had been more careful in managing my money. Nevertheless, I have learned valuable lessons in using time well. And the greatest opportunities for me came during a flight.

Times were when being a passenger was an experience to be savored, with a good magazine and all the peanuts one could eat. Today we are road warriors, connected to our laptops, pagers, and cell phones, earnestly typing reports and managing the office from Terminal D, Gate 36—and eating peanuts.

I decided this flight was going to be like it once was. I settled into my bulkhead seat, on the aisle, about to leave Detroit for Amsterdam. With so much time ahead, I had packed away my work gear in the overhead storage compartment and pulled out my new paperback regaling me with exciting tales of the Civil War. The head-phones piped soothing music. Nine hours of reading and relaxation would be my reward for previous flights of pure labor. This was going to be a delight—until I heard the baby screaming and wailing.

I could imagine the hairs standing straight up on every passenger ten rows up and twenty rows back, silently praying that this child and connected parent would not sit next to them.

With terror in my being, I saw the mother's face flicker with recognition at her row and seat . . . right next to me.

All of us experience crossroads every day in every situation. We can say or do one thing or another. What we choose determines destiny. And something spoke to me that this baby and her harried mother were my destiny.

As the mother struggled to put items one-handed into the overhead while the child furiously kicked, I astounded everyone, no less myself, by standing up and taking the child into my arms.

"This is how my kids love to be held." I smiled, turning the little girl stomach-down on my right arm and bouncing her gently. She and some passengers were slack-jawed.

Surprised, the mother expressed appreciation while she stuffed diapers and wipes around our seats. "Thank you," she exclaimed. "I had prayed to God that I would sit with someone who would understand Ava."

Ava cooed.

For the next 40 minutes Carol related how difficult life had been since her recent divorce, and she added that she never had a chance to work through her pain because

18

of Ava's needs. Now, with a flight headed for her native Netherlands, she hoped to begin anew.

"I don't know what I'll do next," she said, as she quietly rocked a sleeping Ava. "But I hope to meet people as nice as you."

At that moment the lead flight attendant knelt in the aisle next to me. "Sir," she said, "We're going to attach a crib to the bulkhead for the little baby. Do you mind?"

There are crossroads every day. I can choose. Those choices determine destiny.

"No," I said, "I don't mind. Whatever helps."

"I was hoping you'd say that," she said, standing up. "You see, all the flight attendants noticed how kindly you've treated this lady and her baby, and to thank you we'd like to ask you to take a seat up in First Class for the rest of the flight."

Leaning tenderly over sleeping Ava, I kissed her forehead. "Thanks," I whispered.

Cast your bread upon the waters, for you will find it after many days. Ecclesiastes 11:1, RSV.

Victor Czerkasij is director of admissions and recruitment at Southern Adventist University in Collegedale, Tennessee. He is a member of the Collegedale Seventh-day Adventist Church.

COLD COMFORT
By S. L. Bailey

I ALMOST NEVER thought about financially supporting Union Springs Academy. It just didn't seem that I could do anything. I didn't have a high-paying job, and I was usually struggling just to take care of life's necessities.

On that late summer Sabbath three years ago the conference youth director came to my church to share the financial needs of the academy. Even though I didn't have any money that day, I felt God urging me to pledge a specific amount. From my pew I argued with God that I needed something more urgently than the academy needed my money. I needed another refrigerator: mine wasn't keeping food cold, and several items had recently spoiled before I had a chance to use them. A lump-sum paycheck I would be receiving in ten days was already designated to purchase a second-hand unit.

The Spirit persisted. I pledged the amount I was expecting to spend on the refrigerator. "You will have to provide for my needs," I told God. "I need a refrigerator that works."

When I returned home from church that Sabbath afternoon, I found the milk ice-cold. Two weeks after I made my pledge to the academy, I had to turn the control down because food was freezing in the refrigerator compartment. But God didn't stop at that.

19

Several days after making my pledge I was offered a week's work that gave me more than the amount pledged. And when that earlier promised paycheck arrived, it was more than $400 beyond what I had counted on receiving!

God took care of the need—on every level. And through me He helped care for the school He loves as well.

Give, and it shall be given unto you; good measure, pressed down, and shaken together, and running over, shall men give into your bosom. For with the same measure that ye mete withal it shall be measured to you again. Luke 6:38.

S. L. Bailey is a secretary/receptionist in Hudson Falls, New York. She is a member of the Kingsbury, New York, Seventh-day Adventist Church.

HEAVEN'S BANK WINDOW
By Bryce R. Hickerson

IN THE mid-1950s jobs were scarce in our little foothill town in northern California. I had been hired to be a bookkeeper for a small establishment at a very low wage by a penurious employer who often reduced his workers' wages when he heard that there might be the slightest indication of a possible recession coming. Behind his back we called him Laban.

Our family kept a large garden, canned lots of food, and skimped in every way possible. The house we bought had been a repossession, so we were able to get it for a very low down payment and low monthly payments. It definitely was a "fixer-upper," except that we didn't have any money to do the fixing. We did do the best we could with some paint and minor repairs, and we bought a big, secondhand wood stove that kept us comfortably warm during the cold weather. Our front windows gave us a magnificent view of the surrounding hills, which more than made up for the condition of the house.

Each month when I received my paycheck, we always took out our tithe and offerings first. After that we paid our house payments and utilities, and we kept some money out to pay for the gasoline that we would use that month. That left us $70 for food, clothes, and any other expenses that might come along.

My wife would then take our two small children to town, as our food supplies by that time in the month were becoming quite low. She always stopped at the bank first, wrote a $70 check for cash, and then went to the grocery store to buy staple items and other foods that we would use for most of that month. Later in the month we would receive our bank statement and the canceled checks that had been written.

One month, after following our usual financial procedures, the bank statement

20

arrived, but there was no $70 canceled check with the other checks or any record of our having written a $70 check.

I took the statement to the bank and explained that there must be some error, because we knew that my wife had written a $70 check, had received cash, and had done her grocery shopping with it. The teller wrote down the information that I gave her, including the date the check had been written. She said she would look through the transactions of that day and that I could come in later and find out about it.

When I returned, she told me that on that day in question they had no record of any check being written against our account and that no one had come into the bank and written a check for $70 on any account. She also said that their records showed that there were no shortages of funds, and all their transactions had balanced out perfectly. She told me just to forget about it. Of course, she thought we simply had made a mistake.

We knew we had written that check on that day; we had a cupboard full of groceries to prove it and a little cash left over.

We don't know which of God's "thousand ways" He used to provide this much-needed money for us, nor did we ever imagine that when He promised to "open . . . the windows of heaven," one of them would turn out to be a bank teller's window.

Know therefore that the Lord your God is God; he is the faithful God, keeping his covenant of love to a thousand generations of those who love him and keep his commands. Deuteronomy 7:9, NIV.

Bryce R. Hickerson is a retired elementary school teacher in Carmichael, California. He is a member of the Carmichael Seventh-day Adventist Church in Sacramento, California.

A ROOF AND A PRAYER
By Timothy Atolagbe

I GREW UP in a home where the family gathered for prayer every morning and evening. My siblings and I didn't appreciate the blessing of this family routine for many years until one day just before the beginning of the rainy season. The roof on our house needed to be replaced.

My father had made arrangements with a carpenter friend to bring his work crew in the beginning of the week. The carpenters didn't come until Friday morning. They knew that our family were Adventists, and my father made it clear that should they choose to start working on the roof on Friday, it had to be completed before the beginning of the Sabbath at sunset.

My country at that time had no broadcast weather forecasts, so leaving a roof unfinished was not an option. The job would have to be completed in one day.

The men started working just before noon, but in keeping with their Islamic practice, they took a break to go to the mosque for prayers. By the time they returned, they had only a few hours left before Sabbath. At sunset my father expressed his dissatisfaction to the work-crew leader and requested that the work on the roof be stopped until Sunday morning. No one thought that it would rain, because the sky was clear and the rainy season had not really started. However, the possibility that it could rain still existed, so the carpenters asked to be allowed to work a little longer or to return the next morning on the Sabbath to complete the job while our family was at church. My father told the carpenters of his trust that the same God who commanded that His Sabbath be kept holy is able to protect our house in any weather. The men laughed as they left.

That evening our family gathered for worship and prayed that the Lord would hold off any rain until after Sunday when the carpenters would return to complete their job. In the middle of the night I was awakened by loud thunder and the sense that someone was standing in the corner of my room whispering. I soon realized that my father was praying with an open Bible in his hand. He told us later that he had gone around to every corner of our house praying. As the thunderstorm continued, I could hear some of our next-door neighbors knocking at our door, asking if they could do anything to help. My parents thanked them and said we'd be fine. As the thunderstorm continued, we children slept while our parents stayed up praying.

The next morning my father got up a little earlier than usual before family prayer time to inspect our house for damage. We rejoiced and thanked the Lord that there was no damage to our home.

We didn't realize the full extent of God's blessing that stormy night until later in the day when we returned from church. Some men from the neighborhood came to ask my father if he would sell them the "formula" for blowing away the rain. While it had rained hard everywhere else in the neighborhood, it had not rained around our house that night.

God is our refuge and strength, an ever-present help in trouble. Therefore we will not fear, though the earth give way and the mountains fall into the heart of the sea, though its waters roar and foam and the mountains quake with their surging. Psalm 46:1-3, NIV.

Timothy Atolagbe is a medical laboratory technician in Baltimore, Maryland. He is a member of the New Hope Seventh-day Adventist Church in Burtonsville, Maryland.

TIME TO BE LIKE JESUS
By Jerry Page

WORD reached me that one of my staff members was at it again. Jim was spreading false rumors about another couple on our conference team. I'd warned him before about his tendency to gossip, and this time I was extremely annoyed.

I set up an appointment for the next Tuesday. My plan was to go over a list of what he was doing, watch him squirm a little, and then make it clear his behavior needed to stop.

Tuesday came, and I took my time with the Lord that morning. I even asked Him to speak clearly to me from His Word whatever I needed to understand. The upcoming appointment with Jim that morning was not in my mind. But it was on God's mind.

I had been reading through Proverbs, and verses from chapter 12 began to jump off the page at me. "A fool shows his annoyance at once" (16). "Reckless words pierce like a sword, but the tongue of the wise brings healing" (18). "A prudent man keeps his knowledge to himself, but the heart of the fool blurts out folly" (23). "A righteous man is cautious in friendship" (26).

"I hear you, Lord," I prayed. "I am right about the facts with Jim, but I am so wrong in spirit. Help me to be like Jesus when I meet with Jim today." Galatians 6:1 came to mind: "Brothers, if someone is caught in a sin, you who are spiritual should restore him gently. But watch yourself, or you also may be tempted."

As I met with Jim that day, I began by reading Galatians 6:1 and asking him to pray for me to be like Jesus in all my dealings with people. I admitted that I sometimes talk about people behind their backs in negative ways. Then I shared a little of my concerns "gently" with him, and we ended up on our knees, arms around each other, tears in our eyes, praying for each other to be more like Jesus. It was a Spirit-filled conclusion to what might otherwise have been a hurtful confrontation.

Late that evening a pastor called me. He was very angry that some members were spreading false gossip about him. He was going to straighten them out the next day.

Well, isn't God good! He had worked me over just that morning so I could have a better meeting with Jim and also be ready to help a pastor calm down later that evening.

So often I make great time on the freeway of life only to discover I am heading in the wrong direction. Life gets so busy. It seems there is never enough time even to begin to accomplish what I need to do. The temptation is to cut short or skip the time with my Lord and move on to getting something "practical" done.

But I am continuing to learn that if I put my time with God first on my list of priorities, He can accomplish many more of the right things.

I am the vine: you are the branches. If a man remains in me and I in him, he will bear much fruit; apart from me you can do nothing. John 15:5.

Jerry Page is president of the Central California Conference of Seventh-day Adventists in Clovis, California. He is a member of the Oakhurst, California, Seventh-day Adventist Church.

HE MAKES UP THE DIFFERENCE
By Jeanette Rawson

WHAT? You mean to tell me that I've been tithing wrong after all these years?

I remembered when I was young asking my Mother about tithing. My parents were Iowa farmers, and they knew about bookkeeping. She had told me, "You tithe on the net income, which is the income you have left over after all expenses are taken out."

So that's the way I always tithed until a few years ago. An article in the *Adventist Review* about tithing changed all that. As I read the article, I became convicted that I needed to change and start tithing as my husband did. My husband had always tithed on the gross. I thought to myself, *He just doesn't understand. But far be it from me to interfere if he wants to give more of his money to the Lord than he needs to. I'll not stand in his way.*

But the article showed me that I really did need to tithe on the gross. I had not realized that farmers and other investors, understandably, tithe differently because they have invested their money and time up front.

When my next paycheck arrived, I told the Lord, "You're going to have to help pay the bills since I'm returning more tithe." (I can get pretty selfish at times.) I wish I could say that I joyfully gave the extra at that time. I can't. But I did give, knowing I could not keep what the Lord required. Amazingly enough, the money stretched just as far as it ever had.

We were in need of another car to take our son out to college at Walla Walla. Our "good" car had 350,000 miles on it and needed $600 in repairs. We weren't sure where we would get the money to pay for it. So it was a big surprise when, out of the blue, my brother called and told me that he had spoken with my other brother and sister, and they all agreed I should have our mother's car. He said, "You need it the most." And his wife said, "I heard of your concern about getting over the mountains in that car."

God had also known what we needed and certainly made up the difference created by my new understanding of tithing. He has made up the difference with other things too.

The lawn mower we used to care for several acres needed $450 of repairs. A good friend of my husband moved back into town. He told my husband that he wouldn't be needing his riding lawn mower anymore, so he would let us use it. What an answer to prayer!

Yes, God has made up the difference with a couch we badly needed too. Though none of these things were new, He knew what we needed. The Lord continues to make up the difference. Do we still have debts? Yes, but that's because of some of our mistakes of the past. We feel He makes up the difference when our three children are able to attend our Christian colleges, when He gives good health and safety to us and our children; when He provides beautiful sunsets, bright starlit nights, and quiet and peaceful living in the country.

Delight thyself also in the Lord; and he shall give thee the desires of thine heart. Psalm 37:4.

Jeanette Rawson is a teacher and home health aide in Cedar Rapids, Iowa. She is a member of the Covenant Seventh-day Adventist Church in Cedar Rapids.

ONE POTATO AND A HOMECOMING
By Stella Bicky Hill Young

EVERYONE had filed out of the church. I sat alone as the light from the stained-glass windows gave an unnatural glow to my surroundings. I held my husband's $25 tightly in my hand. It was all we had for groceries to feed our family of seven. My thoughts darted through the 25 years I had just spent away from the church that I had loved as a child. Now I was back home, vowing to go all the way with my Lord.

The moment of decision had come. How could I be tested so quickly with such a major decision? I knew $25 would not buy enough food to feed us for the whole week, but if I tried to spread it around in my own power, I knew I would fail. I also knew I had nothing else to give for tithe. I had been gone so long.

My new commitment pounded in my brain; the tears spilled out as I sat there in silence, pleading with God for direction. Soon the answer became very clear as the story of the widow and her mite came to mind. Yes, that is what I would do. I would give the whole $25 to my faithful Lord, who had just welcomed me home again to stay.

Trying to explain to my husband and children what I had done was hard, but surprisingly, they seemed to understand. During the week we used up what remnants we had of food. Then the dreaded day came. All I could find in the house to feed the clan was one large potato.

I cooked the potato and prepared to cut it seven ways, as I called everyone to the table. We bowed our heads in prayer as my husband gave thanks for the food we were about to share. Before he could finish the prayer, the doorbell rang. We quickly chorused, "Amen," and ran to the door in a group.

There stood my new pastor and his wife with bags of groceries in their arms and stacked at their feet. Through thankful tears I asked them how they knew we needed anything, for I had not told anyone of our dire circumstances. They said they did not know and were even afraid we might take offense at their gesture of goodwill. But the urge to bring us food was so strong that they were simply compelled to do so.

Was it a coincidence that they came while we were offering thanks in prayer for one large potato? I know it was not. When I gave the Lord all I had to give Him, I knew in my heart He would never let us go hungry. How did I know? Because in the silent moments in my Father's house and in the glow of the stained glass, I had claimed His promise.

I was young and now I am old; yet I have never seen the righteous forsaken or their children begging for bread. Psalm 37:25, NIV.

Stella Bicky Hill Young is assistant pastor of the Greenville, South Carolina, Seventh-day Adventist Church.

You have a stewardship testimony you need to share and we need to read. See page 224 for details.

The
SECOND
MEETING

Come and hear, all ye that fear God, and I will declare what he hath done for my soul.

Psalm 66:16

John J. Jones

Yvonne Thomas

Ann Heck

Albert E. Hayward

Linda Hicks Dowell

Rudolph Carlson

Dianna Brantley

Gary A. Brodis

Dena Guthrie

Tari C. Popp

A BUILDER KEEPS THE SABBATH AND A BANKER BREAKS THE RULES

By John J. Jones

I WAS a traveling salesman for several years after finishing college. However, after marrying a beautiful young lady, I became tired of traveling and wanted to be home every night with my lovely wife.

There were not many higher-income jobs in my hometown, so I decided to be a home builder. Many people told me that I was crazy. Leaving a well-paying job and beginning another occupation that I knew nothing about didn't seem smart. But Jesus had richly blessed me as a salesman, and I was sure He would bless me in building houses. So I stepped out in faith. Sure enough, I was blessed abundantly.

Within a few years I became one of the top builders in my town and in the entire county. The local office of a large savings and loan association arranged a special financing program with a lower interest rate for people who bought my houses. Meanwhile, regular interest rates began to go higher and higher. Finally the president of the bank called me into his office and told me they would give me and my customers one more year of this special financing program, and then it would be over.

I accepted his offer graciously, bought many lots, and began building several houses at a time. My operating capital was spread thinly. To keep ahead, I had to close on a house every month to survive.

As we approached winter, the weather became severe, with rain, sleet, and snow. This greatly slowed down the outside finishing work on the houses.

The bank had given us a deadline of February 8 for the end of the low-rate financing. We still had three more houses under contract to finish and close. The bank wouldn't give a loan on a house that wasn't finished. The buyers of these houses wouldn't be able to qualify for a loan at the regular interest rate. So I had to finish those houses before the deadline, or I would be stuck with three unsold houses, perhaps for a long time. Regular interest rates were so high by now that people had stopped buying.

I never allowed subcontractors or my own workers to work on the houses on Sabbath. However, many times, when necessary, the workers had volunteered to work on Sunday. Three weeks before the deadline several of the workers approached me and said, "John, your ox is in the ditch, and we've got to get it out. We can work Saturday and Sunday to help you out of this jam. You've got to finish these houses and close on them, or you will lose everything. We don't want to see you go broke."

I thanked the workers for their concern and their offer to work on their days off. However, I explained to them that this was not a life-or-death situation. There was no proverbial ox that had fallen in the ditch and was suffering. They were unconvinced.

My wife and I prayed every day for Jesus to resolve our dilemma. We worked steadily and finished one of the houses and closed it on February 7. After the settlement meeting at the bank, the president told me he would be closing the other two houses tomorrow, February 8. I was shocked. I told him the houses weren't finished.

"I know that," he said, "but we are closing anyway." He was going directly against bank policy. To help justify what he was doing, he said he would hold back a sizeable portion of the money due me until I had actually finished the houses. I was thrilled. Those houses would be sold. I had a reprieve that allowed me to finish the houses after that terrible deadline.

I wondered how he could do this, for he might get in trouble with the home office in Atlanta. He recognized my concern and told me not to worry—everything would work out fine.

We went to closing on the two houses the next day, and to my astonishment the bank didn't even hold back any money from the sale. Apparently the president just trusted us to finish the houses. Jesus had answered our prayers and saved us from financial hardship.

We finished the houses three weeks later, and the buyers were well pleased with them. No one else could explain why the banker was willing to break strict company rules. But we knew that Jesus had intervened.

If you turn back your foot from the sabbath, from doing your pleasure on my holy day . . .; then you shall take delight in the Lord, and I will make you ride upon the heights of the earth; I will feed you with the heritage of Jacob your father, for the mouth of the Lord has spoken. Isaiah 58:13, 14, RSV.

John J. Jones is a general contractor and land developer in Sylacauga, Alabama. He is a member of the Sylacauga Seventh-day Adventist Church.

A WIDOW'S TITHE
By Yvonne Thomas

WHEN I was 24, my husband died of cancer, and I was left with five children ranging in age from seven to twin girls a year old.

Shortly after my husband's death a gentleman who had known me as a child came to the door and asked if I would like to go to church sometime. I told him yes, for I needed something to help me through this awful time.

It was wonderful to learn the truths from God's Word. One Sabbath at church the pastor preached about tithing. He showed us a large board with two columns of numbers. The first column listed rent, food, electricity, clothes, medical expenses, and tithe and offerings, in that order. There was little left for the tithe. The second column listed tithe and offerings at the top and all other expenses listed below. As the pastor spoke, the Holy Spirit was doing His work. Until then I had felt that I was exempt from returning tithe because of my situation as a widow on a small income with five children. How would we live if I took money out for tithe?

As I prayed about this, I felt God was saying, "Test me; My Word is true." So with fear and trembling I placed my tithe in a tithe envelope, not knowing when my children would eat their next meal.

I cannot say that there were not times of hardship, but I can say that God was always true to His Word. One time we had nothing left in the cupboard. I gathered my children around for prayer, and within a few minutes we heard a knock at the door. There stood two ladies with bags of groceries. We lived twelve miles out in the country, so I knew that before I had asked, God was already acting to answer my prayer.

I know what it is to be in need, and I know what it is to have plenty. I have learned the secret of being content in any and every situation, whether well fed or hungry, whether living in plenty or in want. I can do everything through him who gives me strength. Philippians 4:12, 13, NIV.

Yvonne Thomas is assistant dean of girls at Wisconsin Academy in Columbus, Wisconsin. She is a member of the Wisconsin Academy Seventh-day Adventist Church.

GOD'S EVERYDAY WAYS
By Ann Heck

Now THAT you're retired, what can we do to serve the Lord more than we are doing?"

My husband Joe had recently retired. I thought it was time we did something big.

"We have lots of land," he said, "and we are teachers. Why don't we start a self-supporting academy?"

This was a big idea, the kind I was looking for. But it wasn't to be. So I continued to be active in church and community service, and I was blessed by the results. Still I was looking for that "something big."

We were invited to teach in the South Pacific but were unable to do so at the time, so we spent the next three years teaching church school for our church. After two families moved, the school was closed.

Shortly after this I saw an ad on the back of the South Pacific Division *Record*: "Teach English in China for a year." I had dreamed of being a missionary in China since I had heard one speak in church when I was seven.

Praise God! He wants me to teach English in China. My dream would come true. I could do something big for God.

Seven months later we were teaching English in China, not just one year but two. Our students saw something different in us and asked us what it was. We were able to share with them the truth that sets us free.

Now I am back home, serving the Lord in all the everyday ways He sets before me. And He rewards me with simple pleasures. Who can top the joy of showing God's love to an alcoholic who, through the power of God, is now sober and baptized? What a blessing to hear someone tell you that because you showed him God's forgiveness, he now really knows that God loves him after all! What can beat seeing the joy on a young student's face when a new concept is finally understood? What better way to spend my time than studying the Bible with a friend, or sharing breakfast with singles on Sabbath mornings, or listening to a lonely person? These are the everyday ways God uses me to bless others—and me.

God has shown me that it isn't the occasional big things we do for Him that bring the biggest blessings. It's the little things He calls us to do every day.

And we desire that every one of you do shew the same diligence to the full assurance of hope unto the end: that ye be not slothful, but followers of them who through faith and patience inherit the promises. Hebrews 6:11, 12.

Ann Heck is a retired schoolteacher in Talkeetna, Alaska. She is a member of the Sunshine Seventh-day Adventist Church in Talkeetna.

NOTHING TO HIDE
By Albert E. Hayward

WINTER was approaching, and my wife and I had just been given notice to vacate the small cottage we were renting.

After a fruitless search for an affordable place that would meet our needs, God opened the way for us to purchase a new mobile home. He also provided a place for us to set it up.

Two problems for which we had no money came with the trailer: an unreliable well and a poor septic system.

Because I was a veteran of the Second World War, I was advised to contact the Department of Veterans Affairs and appeal for funds, which I did. When their representative came to see us, he requested that we itemize where every cent of our family finances went to, which we agreed to do. He told us he would have to present the information to a committee, and he promised to return to get our report.

Several days later, when he came back, I saw a look of consternation come over his face as he studied our list. "What is this 'tithe' that you have at the top of the list?" he asked.

I explained to him that tithe was ten percent of all money we received, and that we returned it to God through the church. "My church would be lucky to get a dime," he replied. He asked us whether there was some item on the list in which we could hide the tithe.

"No," we said, "it is God's."

"You've given me a tough job," he said as he left, clearly frustrated. "I doubt you'll get any money."

Two weeks later he returned, with a surprised look on his face. As he got out of his car, he pointed to heaven. "Somebody is really taking care of you," he exclaimed. "You're getting the money you need. You'll be receiving a check shortly in the mail."

Years later the well purchased with those funds still flows. It has never failed, even when surrounding wells went dry.

Blessed is the man who walks not in the counsel of the ungodly . . .; but his delight is in the law of the Lord, and in His law he meditates day and night. He shall be like a tree planted by the rivers of water, that brings forth its fruit in its season, whose leaf also shall not wither; and whatever he does shall prosper. Psalm 1:1-3, NKJV.

Albert E. Hayward is a retired medical professional in South River, Ontario. He is a member of the South River Seventh-day Adventist Church.

....

THE HOUSE GOD PROVIDED
By Linda Hicks Dowell

WITH two little girls, and a third child on the way, our young family was fast outgrowing the small three-bedroom trailer we occupied. Closets were overflowing. Dresser drawers and shelf space were filled to capacity.

But space wasn't the only need. As stories reached us of little children being injured by older children near the less-than-ideal trailer park where we lived, my mother-in-law advised me to keep our girls indoors.

"Just let them watch more TV to help keep them busy," she said.

I had recently felt convicted to keep TV-watching to a minimum and to instill in my children a love for the outdoors. I couldn't consider an option such as my mother-in-law had suggested. Beginning with our first child, my husband and I had sacrificed so I could stay at home and give the children personal attention and the best upbringing possible. I believed these children were a gift from God, and I needed to do all I could to raise them for Him.

One evening during a short devotional time at the end of my day, I mulled these matters over. Suddenly my whole attention was drawn to a verse in the chapter I was reading.

"Therefore I say unto you, what things soever ye desire, when ye pray, believe that ye receive them, and ye shall have them" (Mark 11:24).

Deeply impressed that in these words God was speaking to me personally, I began to pray for a house in which to raise my children for Him.

"It doesn't have to be new," I told Him. "It doesn't have to be ideal in appearance or layout." I just wanted someplace, wherever He saw fit, in some quiet neighborhood, with lots of space in which my children could explore nature.

As the days went by, another Bible promise was impressed upon me: "Seek, and ye shall find" (Matthew 7:7).

Though we trusted God's leading, my husband and I decided it might be presumptuous to even consider looking at newer homes. We therefore turned our attention to houses some call "white elephants." We made appointments and viewed several such houses. In each house, some major defect eliminated it from our consideration. One house needed a new furnace. Another had only one bedroom that didn't need extensive remodeling. And so it went.

After another fruitless viewing, we were standing by our car late one afternoon feeling quite discouraged. But a last glance at the housing magazine we had in hand led me to the description of a house I hadn't noticed before. The description included terms like "three and a half years old," "full basement," "nearly an acre of land." And the price tag was an unbelievable $29,500! That was much less than any of the "white-elephant" houses we had looked at. I pointed out the advertisement to my husband, and we read it again, not daring to believe that such a house could be available.

According to the description, it was located about three blocks from where we were standing. We decided it would be a shame not to take a look.

We parked in a cul-de-sac and began our walk down a 300-foot driveway. The three-bedroom brick-and-siding house was located at the back of a small housing community. It faced a pasture and had pine trees in the right half of the front yard. A small creek ran across one corner.

As I was drinking in the view, it was as if God said to me, "Linda, you don't have to settle for a 'white elephant'; I'm going to give you this house!"

We contacted the realty company, filled out an application, and left $100 earnest money to hold it for 30 days. The next month was a real trial of faith for us. A prospective buyer for our trailer changed his mind halfway through the month. Our bank was unwilling to lend us the rest of the money necessary for closing. Two other persons also filled out applications and left earnest money on the house we wanted to buy.

One day before the planned closing, our trailer sold. The realtor involved in selling us the house had never met us before and wasn't obligated to us in any way. She knew of our financial situation, but unexpectedly gave us a personal loan for the rest of the money we needed to close.

We lived in that house for eight years. The children and I explored every inch of the surrounding fields and woods. We had many picnics at the side of one or the other of two nearby ponds and family worship times on our front porch, with cicadas serenading us throughout.

Over the years we lived in several different homes, but none stands out like the house of this story. To this day my children and I remember with awe and gratitude the house God provided when we made principled decisions to live as we believed He had called us to.

And all thy children shall be taught of the Lord; and great shall be the peace of thy children. Isaiah 54:13.

Linda Hicks Dowell is a registered nurse for John Peter Smith Hospital in Forth Worth, Texas. She is a member of the Fort Worth First Seventh-day Adventist Church.

CAST YOUR NETS
By Rudolph Carlson

IT WAS an important event when my father, a commercial fisherman, first trusted me with my own fishing crew during the annual spring smelt run on the north shore of Lake Superior.

After working hard most of one Friday night with little to show for it, I surprised myself that I was still willing to drag myself out of bed to go to church. I was just getting acquainted with Seventh-day Adventists, and my curiosity about what they believed wouldn't let me sleep on Saturday morning. Anyway, I could always take a nap later that afternoon.

For some reason on that Sabbath the idea stuck in my head that God challenges us to a partnership with Him in financial affairs. While somebody prayed over the offering, I made a deal with God. I said, "God, let's be partners on tonight's catch. I will give You not only ten percent of what I make; I'll make You a true partner and split it down the middle, 50/50."

My crew started setting up for fishing a half hour after sunset, as required by law, just as we had for several previous nights of unsuccessful fishing. We anchored our rectangular fifteen-by-ten-foot fish corral in the river with its three-foot opening facing the river mouth. The corral was made of a metal mesh welded to an iron frame with two ten-foot mess gates extending out diagonally from the opening on each side. The fish swim in, and they don't swim out. The fishermen use a dip net to scoop out the fish and then put them in boxes that are stacked seven high on a semi-trailer.

After everything was ready, one of us stayed by the water, monitoring the fish corral, while the rest of us climbed into the cab of the truck to keep warm and try to sleep. At about midnight my turn came to watch for fish. So far we hadn't seen a thing.

I hadn't been watching more than five minutes when all of a sudden the corral started to move upstream! I looked inside, and in it were several large game fish that I had to scoop out and return to the river as the law mandated. The more I worked, the more I kept asking myself: Why are all of these large fish coming in? So I turned and looked out into the lake in search of a clue.

There, barely in sight, was what appeared to be a single wave heading for the river's mouth. I pulled up my hip waders and ran out into the lake to take a better look. The wave was about eighteen inches high, and to my amazement was made of fish swimming on one another's backs. I stood there gazing in amazement until the wave hit me and almost knocked me down. Now I knew where all of those game fish came from. They were being herded up the river by the advancing horde of smelt. I ran back to the truck and woke the other crew members. We fished as hard as possible. The smelt came in so fast that we had the first truck loaded in no time. As it pulled away to make room for the second truck, its axle broke from all the weight it was carrying.

That was the most fish I had ever seen before or since. The next Sabbath the Lord and I split $1,400, and He's been my partner ever since.

He called out to them, "Friends, haven't you any fish?" "No," they answered. He said, "Throw your net on the right side of the boat and you will find some." When they did, they were unable to haul the net in because of the large number of fish. John 21:5, 6, NIV.

Rudolph Carlson is a teacher and principal at North Woods Adventist Elementary School in Hutchinson, Minnesota. He is a member of the Hutchinson Seventh-day Adventist Church.

THE BATTLE BELONGS TO THE LORD
By Dianna Brantley

THE CHOICE was clear: Either I would work on the Sabbath, or I would lose my job.

As a civil deputy sheriff in a county police department, I had never had a Sabbath conflict before. Now I was being told that I would have to work the evening shift, which included Friday nights.

I met with my immediate supervisor and informed her that I couldn't work on Sabbath because of my religious beliefs. Though sympathetic, she explained that the decision was out of her hands. I would have to talk with the commander.

I prayed, asking Jesus for strength and endurance. I also shared my decision with my husband, knowing that he would support my convictions. Together we sketched the plan: I must talk to my commander and explain the situation, then leave it in God's hands. My husband also reminded me that even though I had been with the police department for almost 20 years, God had supplied me that job. If necessary, He could get me another one.

Filled with these thoughts, I summoned my courage, put on my breastplate, and walked into the commander's office, ready to do battle.

After nearly two hours of discussion, the commander underlined his authority. He was the commander, and I had to follow his orders or lose my job. With a smile, I reminded him that Jesus was also his commander and that he couldn't operate without Jesus' permission.

The next Monday morning my supervisor approached me excitedly, smiling from ear to ear. Out tumbled the news: The commander had contacted her over the weekend and asked her to inform me that he had changed his mind. I would now be able to work anytime and anywhere I chose.

Strange and abnormal things had happened in his household over the weekend, he told my supervisor, and the only thing he could attribute them to was our conversation, which had weighed heavily on his mind. My supervisor was delighted at the turn of events. She too was a Christian and glad for the chance to be a bearer of good news.

Jesus saw to it that the commander and I later became very good friends and I no longer had to worry about keeping the Sabbath.

The battle is not yours, but God's. 2 Chronicles 20:15.

Dianna Brantley is a civil deputy sheriff for the Miami Dade Police Department in Florida. She is a member of the Miami Bethany Seventh-day Adventist Church.

PACKING A LUNCH AND WAITING FOR GOD
By Gary A. Brodis

WHEN I RECEIVED my first allowance as a child, my mother taught me that one tenth belonged to God. Her example showed me the importance and the blessing of regular faithfulness to God with our money.

When Jean and I married, we vowed to give regular tithe and offerings. We moved to Vermont, bought a house, started a family, and I began a new job. That job came to an end just before Christmas. The Lord provided another job with good pay for the next five months, but it also brought conflicts over the Sabbath and my Christian beliefs. During this time I felt impressed to work for myself in carpentry, remodeling, and repairs.

In May 1980 God and I went into business. Witnessing opportunities multiplied. Work came regularly. Money flowed comfortably. However, by winter work stopped. Wisely we had saved for such times. With Jean now caring for our two children and not working outside the home, the full financial responsibility fell upon me.

Some weeks, no money came in. We resolved to continue to support the church program regardless, as we had before. At last the time came when our savings reserve was gone. Jean and I talked. Did we believe God had directed us into business on our own? Yes. Had we been faithful in tithe and offerings? Yes. Would we trust and prove Him now? Yes.

Monday morning, with no prospects of work, we got up, prayed, and dressed for work. While I ate breakfast, Jean packed a lunch. We would be ready for God's answer to our prayers. Only minutes after breakfast the phone rang. "Would you be willing to shovel snow, cut brush, repair, and paint?"

So it was for the weeks ahead. Sometimes the work lasted two hours, sometimes three days. Whenever the job was over, Jean and I would pray again, I would dress for work, and she would prepare the lunch. Not once did I go even one day without work the remainder of that winter. In the 20 years since, there has not been a total of five days that I have not had work for pay.

Has God fulfilled His promises? We are all in good health. We still own our first home. We have been able to send our children to Seventh-day Adventist schools through college. We have traveled to all 50 states. We have been able to hire others in need of work. We have had many opportunities to tell of God's blessings and encourage others to step out in faith and start businesses with God as their partner. They too have prospered.

Throughout my life I have seen unexplained timing of phone calls, checks in the mail just when we needed money, and a long list of other providences that confirm my belief in God's direct blessing as a result of faithful stewardship.

Therefore take no thought, saying, What shall we eat? Or, What shall we drink? Or, Wherewithal shall we be clothed? (For after all these things do the Gentiles seek:) for your heavenly Father knoweth that ye have need of all these things. But seek ye first the kingdom of God, and His righteousness; and all these things shall be added unto you. Matthew 6:31-33.

Gary A. Brodis is a self-employed builder in Putney, Vermont. He is a member of the Brattleboro, Vermont, Seventh-day Adventist Church.

TRAPPED IN A VACATION
By Dena Guthrie

A WASP droned around the warped screen door of our old family cabin. "Well, at least it's something live and moving," I fretted. How on earth had five acres at the end of a paved road and this old plywood shack we called "the Cabin" become our permanent address? Was this the price for clean air and quiet nights? Maybe it was too high. Maybe we should reconsider our good jobs and large church family back near Los Angeles.

Early each morning my physician husband drove away to the wonderful world of people and his healing mission, leaving me to consider my options. His clinic didn't need my nurse-practitioner skills, and it was two hours round-trip to any other job opportunities.

"Lord," I cried, "I used to love coming up here to the Cabin on holidays. Now I feel trapped in a perpetual vacation from which I can't escape! Surely You have some specific mission for me way up here in the foothills of the Sierras. Please show me what it is. I give back to You my time (I have too much of it, Lord!), my professional skills (they're rusting fast, Lord!), and my influence (can we get past the wasp, Lord?). I'm Yours to use. Please use me, and please let it be soon, or I think this wasp is going to drive me over the edge!"

Later we put in a phone, and my mother called: "You ought to consider running a healthy lifestyle program at your little mountain church," she enthused. "We're running one at our church here in Wichita, and it's turning peoples' lives around."

I wasn't sure. After all, my expertise was in primary care, not prevention. "Lord, is this what You have in mind for me?"

I hadn't ordered them, but one day two heavy boxes of health-education materials arrived at our door. Was Mother scheming? I refused to open them. What if I couldn't get people out to the program? What if I lost money trying? What if I made a fool of myself? I skeptically eyed those boxes for many days. Finally, with a prayer for wisdom and courage, I ripped them open.

Actually and unwittingly I was unwrapping God's answer to my prayer for a mission with meaning. Since then more than 100 people have graduated from our lifestyle program. Our little church parking lot is never so full as when we are in the middle of our health classes. People with diabetes, high blood pressure, obesity, and high cholesterol have reduced or eliminated their medications and are thrilled with how they feel!

Mission? Influence? Friends? All have flourished as I've walked with God through His revised plan for my life.

The little green cabin has a new coat of paint now. The inside is remodeled bright and cozy. The despair that once gripped my soul has flown away with the wasp. God turned my vacation trap into a mission with meaning. And it's been the trip of a lifetime!

For I know the thoughts that I think toward you, says the Lord, thoughts of peace and not of evil, to give you a future and a hope. Jeremiah 29:11, NKJV.

Dena Guthrie is an adult nurse practitioner and owner of Healthy Happenings in Coulterville, California. She is a member of the Groveland, California, Seventh-day Adventist Church.

FAITH AT THE MALL
By Tari C. Popp

SHE WAS ten years old, going on sixteen, and school was about to begin again. As was our tradition, I had set aside a day when just Lauren and I would go shopping for school clothes. We both looked forward to this appointment each year, but lately I had become concerned as I observed her increasing appetite for new things and the latest styles.

Deciding to be proactive, I helped her make a list of the clothes she needed for school, estimated what I felt each item would cost, and gave her $150 to get the job done. The money was hers. With my guidance, she was going to spend it on things she needed.

As we headed to the mall I felt excited about the great learning experience Lauren would have. I believed I had been fair in deciding her budget, but she would have to think her choices through carefully. There wasn't any extra for extravagances. And then in the middle of this great parenting moment, I remembered that we had forgotten about tithe. She hadn't returned tithe on these funds.

Oh, how I struggled for the next few miles! Ten percent in tithe would leave Lauren with only $135. I didn't think she could find everything for that amount, and I was tempted to remain silent. Lauren knew she had a limited budget, and I feared she would be upset if I reminded her of her responsibility. Yet hadn't I wanted this to be an education, and hadn't God abundantly blessed Doug and me as we returned our tithe and offerings over the years? Why shouldn't I let Lauren experience the same?

I took a deep breath and explained to Lauren what we had both forgotten. With the simple faith of a child, she quickly concurred and even suggested she add an extra $5 for offering. Silently I asked God to bless her willing spirit and the $130 she had left.

As the day progressed, we were delighted to find pants on sale, shirts marked down, and accessories discounted. We were finding and agreeing (a blessing in itself) on everything. Yet one item remained on the list: Sabbath shoes. I knew there wasn't enough money left for the adult-sized pair she was now requiring. We went from store to store with no success.

Finally we headed dejectedly into the last department store. Knowing Lauren needed these shoes, I pondered the idea that maybe I should supplement her budget by the amount she had set aside for tithe and offerings. Just then, however, she excitedly interrupted my thoughts and told me she had found some shoes that even I would like! Sure enough, compared to the styles we'd seen that day, these looked wonderful. But what thrilled us even more was the sticker attached to the bottom of the shoes. We quickly calculated that the 50-percent discount shown there was exactly the amount of money Lauren had left.

I had wanted Lauren to learn to shop wisely, and she had. By putting God first, she saw her remaining money used most efficiently and discovered the joy and blessing of becoming a financial partner with God.

Favour is deceitful, and beauty is vain: but a woman that feareth the Lord, she shall be praised. Proverbs 31:30.

Tari C. Popp is a trust officer for the Planned Giving and Trust Services department at Andrews University in Berrien Springs, Michigan. She is a member of Pioneer Memorial Church in Berrien Springs.

You have a stewardship testimony you need to share and we need to read. See page 224 for details.

The
THIRD
MEETING

Jack Stout

Valerie Hamel Morikone

Nancy Arellano

Dennis T. Ranalla

Matt Fivash

Charlotte Groff

Ann Morrow

Stanley S. and Bennie Beth Will

Diane Gordon

Thomas J. Mostert, Jr.

SEVEN MONTHS OF MIRACLES
By Jack Stout

IN OCTOBER 1997 our church members decided we wanted a new church building. A man came to show us how to raise the money. He suggested that we go home and pray about how much we could commit toward the building fund.

When I got home, I went into my bedroom and prayed. I felt impressed to commit $30,000. I reasoned with the Lord that we couldn't come up with that much money, even though it was to be paid over three years. I prayed again and still felt impressed to commit the same amount. I figured God knew something that I didn't.

We didn't have many bills. Our simple house was paid for. We had a van payment of about $500 a month and the kids' tuition of about $700 a month. Our business was going okay—not really well, but not too badly.

In December a realtor friend of mine called and asked if we were still searching for a house farther out in the country. I told him that we had been looking earlier in the year, but due to some new commitments, I wasn't thinking of buying any longer. He said it wasn't going to cost anything to look. He said the owners of a certain house had to move because they couldn't afford to keep it.

The next day my wife and I drove by the house. It was just what we had been hoping for: a two-story house, only a year-and-a-half old, situated nicely in the middle of 30 acres. I told my wife that if the Lord wanted us to have it, He'd work out the details. I made my offer and then a couple of counteroffers, but the owners had too much money in it and declined. So we forgot about it for a month or so. Then we started thinking about that house again, and I made another offer. This time it was accepted. Our bank approved the loan, and we moved in about the first of May.

Before long I began to have some major worries. There was a reason. No sooner had we bought the house than our business took a big dive. I began having thoughts that we might lose the house if we couldn't make the payments of $1,037 a month.

In July our cash flow was so low that I told my wife I was going to stop making weekly payments on our church commitment until our income improved. About a month later I thought, *This is crazy. God should be my priority.*

I started making weekly payments again for the new church, not knowing where the next payment was going to come from. I also started praying that God would help me get out of debt. Almost immediately our business increased, reaching its highest levels ever.

By October we paid off our van, which was about $13,000. Praise the Lord!

We paid our children's tuition without any difficulty. Praise the Lord! In November we paid off our building commitment two years early. Praise the Lord again! In February, nine months after moving, we paid off our new house more than nine years ahead of the mortgage schedule. Another praise the Lord! I never would have believed it. God taught me three important things during this time:

1. You can't outgive the Lord.
2. The Lord can do mighty things in a very short time.
3. You must have faith to step out and honor your commitments to God.

Now, I know that the Lord doesn't always choose to do things this way. But this is my story. I hope and pray that by His grace my faith in Him would be just as great no matter how He led. To God be the glory!

Taste and see that the Lord is good. Psalm 34:8.

Jack Stout owns a satellite television business in Muskogee, Oklahoma. He is a member of the Muskogee Seventh-day Adventist Church.

FRIENDSHIP OVER RICE AND BEANS
By Valerie Hamel Morikone

IT SEEMED like the beginning of an ordinary Sabbath day. We drove the 50 minutes to our small church to arrive early. My husband dropped me off and, as usual, continued on to a church member's house to see if anyone needed a ride.

Alone at the church, I busied myself with various tasks, turned on 3ABN, and was folding the morning's bulletins. I heard the front door open and shut. Since I hadn't heard or seen a car drive past the church windows, I nervously walked to the foyer to see if anyone might be there.

A man wearing a black cowboy hat and a white shirt with blue jeans and cowboy boots stood there.

"May I help you?" I asked cautiously.

"I've come to attend church," he said.

During the service I thought about this visitor, whose name was Howard. Did he need a place to go to for dinner? Would anyone invite him? Maybe we should invite him, but we live so far from the church! Besides, I argued with myself, I don't have anything special prepared to serve to company.

When the service was over, my conscience was a bit relieved to realize that Howard had left. But my husband mentioned that we should have asked him over for dinner. We soon left for home, but at a nearby intersection my husband suddenly asked, "Isn't that the visitor?" He pointed to a vehicle crossing in front of us. Making our turn, we followed and decided it was Howard.

Again my husband mentioned inviting him over for dinner. My thoughts screamed "No," but my heart told me that the Lord was giving me another chance. I quickly said yes. We caught up with Howard, driving alongside his car. My husband began making motions from a pretend plate up to his mouth as if eating, and then pointing to ourselves. Howard began nodding, so we pulled in front for him to follow us home. His car began having trouble, so he parked beside the road and got into the car with us.

Arriving home, I nervously began laying out what I had planned for our simple dinner. Brown rice, black beans, some fresh and cooked vegetables, and home-baked bread. It was nothing special.

Howard gave himself generous helpings and said that his favorite food was beans and rice. What I had been afraid to serve to company was just what this man enjoyed eating. God was wanting me to share even the ordinary, simple things with others.

On the drive back to get his car, Howard told my husband that he had become acquainted with Adventists when he became friends with a man who was a church member. The Adventist friend moved away, so Howard made a trip to visit him in another state. Through this friendship he made the decision to join the church. But when he returned home and attended the local Adventist church, he didn't find the friendship that he craved, so he quit going. He was in our state visiting relatives and decided to attend our church this particular Sabbath.

Was I ever glad, then, that we had extended the hand of hospitality to this stranger, regardless of whether I felt prepared to entertain!

And the Lord said unto him, What is that in thine hand? Exodus 4:2.

Valerie Hamel Morikone is a homemaker in Williamson, West Virginia. She is a member of the Williamson Seventh-day Adventist Church.

A MOTHER'S LESSON
By Nancy Arellano

NO WAY!" I told my husband. We had recently been baptized, and he had just told me that we needed to add tithing to our already-overloaded budget. As a child, he had been taught Christian principles, including the importance of stewardship, by his ever-faithful mother. To please him—and the Lord—I tried for the next six months to return tithe and offerings—*if* I had money left over from our bills. Our financial situation seemed to get worse.

In the meantime an older couple in our church shared their story with us. During the Depression they were forced to make a choice between returning tithe or buying coal to heat their home. Stepping out in faith, they chose to return the Lord's tithe.

Very shortly after their decision a coal train derailed near their home, and the railroad company offered the coal free to anyone who wanted to clean it up. That was the kind of story the Holy Spirit knew would help my hesitant heart. I decided to truly put God first. We would return tithe and offerings first and then pay bills with what was left.

Slowly, over many months, I came to realize that while we didn't have more money, we didn't seem to have less either. Not only that, but our old appliances kept going and going. Our rusty cars kept running without repairs, and our weekly allowances seemed to last.

Several years later, when my husband quit a good-paying job to start his own business, we decided to apply tithing principles to our new company by setting aside a certain percentage of our profits for charitable work. Eventually, through God's blessing, we were able to start a small not-for-profit corporation (funded by our new business) to help young people with educational scholarships as well as to assist low-income families with specific needs.

There were times when our company began that it seemed we couldn't afford to pay our own salaries. But each time we would get a "miracle" sale that would be just enough to keep us going. Fifteen years later we've grown from three employees (my husband, daughter, and I) working out of our home, to more than 140 employees working all across the United States and in several foreign countries.

God has been good to us! He's chosen to let us prosper a little at a time as we've gradually learned to be better stewards. We've come to realize that everything we have is from God and that He cares about all aspects of our lives.

God is in control—just as a mother taught her son many years ago.

As for God, His way is perfect; the word of the Lord is proven; He is a shield to all who trust in Him. 2 Samuel 22:31, NKJV.

––––––––––

Nancy Arellano is a homemaker in Chesterfield, Indiana. She is a member of the Anderson, Indiana, Seventh-day Adventist Church.

THREE TIMES FIRED
By Dennis T. Ranalla

WHEN I was 30 years old, I again gave my heart to Jesus and was rebaptized into the church. I truly wanted to be a partner with God, so careful stewardship of all of God's blessings became very important to me.

About this time God opened up a job for me at a large hospital. When I accepted the job, I made it very clear to my employers that I did not do scheduled cases on Sabbath. They said that was fine. After I had worked for about a month, my supervisor asked me to do some scheduled cases on Sabbath. I said I couldn't do that and reminded him of the agreement.

He asked me to come to his office. We sat down, and he told me a story about a rabbi who disappeared every Sabbath day. No one knew where he went. This happened Sabbath after Sabbath, so one day someone decided to follow him. The rabbi went into the woods where an old woman lived by herself. The rabbi changed into work clothes and cut and stacked wood all day long. At the end of the day he changed his clothes and went his way.

My supervisor asked me what I thought about the rabbi's doing good on the Sabbath day. I told him that was between him and God. He said I would be doing good by working on the Sabbath. I said I felt uncomfortable with that.

"Okay," he said. "You're fired."

The next morning I was called at 6:30 and asked to come to work. At 2:30 in the afternoon I was told, "You're still fired, but come to work tomorrow." I worked that day, and at the end of the day I was told not to come anymore. The next morning I was called at 7:00 and asked to come to work, so I worked that day, and at the end of the day I was told, "You're really fired." The following morning at 6:30 I was again called and asked to come to work.

That afternoon I was invited to be a guest in my supervisor's office. This time he told me he had worked out the schedule so that I wouldn't have to do scheduled cases on Sabbath. I would just have to take call and do emergencies. And I was no longer fired.

I worked at that hospital eight years, and did only emergencies on Sabbath. Our heavenly Father gives and takes positions. That was 22 years ago, and He is still faithful in providing me with work.

I have been young, and now am old; yet have I not seen the righteous forsaken, nor his seed begging bread. Psalm 37:25.

Dennis T. Ranalla is an anesthetist in Dallas, Oregon. He is a member of the Inchelium, Washington, Seventh-day Adventist Church.

REAL NEEDS, GOD'S WORDS
By Matt Fivash

HEAD ELDER! *How do I get myself into these things?*
It started innocently. I had opened my mouth with a few ideas about how to care for our little church. Then the pastor asked if I'd help as an elder. I agreed, but only if the need was real, and I didn't think there was any real need for my services.

And becoming head elder certainly wasn't on my agenda, not after my ministroke. It's been difficult learning to speak again. The words still come slowly. Occasionally the right word waits, it seems, for seconds before my brain permits me to say it. When the words come, they seem to be voiced before I can be certain they are the right ones. Many times I pray that my words make sense to those listening.

In light of this I wondered how I could really help in any meaningful way. But since then I realize I have served our little church as a cook, a speaker, an accountant, a counselor, a musician, and a lot of other things. But I wonder if anyone has found the Christian walk better, or easier, or been drawn closer to God during my watch? Have I been a good steward in God's house?

As a mathematician who sees the world and the Bible from different perspectives, I worry that I've just muddied the waters, that somehow Jesus and His love have been missed. Many times in the small hours of the morning I find I'm thinking about my little church. Did I bungle an opportunity? Did I say the wrong thing? Have I have driven someone away?

I am thankful that God has ways to let me know how I'm doing. Although I can't quite recall the first time a certain couple stopped by our church for a sermon, they've become members. One Sabbath my wife and I asked them to our home for Sabbath dinner. (Isn't this part of the first elder's job?) After lunch I listened to their testimony with numbed surprise. They told of their search for a church home and how those sermons of mine seemed to draw them to our church.

I had to recheck my notes. Did I really speak those words?

I pray that God will give me the courage and the joy to speak and work for Him in whatever way He asks.

Now therefore, go, and I will be with your mouth and teach you what you shall say. Exodus 4:12, NKJV.

Matt Fivash is a statistical researcher for the National Cancer Institute in Frederick, Maryland. He is a member of the Catoctin View Seventh-day Adventist Church in Thurmont, Maryland.

GOD'S ECONOMICS
By Charlotte Groff

YOU CAN'T have more money now than you had last year!" snorted my uncle. "I was a sales manager for 30 years, and I know you can't make less money, give more to the church, and still have more left over—it's just impossible!"

Teaching jobs were scarce that year. The only one available paid $300 less in annual salary than my previous position and involved added transportation costs. With many misgivings, I signed the contract and looked for ways to economize. I had always returned my tithe, but offerings consisted of "wallet-potluck" on Sabbath mornings. Faced with less income, I decided to return a double tithe using the second one for budgeted offerings.

A few weeks into the program, I noticed that something was different. Previously, with the larger salary, I had never been able to save money. Now my bank account grew steadily.

When I mentioned this increase to my unchurched uncle and showed him my bank book, he shook his head in disbelief. "I just don't understand it," he murmured. "Economically it can't happen!" Though a career businessman who understood dollars and cents, he didn't understand that God's economics defy common sense.

During that year, I never missed the cut in salary. As a bonus, the job that looked rather unpromising at first developed into a fine educational position which has lasted more than four decades.

Through the years the tithe has grown, too. In the beginning, it was returned on "take-home pay" only; later, a first tithe was returned on gross income and a second tithe on "take-home pay." Later still, both tithes were returned on gross income. Finally, it has grown to much more than double tithe.

I truthfully can say I have never missed a penny of that money. Returning it is no credit to me. God has done a miracle by stretching the remaining funds far more than I could ever ask or think.

Moses' promises to Israel are still being fulfilled to us today.

The Lord shall open unto thee his good treasure, the heaven to give the rain unto thy land in his season, and to bless all the work of thine hand: and thou shalt lend unto many nations, and thou shalt not borrow. Deuteronomy 28:12.

Charlotte Groff is a reading specialist for Coloma, Michigan, Community Schools. She is a member of Pioneer Memorial Church in Berrien Springs, Michigan.

WILLING SPIRIT, EMPTY TANK, FAITHFUL GOD
By Ann Morrow

THE evangelistic series begins in Marion next week. Would you be willing to sing?" An anxious-to-serve newlywed, I impulsively agreed, forgetting that my agreement also committed my new husband and our old blue Ford.

So for the next six weeks we traveled 60 round-trip miles six days a week on the tiny budget of two university students. We loved the Lord and expected Him to provide whatever we needed to fulfill this commitment.

The first three weeks flew past uneventfully, but by the fourth week we were down to $1.40 between us. Sunday as we prepared to go to the meeting, the gas gauge pointed toward "E."

Every time the car sputtered and stopped, I tightened my eyelids and silently prayed harder. Pushed by feelings of anxiety and guilt, I placed a hand on Lester's arm. "Honey, maybe we should phone and tell them we can't get there tonight—God knows we tried."

"Ann, why don't we give it one more try, before phoning?" He took my hands into his large ones and said a brief prayer.

"Please, Father, help us."

Thirty minutes later we rolled to a stop in front of the Marion Theater. The words "End-Time Prophecies" spelled out in lights illuminated the darkness. We made it on time, but we still needed to get home.

"Honey, I don't know how He'll do it." Lester locked the car door and took my arm.

"But God does," I said. We laughed and went inside.

The meeting went by quickly. A number of people came forward for Bible study and baptism. As we left the theater, that old foe anxiety made another attack. This time I ignored him. The car started up with a purr, and I settled back, waiting on the Lord.

Less than five minutes later Lester pulled into a gas station and told the attendant, "Fill-it-up." At my surprised expression he laughed.

"God came through again. Just before you got up to sing for the first time, Ross our church brother and friend, slipped this into my hand and said, 'God told me you might need this.'"

Lester pulled from his coat pocket an envelope containing five ten-dollar bills.

You of little faith, why are you talking among yourselves about having no bread? Do you still not understand? Don't you remember the five loaves for the

five thousand, and how many basketfuls you gathered? Or the seven loaves for the four thousand, and how many basketfuls you gathered? Matthew 16:8-10, NIV.

Ann Morrow is a teacher and freelance writer in Columbus, Ohio. She is a member of the Ephesus Seventh-day Adventist Church in Columbus.

A WEEK'S PAY AND A HOUSE OF FURNITURE
By Stanley S. and Bennie Beth Will

WE WERE married in June 1944, and I began almost immediately pastoring the Charleston, South Carolina, Adventist Church. Pastoral pay was $27 a week, and Bennie Beth wasn't getting paid for her full-time work as a pastor's wife.

When the annual Week of Sacrifice arrived that fall, we wrestled with the suggestion that each family give a week of salary to this offering. We had no reserve to speak of except a $100 gift that Bennie Beth's parents had given us as a wedding present, another $100 given us by the Charleston Church, and a very small amount in the bank that we had been able to save. We had only a few pieces of furniture: an old icebox, a bed, a table and a few chairs, a desk and some books.

Before the Week of Sacrifice offering we discussed our gift and what it would mean to us. Our tithe for the month would be $12; the sacrifice offering came to an additional $27. With Sabbath school-church expense offerings added, the total came to $60. We would be left with about $40 to pay the rent, food, gasoline, and utilities for the rest of the month. We wondered whether we could do it.

But we made up our minds and wrote a check for $60, turning it in on the Week of Sacrifice Sabbath. We had decided to trust God and His promises.

The next Monday Stan walked to the grocery store to buy a loaf of bread. While there he overheard a conversation between a serviceman's wife and the clerk.

"Do you know anyone who might buy some furniture?" she asked him. "We have to move."

Stan spoke with the woman, asked about the furniture and the approximate asking price, and received the street address. That morning we drove to her home. She had furniture for three bedrooms, a living room (including a piano), and kitchen appliances. We bought all of the furniture for $300. We kept what we needed (about $100) and sold the rest.

God honored the faith of a young couple in ministry, and He made arrangements for some much-needed furniture. That experience confirmed our belief in the promises of God. It has helped us through 52 years to return a full, honest tithe and to be generous in giving.

A generous man will prosper; he who refreshes others will himself be refreshed. Proverbs 11:25, NIV.

Stanley S. and Bennie Beth Will are retired in Naples, North Carolina. They are members of the Arden, North Carolina, Seventh-day Adventist Church.

KEEPING MY PROMISE
By Diane Gordon

I HADN'T bought groceries for some time. Now the cupboards were almost bare, and I knew I had to find some money somewhere to buy a few essentials. In 1985, things on our Alberta farm were very tight. We managed to pay our bills, but it wasn't easy. I planted a big garden, did a lot of mending and sewing, and always checked the secondhand stores before buying new clothes. Despite my best efforts, things seemed to be getting worse and worse.

A few years earlier I had renewed my commitment to the Lord after leaving the church for nearly fifteen years. My non-Adventist husband did not understand my new lifestyle and values. When I refused to help in extra farm chores on the Sabbath, he would shrug his shoulders and say he hoped that this was a passing fad.

Tithing was a problem. To avoid conflict, I had resolved to give to the church 100 percent of my monthly government family allowance check, as this was my money to spend as I wished. But in this crisis, when I found the latest family allowance check in the bundle of mail, I didn't know what to do. Yes, I had promised God to return all of this check to the church, but if I did, I wouldn't have money to buy groceries. And there was no promise of other money in the immediate future, either.

I struggled all morning unable to make a decision. Finally, at noon I endorsed the check and sealed it in a tithe envelope for offering on Sabbath morning. I would keep my promise to God regardless of our needs. I then took my three children in the car and drove to town. I had arranged for a small, personal accounting job to work on for the next few weeks. This would give me some money in a month or so.

When I picked up the set of books, the lady insisted that she prepay me for the job! Never before or in the years since have I been paid in advance for an accounting job. But this time, when I really needed the money, God honored my commitment to Him and provided me with grocery money in a way I never would have guessed.

For with God nothing shall be impossible. Luke 1:37.

Diane Gordon is a bookkeeper in Killam, Alberta. She is a member of the Sedgewick, Alberta, Seventh-day Adventist Church.

LAST DOOR, FIRST CONTACT
By Thomas J. Mostert, Jr.

IT WAS a typical hot, humid, summer Sabbath afternoon in Florida—a very good day to stay inside and keep cool. But during the church service that morning a leader had asked for volunteers to distribute Bible-course enrollment cards to an assigned territory that afternoon. My teenage heart had been touched with a helpful spirit, and I raised my hand. But now my interest in things evangelistic had wilted with the rising temperature. I regretted my decision, but I kept my promise and joined the group for a miserably hot afternoon of missionary work.

We were instructed to ring the doorbell of every house in our assigned area and try to talk to as many people as possible. If no one answered the bell, we were to leave the enrollment card in the door. In clear and ominous tones we were told, "Whatever you do, don't skip a house, because you never know who might be waiting for your visit."

The organizers dropped me off by myself to cover a six-block territory. By the sixth block I was a very hot and tired teenager, dying for a cool drink. I had dutifully contacted every house except this last one—a garage apartment at the end of a long, coarse-gravel driveway. It didn't look as if anyone was home. The curtains were drawn, and there was no sign of anyone in the yard.

"I'll just skip it," I said to myself. "It's not worth the trouble. The leaders are probably waiting to pick me up anyway. I shouldn't keep them waiting. But—what if someone is in that house waiting for what I have to offer?"

Wearily I trudged up the long driveway and up the steep stairs. I knocked timidly on the door, hoping no one would answer. As I turned to leave, the door opened.

Three months later, at a baptism, the congregation heard the story of a woman who had been praying for God to send her someone who could help turn her life around. I stood proudly to acknowledge that I had made the first contact.

"Well done, my good servant!" his master replied, "Because you have been trustworthy in a very small matter, take charge of ten cities." Luke 19:17, NIV.

Thomas J. Mostert, Jr. is president of the Pacific Union Conference of Seventh-day Adventists in Westlake Village, California. He is a member of the Thousand Oaks, California, Seventh-day Adventist Church.

The FOURTH MEETING

Come and hear, all ye that fear God, and I will declare what he hath done for my soul.

Psalm 66:16

Randall Murphy

Edwin C. Beck

Larry Owens

John Moyer

EuGene Lewis

Olla Gillham

Frank Barton

Victor Chant

Blanche Yates

Douglas L. Inglish

HE KNOWS MY SHOE SIZE
By Randall Murphy

I WAS teaching church school on the eastern shore of Maryland in the 1960s. My wife, Marty, and I, with our two small boys were trying our best to live on one income, because we thought it best that the boys be at home with Marty. Money was tight, but we had also committed ourselves to be faithful with tithe and as generous as possible with offerings.

I was asked by our pastor to preach the religious liberty sermon in the Forest Grove Church, near Dover, Delaware. During the appeal, at the end of the sermon, I pledged $10 to purchase Religious Liberty Bonds and encouraged others to match or to do what they could for the cause.

Marty's head snapped up when I announced "our" pledge. She pointed to my shoes, and I clearly understood her message. The only $10 we had available was the money we had been saving for two months to buy me a much-needed pair of dress shoes. I nodded my understanding, and she later said we would just start saving all over again and that I would need to keep putting new cardboard in my shoes until we could afford new ones. We never mentioned our plight to anyone.

The next week one of my eighth-grade students came to school early with a big sack in hand. "Mr. Murphy, what size shoes do you wear?"

"I wear 9½ D. Why?"

"Mom went to a shoe sale and bought me some shoes, but my feet have grown, and I can't wear them. No one in our house can wear them. Mom wondered if you would be offended if we gave them to you. She said that if you couldn't wear them, I was to give them away to someone who could wear them. I'm glad they are your size, because Mom got them at a sale and can't take them back."

I looked into the sack and found a brown pair of wing tips and a black pair of slip-ons, size 9½ D. The styles fit me perfectly, and so did the shoes.

"Why Eddie, I would be glad to have them. Please thank your mother for shopping for me. How much do I owe her?"

"I don't think she'll take any money."

I tried my best to convince Mrs. Urie to let me pay for the shoes (where I would get the money was another issue), but she and Don would have nothing to do with my paying. Several months later I told them of our pledging the shoe money for religious liberty and how God had used them to supply doubly my dream of a much-needed new pair of shoes.

But my God shall supply all your need according to his riches in glory by Christ Jesus. Philippians 4:19.

54

Randall Murphy is president of the Mountain View Conference of Seventh-day Adventists, in Parkersburg, West Virginia. He is a member of the Parkersburg Seventh-day Adventist Church.

GOD'S PLAN IS ALWAYS BEST
By Edwin C. Beck

WHEN I WAS called to be a conference president, I tried to do my homework. Before accepting the position, I asked the union president to assess the challenges for that conference. There were two main challenges, he said: One was the need for a strong evangelistic outreach, and the other was to solve the education problems. Maintaining the academies—especially the boarding academies—was draining too much of the conference financial resources.

I accepted the challenges and began my work. Within a year the education department outlined to the conference constituency meeting what the schools needed for both operation and capital. It was clear that the conference didn't have sufficient money to meet these needs. Constituency-meeting delegates, lay advisory members, and believers around the conference were asked to make this a matter of earnest prayer.

Although the matter had been studied for the past fifteen years, the session again appointed new study groups. Their report found that the conference was supporting two boarding academies that were each half-utilized; either one by itself was large enough to accommodate all the boarding students in the conference. After considerable prayer and another two years of study, delegates voted to close one boarding academy.

The decision didn't go over well with some constituents. Closing an academy is never a popular chore, and no one is anxious to do it, for these institutions have very loyal supporters in former students, parents, and community people. However, at a second special constituency meeting, delegates again overwhelmingly voted that one academy must be closed and chose to close the one nearest to a day academy. After all the study and all the prayer, we could only accept that the decision was the Lord's leading. It was my job to carry out that decision. However, constituents who owned houses and lived near the closed academy were understandably very upset. And, quite naturally, the blame fell upon me as conference president.

At the next regular conference session the delegates felt that, although what had been done was needed, the conference needed a new leader to heal the wounds caused by the academy closure. I found myself hurt and without a job, feeling let down and betrayed. Still, I chose to believe that God had not forsaken me.

A few months after the shock I received a call from the General Conference to be church-growth coordinator for the Far Eastern Division. My wife and I had returned from mission service nineteen years before, and we now eagerly accepted the invitation to return and take up responsibilities in the new region.

The work of training pastors and lay elders for church nurture and growth was the most rewarding of my entire ministry. Leading pastors and church elders to effective outreach ministry in evangelistic meetings, and seeing thousands of souls accepting Christ was just the experience I needed.

The academy whose closure had caused so much pain to so many people has become, with the loyal support of its constituency, a self-supporting school. It is proving to be a blessing to a large number of young people.

God does bring tremendous blessings when we follow His leading, even if it seems too painful and difficult to do.

Trust in the Lord with all your heart, and do not rely on your own insight. In all your ways acknowledge him, and he will make straight your paths. Proverbs 3:5, 6, NRSV.

Edwin C. Beck is a retired pastor and administrator in Mesa, Arizona. He is a member of the East Mesa Seventh-day Adventist Church.

THE END OF "FUN" AND THE BEGINNING OF FAITHFULNESS
By Larry Owens

THE first time I tried to be independent, I moved out on my own and got an apartment with a friend. Everything was great for a while. Fun, fun, fun. That is, until the bills started piling up. They were hard to deal with. I was always shuffling to pay this one now and putting off that one for later. It got to be a headache.

I went home to visit Mom and Frank. They challenged me to move back home, get another job, and set my feet back on the ground again.

"Okay," I said. "I'll do it if I can find a job tomorrow." The next day I gave it a good shot. By noon God gave me a job at Empire Pipe & Supply in Trusville.

So I started over, back at home. This turned out to be the best thing for me. My family helped me with a budget. I had never used one, so it was tough. The number-one item on the list was tithe. As a kid, I had known about tithing but never seriously practiced it. Tithe was always later, some, or not at all. Now, starting over, I learned that the right way to set up a budget is to put God first. That principle was planted very well—so well that in my marriage to Becky it was the way our budget was set up from the start.

One time we got into some financial problems. A check bounced; that started a few others doing the same. It looked bad. So we sat down to figure out what to do. Becky suggested holding tithe over to the next week so we could cover a few more bills and hopefully catch up. It could work. But I shared with her that "it's not ours to hold till later, and there has to be a better way."

We decided to return our tithe on schedule. We called up some of the creditors and explained that we were going to be late with their money. That wasn't easy. But God helped us.

That week we received a letter from our car insurance company. Oh no! Another problem, we thought. But inside was a check repaying us for an overcharge. Who ever heard of such a thing?

After returning tithe on that insurance check, we still were able to cover our needs for that week, and we learned a lesson we will never forget.

For to this end also did I write, that I might know the proof of you, whether ye be obedient in all things. 2 Corinthians 2:9.

Larry Owens is a production manager for Keebler Bakery in Cleveland, Tennessee. He is a member of the Bowman Hills Seventh-day Adventist Church in Cleveland.

BETWEEN FAITH AND DESPAIR
By John Moyer

AT THIRTY-SIX years old, I found the prospect of attending college intimidating. It had been eighteen years since I had graduated from high school. Our family had grown to include five healthy, active boys. We had very little money but a strong belief that God was calling us into the ministry.

We followed the example of Moses for a while, reminding God of how big the problems were and how little we had to contribute to the project. However, doors started to open that only reinforced the call for us to step out in faith and to walk as far as we could see His leading. The staff at Southern Missionary College (now Southern Adventist University) were most supportive, encouraging us that if God was leading us in this direction, He surely would provide for our needs.

Several weeks before classes started, we moved into college housing, and I found a job. Soon I received a letter from the school reminding me that a $1,000 registration fee had to be paid before I could start classes. In addition to that, four of our boys would need to be enrolled in school (three in elementary and one in academy). It didn't take a CPA to figure out that my paycheck was not going to cover all of this amount.

For the next two weeks I alternated between faith and despair. I was sure that God was leading, but I couldn't see how He could accomplish this task. A well-meaning friend suggested that I borrow the money, but after praying about this possibility, I didn't feel right about doing it. As the deadline approached, my anxiety level increased. My wife kept reminding me that we were following God's leading while doing everything that we could, and that we could trust Him to provide whatever we needed.

Just a few days before the money was due, a letter came from a friend back home. The line I will always remember was "God has impressed me that you needed this."

In the four years that we were in college, I experienced the same test and God's faithfulness many times. And when graduation day came, we were able to leave school with no debts and a greater trust in God's leading and ability to provide.

Trust in the Lord with all thine heart; and lean not unto thine own understanding. In all thy ways acknowledge him, and he shall direct thy paths. Proverbs 3:5, 6.

John Moyer is secretary of the Oklahoma Conference of Seventh-day Adventists in Oklahoma City, Oklahoma. He is a member of the Central Seventh-day Adventist Church in Oklahoma City.

THREE PLEAS, ONE ANSWER
By EuGene Lewis

IN THE SUMMER of 1986 I moved my family to Huntsville, Alabama, so that I could take the ministerial course at Oakwood College. I felt I had been called by God to begin this new career.

The move and educational expenses depleted our financial resources. However, we managed to be faithful to God in our tithe and offerings. The importance of being faithful became a reality to me on December 23, 1986.

Early that morning my youngest son, who was two at the time, asked, "Dad, where are the presents that are supposed to be under the Christmas tree?"

His big brown eyes and tender voice broke my heart. After returning our tithe and offering, we had no money left to buy presents. In fact, I was even short $200 on the rent. What was I to do? I didn't know how to tell a two-year-old there wouldn't be any presents at Christmas. My heart ached.

At the time I was working as the associate pastor of the College Church. I locked myself in the church sanctuary and prayed as I had never prayed before. I pleaded with God about three specific things: (1) My call to the ministry was embarrassing me before my family. Why? (2) I needed $600 to cover our rent and Christmas expenses. (3) I would continue to serve Him even if He didn't grant my request, but He had to give me the strength to face my family.

After praying I went about my church duties, but throughout the day I looked for God to answer my prayer. When He hadn't answered my prayer by 8 p.m., I stopped looking. I gave up.

Just then Elder Ward, the senior pastor, stopped by my office and asked me to attend the Christmas party being held in the church cafeteria. I didn't feel like going, and I told him so. He asked me to stop by and see him in his office before I went home.

As promised, at 10 p.m. I went to see Elder Ward. We chatted about church events for awhile. Then he thanked me for my service, and handed me an envelope. I took the envelope, placed it inside my coat pocket, and forgot all about it. The cloud that had hung over my head since morning had gotten heavier. I felt defeated. It was time to face my family, and I would do so empty-handed.

As I got into my car a voice out of nowhere spoke to me: "EuGene, the envelope! The envelope! Open up the envelope!" I opened it, and to my surprise I found $600. God had arranged for the exact amount I had prayed for that morning. He had chosen to bless me in spite of my failure of faith.

Then you will call upon me and come and pray to me, and I will hear you. Jeremiah 29:12, RSV.

EuGene Lewis is senior pastor of Emerald City Community Seventh-day Adventist Church in Seattle, Washington.

....

PRAYER, PATIENCE, AND PERSEVERANCE
By Olla Gillham

IT WAS A wonderful day. As Raymond, Jennifer, and Helen stepped into the baptismal tank, I couldn't stop my tears. My mind raced over the seven years that I had known Raymond. How I remembered the many scenes in the battle that had raged over his soul.

It seemed only yesterday that my quiet night had been disrupted by the shrill ringing of the telephone at a time that I usually don't receive calls. I hoped it was Raymond calling to give a glowing report of the new start he had made for God in Oklahoma as he had promised just a few days earlier.

It was Raymond, all right. He was making his one allotted call from the jail in Altus. Almost methodically I answered his questions. Yes, I would notify his family in Tulia. Of course, I would write. I assured him that I would keep him continually before the Lord in prayer and that I would visit him just as soon as arrangements could be made.

How could this happen after all the prayers and effort that had been spent working for Raymond's salvation? My heart sank, and I acknowledged that only the power of the Holy Spirit could salvage this soul that had become so precious to our little group of believers. We had hoped that he and his family would become the firstfruits of our efforts in Tulia.

"Why?" I asked the Lord. After all, we had studied with Raymond and his wife, had helped them remodel a small frame house so that their family could find independence, and had been joyful as they worshiped with us almost every Sabbath for a year. Things had seemed to be going well, and they had even requested baptism. We had looked forward with eager anticipation to that day.

But the home had broken up. Raymond had returned to drink and drugs. I wondered why God would let this precious family slip away so quickly after all our prayers and effort. Raymond was in jail.

Our little group continued to pray. I continued to correspond as I had promised. Our hopes revived as I received letters from him expressing his love for God and the Adventist message. Soon he was working with others in the jail, and they were writing and asking questions about God. Again we hoped that as soon as he was released, he would turn his life completely over to God and be baptized.

When Raymond was released, we were saddened as he returned to his old ways. It seemed that he was making a studied effort to ignore us. I continued to search for occasions to speak a friendly word and to remind him of God's love.

On his 30th birthday, Raymond and his new friend, Jennifer, came to church. He expressed his need of God's help in overcoming his problems. From that day on, Raymond and Jennifer faithfully attended services. He finally did leave his old life behind, and he says, "God healed me!" He and Jennifer were married.

And now Raymond, Jennifer, and Helen, Jennifer's sister, were being baptized. What else could I do but cry tears of joy? And as if that weren't enough, the same day Raymond and Jennifer also dedicated their infant son to God.

Cast thy bread upon the waters: for thou shalt find it after many days. Ecclesiastes 11:1.

Olla Gillham is retired from teaching in Adventist schools. She lives in Tulia, Texas, and is a member of the Tulia Seventh-day Adventist company.

STARING OVER AND DOING IT RIGHT
By Frank Barton

MY WIFE and I both came out of bad first marriages. I was a Catholic, and she was in the Assembly of God. We both had had unpleasant experiences with churches. We didn't know where to turn, but we decided to try to find Bible truth and not just accept whatever somebody was preaching.

When we got married and started thinking about attending a church, my wife said to me, "Would you mind returning tithe on my paycheck? You can do what you want with yours." I told her that we had made a commitment to serve the Lord in our marriage, so even though I didn't have enough money to pay the past month's rent, we were going to tithe on both of our salaries.

The Lord soon led us to the Adventist Church. He has blessed us for our commitment to follow Bible truth and to use the opportunities that He places before all of us to have a part of His ministry through our tithe, offerings, and time.

On many occasions we were thrilled to hear of opportunities and needs in other parts of the world to advance the Lord's work. We felt impressed to give money without calculating the consequences on our own lives. But it seemed that no matter how much we committed to these various projects, we were never without our own needs being met.

Even though we were starting a new life in middle age with five children to support, no home, and many bills, the Lord continued to bless us so much that in twelve years we were able to buy ten acres, a home, and vehicles, and to have them all paid off. I was able to retire at 55 and volunteer full time to building a prison-ministry program in the Florida Conference. In eleven years the Lord has made it grow to 500 volunteers working throughout the conference and affecting about 80 institutions.

In 23 years of marriage, we have never missed paying a bill on time. The Lord has continued to bless us to such an extent that we have lived completely debt-free for about twelve years.

Seek ye first the kingdom of God, and his righteousness; and all these things shall be added unto you. Matthew 6:33.

Frank Barton is the coordinator for Florida Prison Ministries with the Florida Conference of Seventh-day Adventists. He lives in Leesburg, Florida, and is a member of the Lady Lake, Florida, Seventh-day Adventist Church.

"WHAT DO YOU THINK YOU ARE DOING . . .?"
By Victor Chant

IN 1975 the Zambian government announced that a period of military training would be required of all high school graduates at the close of that school year. As we approached the time, students sought out several of us faculty members, asking how they should practice their faith in a military camp. The Seventh-day Adventist Church had already appealed to the government for consideration on two issues—the Sabbath and bearing of arms. The answer that came back was unequivocal: church leaders ought to mind their own business and not interfere, or churches would be closed throughout the country.

Teachers and administrators were in a quandary about how to advise the students. We searched the Bible and the Spirit of Prophecy with much prayer, looking for answers to this crisis. When pressed, I began advising students that they would probably have to break the Sabbath and just do what they were forced to do during the months of training. It was the coward's way, but first and foremost I wanted to help save the church in Zambia and keep the young people from hardship.

While we were prayerfully considering all of this, a visitor from the General Conference arrived on campus. A special meeting was called for the staff to meet the visitor. As I sat there in the back corner of the staff room, listening to the presentation, a clear, distinct voice spoke to me: "What do you think you are doing, telling the students to break the Sabbath?"

My cowardly position passed before me, and I saw what I was doing. How could I represent Jesus if I wasn't willing to suffer for Him? I walked out of the staff room that day ready to face prison, deportation, or whatever came my way. I knew that I would speak boldly and encourage the students to keep the Sabbath, no matter what might happen.

I had walked only a few yards when a couple of students approached me to talk about their military training and what they should do about the Sabbath and their belief in God. I shared the message I had heard and encouraged them to stand for truth and to be willing to suffer whatever might happen to them.

As time passed and our students were taken to military camps, nothing happened to me, even though my name was sent to the government as a security risk because of my witness to the students. I never was deported, nor did I face any hardship. The miracles and triumphs experienced by the students in the camps they were sent to over the ensuing years bear testimony to the power of God to deliver and triumph with His truth. Only eternity will reveal the victories of those students and others who saw God at work in their lives.

Not that I have already obtained this or have already reached the goal; but I press on to make it my own, because Christ Jesus has made me his own. Beloved, I do not consider that I have made it my own; but this one thing I do: forgetting what lies behind and straining forward to what lies ahead, I press on toward the goal for the prize of the heavenly call of God in Christ Jesus. Philippians 3:12-14, NRSV.

Victor Chant is a teacher and counselor at Fraser Valley Adventist Academy in Aldergrove, British Columbia. He is a member of the Abbotsford, British Columbia, Seventh-day Adventist Church.

ABANDONING MYSELF TO GOD
By Blanche Yates

I'M SORRY, but we can't use you," the store manager said as he shook his head. "Everyone here works every other weekend—no exceptions."

Putting on my bravest smile, I thanked him and headed for the exit. I'd been beating the pavement looking for a job for several weeks. It seemed that I'd tried every business within a 50-mile radius of home. Either they didn't need help or they worked on Sabbath. The constant rejection was hard for a nineteen-year-old to take.

As I got into the car, I looked at my watch and realized that it was close enough to Sabbath that I'd better head for home. I had no more money for gas. The only money in my wallet was the $30 I'd set aside for tithe and offering. I pondered as I drove home if it wouldn't be wiser to use some of that for gas. Perhaps I could use the offering and not the tithe.

I'd been praying for work, and I'd been persistently looking. But without gas money I couldn't even continue to job-hunt. I felt burdened and unsettled. All of my life I'd returned tithe and offering. It was a "given." But now, for the first time, I faced a strong temptation to borrow some of it.

The struggle continued. But as I arrived at church on Sabbath morning, I made up my mind. I quickly filled out a tithe envelope and sealed it. A special peace settled over me as I dropped it into the offering plate in church. The burden was lifted. For the first time I felt the sweet joy of abandoning myself to God. I sang as I drove home from church.

About an hour after Sabbath lunch the phone rang. I recognized the voice of the last store manager I'd talked to on Friday. He talked excitedly. "I just realized that you said you'd be willing to work every Sunday if you could have Friday nights and Saturdays off. Is that true?"

"Yes, that's true."

"Could you start tomorrow morning at nine?"

I had to choke back tears.

"I'll be there."

Bring ye all the tithes into the storehouse, . . . and prove me now . . . , if I will not open you the windows of heaven. Malachi 3:10.

Blanche Yates works at Eden Valley Institute in Loveland, Colorado. She is a member of the Eden Valley Seventh-day Adventist Church.

JACKHAMMER FAITH
By Douglas L. Inglish

THE SUMMER before I began graduate studies at the University of Arkansas, money was tight. By the time I finished a teaching contract on June 15, no summer jobs were available and my graduate-fellowship money would not become available until classes began in late August. Our meager savings were eaten up by moving costs. Susan my wife could not find a job, and the only work I could find was at a temporary employment agency. Every morning I would call at six o'clock, and if they had work for me that day, they called back. I was fortunate when I got two or three days of work a week.

One evening Susan showed me that our checkbook balance came to $12 and some cents. We had little food in the apartment, rent was due the following week, and after that would come the utility bills. It was clear that something had to happen now, or we would not last until school started.

That night when I said my prayers, I kept them shorter than usual. "Father, I'm in this place because I heard You call me to graduate school. We have no more money. I have been faithful with my tithe, and You promised You would take care of me. It's time for You to keep Your Word."

The next morning I didn't call the agency. They called me, at 5:55 a.m. "Doug, we have a job for you. It's twelve hours a day, seven days a week, which means plenty of time-and-a-half pay. It lasts all the way until school starts for you in the fall, and you start as soon as you can get here and pick up your time card. Do you want it?"

It was Tuesday, and I figured I could get in four solid twelve-hour days before they fired me for not working on Sabbath. "You bet!" I fairly shouted, racing out to my VW Bug almost before I hung up the phone.

The work was miserable. I broke up concrete all day with a jackhammer. The only respite from that bone-jarring work came when I had to push a wheelbarrow full of rubble onto a truck. At the end of the first day they fired one of the temporary workers for not hustling on the job, perhaps to make a statement to the rest of us. So I really put my back into it, hoping to last even to Sabbath.

Friday, after I clocked out, I went to the foreman. "Sir," I began with what I hoped was a tone of conviction, "I am a Seventh-day Adventist, and tomorrow is the Sabbath. I won't be here to work, but I need this job. Will I still have it on Sunday?"

He cocked his head to one side and said, "The job's for seven days a week." When he said nothing more, I pressed the issue. "Can I come back Sunday?" He shook his head and said, "I don't know."

With no more assurance than that, I kept the Sabbath. When I clocked in Sunday morning, the foreman said nothing. After another painful week with the jackhammer, I approached him again on Friday.

"I am keeping the Sabbath again tomorrow. Will my job still be here for me Sunday?"

He gave me the same quizzical look he had the week before and then said, "If this is going to be the way it is every week, I'm not sure we can use you."

With nothing to lose, I again asked, "Will you take me on Sunday?" Again, his noncommittal "I don't know" ended our discussion.

Every Friday I told the foreman I would not be in on the Sabbath, asking to be back Sunday. He never gave me any more assurance of work than a simple "I don't know," but he never fired me when I returned on Sunday morning.

As it turned out, my arthritic knee couldn't keep up the pace all the way until school started, and I had to quit. But by the time it gave out, Susan was working, and my overtime pay was enough to carry us to the start of graduate studies.

Knowing such a God who answers so suddenly in time of need and sustains so faithfully when we have no other assurance, how could we deny His claims on our time or finances?

I know the blessing of tithing, and I know the blessing of the Sabbath. I commend them to anyone willing to receive them.

Them that honour me I will honour. 1 Samuel 2:30.

Douglas L. Inglish is pastor of the Muskegon, Michigan, Seventh-day Adventist Church.

You have a stewardship testimony you need to share and we need to read. See page 224 for details.

The FIFTH MEETING

Come and hear, all ye that fear God, and I will declare what he hath done for my soul.

Psalm 66:16

A. Monise Hamilton

Rick Dahlberg

Lee-Roy Chacon

Viki Blanks

Denzle Harrison

Marcia H. Singleton

Joan Manzella

Jeanette S. Baldwin

Raj Attiken

Curtis Thurber

JUST SAY "NO"
By A. Monise Hamilton

IN RETROSPECT, I guess it did seem like a ridiculous idea. How could I, a nonworking, full-time student and single mother, even wish to attend the track-and-field event at the 1996 Olympic Games in Atlanta, Georgia? But then, in retrospect, it wasn't the first time I had believed in something that was deemed ridiculous. After all, I had recently moved to Berrien Springs, Michigan, to enter the seminary at Andrews University, only eight months after being baptized as a Seventh-day Adventist.

My dream-come-true, all-expense-paid trip began on Friday, July 26. That night, standing on a street corner in Atlanta, surrounded by thousands of equally excited people from all over the world, I recounted to myself the miracle that had occurred.

When the Olympic Games had begun a few days earlier, I still had no idea how—or if—God would answer my prayer. On Tuesday my sister had called to say that she was going to Atlanta with her employer for a business venture in connection with the Olympics.

"Do you think your sister would like to go with us?" he had asked her out of the blue. By Friday I was on my way.

My uncontainable excitement made it difficult to choose from the dizzying array of exciting things to do that first night. My niece and her friend, who had arrived a week earlier, suggested we go to Centennial Park. Packed with a great variety of entertainment attractions, Centennial Park was the "hot spot" of Olympic tourism. "There'll be a lot to do there on a Friday night," she said. "Wanna go?"

Friday night? Did she just say *Friday night!*" In all of my excitement I had forgotten it was the Sabbath.

And that's when the battle began. *I could still go,* I reasoned. *I'd be only walking around. How is that not keeping the Sabbath holy? Plus, I may never have this opportunity again! God couldn't possibly expect me to miss out on all the fun, when I'll be here for only four days. As the lone Sabbathkeeper in my group, what am I supposed to do while they're out having fun? Certainly God will understand. After all, He's the one who blessed me with this trip.*

My mind was made up. Standing just two blocks from the park, I could hear the concert music and could see the lights from a laser-light show. I couldn't resist any longer. I was going to Centennial Park.

"So, do you wanna go?" my niece asked again.

"No," I answered.

"No?"

Did I just hear "no" come out of my own mouth? Shocked by my answer, I realized that in my weakness God had "set a guard over my mouth" and had spoken for me. I didn't understand His interference. But I told my niece and her friend that Centennial Park would have to wait until Saturday night. They decided to visit an attraction on the outskirts of Atlanta. Disappointed and irritated, but now convicted to do what I knew was right, I walked back to the hotel and spent the evening alone.

A little more than four hours after my sudden change of plans, a bomb went off in Centennial Park, killing a woman who was attending a concert and injuring dozens of others. The force of the explosion was so strong that I felt and heard it three blocks away in my hotel room.

In the aftermath of the panicked chaos and terror of being evacuated from downtown Atlanta, I understood God's interference.

See, I am setting before you today a blessing and a curse—the blessing if you obey the commands of the Lord your God that I am giving you today; the curse if you disobey the commands of the Lord your God and turn from the way that I command you today by following other gods, which you have not known. Deuteronomy 11:26-28, NIV.

A. Monise Hamilton is assistant director of university relations at Andrews University in Berrien Springs, Michigan. She is a member of the Highland Avenue Seventh-day Adventist Church in Benton Harbor, Michigan.

"OKAY, LORD! HERE IT GOES"
By Rick Dahlberg

AFTER straying far from God's church, I had stopped returning tithe regularly if at all. But now I had a new commitment to the Lord and a new job. The job paid just $6 per hour, and with an expensive new car, rent, food, and other living expenses, it seemed that it would be only a matter of time before I would have nothing left.

But the Spirit began urging me to start tithing again.

It seemed impossible. How could I do it? Still, I knew it was the right thing, so I said, "Okay, Lord! Here it goes, into the offering plate."

Sure enough, six months later I had nothing left to make the car payment at the end of the month. "Lord, what am I going to do?" I prayed. "I don't have enough! You're going to have to do something!"

That next Friday was a payday, and in my check I received an additional $320—just enough to cover my car payment! I went to the boss to ask if he had overpaid me.

"No," he said. "We're very pleased with your work, so we have decided to give you a raise."

Two years later I felt convicted to return tithe on my gross income as opposed to tithing only the net. Again, I wondered how I could do this, for I was still barely making the ends meet as it was. This would mean less spending money, or none at all. Things were really going to be tight, I thought. But in Malachi 3:10, God promised He would bless me. Again I said, "Okay, Lord! Here it goes, into the offering plate!"

Within a year I had earned nearly $30,000. The next year, nearly $40,000. I paid all my debts and had money to spend. Isn't God good?

Taste and see that the Lord is good; blessed is the man who takes refuge in him. Psalm 34:8.

Rick Dahlberg is pastor of the Sherbrooke, South Stukely, and Waterville Seventh-day Adventist churches in Québec, Canada.

....

RAW VEGETABLES
By Lee-Roy Chacon

MY ALLERGIES were out of control, my body was itching all over, and I was suffering frequent asthma attacks. I was able to sleep only two or three hours a night, had no energy, had constant headaches, and was not able to concentrate. I had difficulty with bowel functions and would get sick often.

A physician put me on allergy shots for about three to four months. The shots helped with my allergies, but the itching continued, as did my sleeplessness. Another doctor tested different antibiotics on me. Nothing seemed to help. I was desperate. A psychiatrist told me that my load was too much and that I was depressed. I was willing to do whatever it took to get well.

Eventually I was referred to a doctor who practiced 300 miles away from my hometown. He ran different tests, and his final analysis was that I had become allergic to different foods. My body was now reacting to corn, dairy products, grains, soy sauce, mushrooms, peanuts, and legumes. Whenever I ate an apple or pear, I had a hard time breathing, for I was allergic to the pesticide that is used on fruit. I was allergic to cats, dogs, pollen, tumbleweeds, and dust, which was not good, since I live in Texas. The doctor said that my immune system was very weak.

"When your immune system is weak," the doctor explained, "you get food and inhalant allergies, emotional stress, and your body is full of toxins. You'll probably complain of fatigue, headache, depression and develop yeast or fungus infections of your skin and nails, and have rectal itching." He said I had a condition called yeast candidiasis.

Candidiasis is a fungus disease that can affect any system in the body, but it primarily affects the gastrointestinal, nervous, endocrine, and immune systems. Candida overgrowth is often caused by overuse of antibiotics. When yeast multiplies, it puts out toxins, which circulate through the body, weaken natural defenders, and cause sickness. Candida also manufactures a type of alcohol that can cause its sufferers to feel constantly "hung over." When the liver is overloaded with toxins, it is not able to filter blood properly.

In August 1999 the doctor put me on a diet of raw vegetables for 90 days. I wasn't allowed to eat packaged and processed foods, breads or other baked goods, cheeses, condiments, sauces, malt products, or mushrooms. I was not allowed to eat melons, fruit juices, or dried or canned fruits, because fruits would multiply the sugar in my blood. All I could drink was water.

That first week of raw vegetables was the hardest. I had been raised on a farm and was used to eating very well. So I went through different emotions. Mostly I was angry. I was constantly hungry and irritable at home. My body began to stink badly, because it was getting rid of all those toxins.

I began reading *Counsels on Diet and Foods*. These statements had a new meaning for me: "A failure to care for the living machinery is an insult to the Creator." "Every careless, inattentive action, any abuse put upon the Lord's wonderful mechanism, by disregarding His specified laws in the human habitation, is a violation of God's law" (pages 16, 17). "Obedience to these laws must be made a matter of personal duty. We ourselves must suffer the ills of violated law. We must answer to God for habits and practices" (pages 18, 19).

I thought I had been a good steward, and perhaps I had been in other areas of my life. But now I was suffering from my bad health habits and dietary practices. I prayed a prayer similar to this: "Lord, forgive me for abusing Your holy temple. Give me the power and strength to overcome. I give my life over to You. I give my cravings and my diet to You. Help me to get well soon."

The Lord granted my request and helped me overcome. Within ten days I was healed. My yeast candida was gone, my allergies were under control, and I was no longer depressed. I could sleep at night, and I had more energy. I felt better than I had in a long time. In the process I lost 22 pounds. At five feet, three inches tall, I could afford to lose some of my 140 pounds. Now I weigh 118 pounds.

I praise the Lord everyday because He has healed me. As a good steward of my body, I have to work in conjunction with His will to overcome long years of poor practices. I still have to be careful about what I eat. I rejoice in the Lord's help and strength every day.

What? Know ye not that your body is the temple of the Holy Ghost which is in you, which ye have of God, and ye are not your own? For ye are bought with a price; therefore, glorify God in your body, and in your spirit, which are God's. 1 Corinthians 6:19, 20.

Lee-Roy Chacon is executive secretary of the Texico Conference of Seventh-day Adventists in Amarillo, Texas. He is a member of the Amarillo Spanish Seventh-day Adventist Church.

GENEROUS WITH SOMEONE ELSE'S MONEY
By Viki Blanks

I'VE NEVER found it easy to give. I put my requisite tithe and offerings in the collection plate, but find it hard to dig deep into my pockets for anything extra.

One Sabbath, just prior to the offering, one of the deacons read the story of the widow and her mite. It moved me so much—I really heeded the Holy Spirit's nudging—that I started searching for something extra to give. Miraculously, I found a ten-dollar bill in my purse that I didn't know was there. I impulsively threw it in the offering plate and sat back, feeling generous.

The next day, my mother asked me to pick up some snacks for my son's class with the $10 she had given me. I realized that I had used her money to make my "generous" gift.

I paid for the snacks with my own money and grimly vowed never to be swayed toward impulsive generosity again. After all, I thought, God doesn't expect us to give more than we can afford.

Thankfully, this was just a fleeting bout with selfishness. As I thought about the real meaning of the story of the widow's mite, I also remembered that Jesus didn't stop giving until He bled and died.

Though I'll probably never claim giving among my spiritual gifts, I'm learning to cheerfully give from my heart when the Spirit nudges. And I'm thankful that I have a Father who teaches me His lessons with love and humor.

But this I say, He which soweth sparingly shall reap also sparingly; and he which soweth bountifully shall reap also bountifully. Every man according as he purposeth in his heart, so let him give; not grudgingly, or of necessity: for God loveth a cheerful giver. 2 Corinthians 9:6, 7.

Viki Blanks teaches grades 6-8 at Pensacola Seventh-day Adventist Junior Academy in Pensacola, Florida. She is a member of the University Parkway Seventh-day Adventist Church, in Pensacola.

CHALLENGING GOD
By Denzle Harrison

I WAS a third-year accounting major at Oakwood College and not sure what I would do when I graduated. I asked a senior chemistry-major friend what he was going to do when he finished. He was an honor student and certainly had a bright future ahead of him. I was not prepared for his answer.

"I'm going to be a student missionary," he said.

I laughed to myself. Why would he want to do something like that, especially after graduation? But neither Robert nor I had any idea the impact his response would have on my life.

For the next several months of my junior year the Holy Spirit spoke to me, directly instructing me that I would become a student missionary. I tried to ignore it, but I could not. So I posed a challenge to God:

"If You want me to become a student missionary, then You will have to meet the following requirements:

Allow me to work in accounting (all the student missionaries I knew taught Bible or English).

Send me to a Spanish-speaking country (most student missionaries went to such places as Korea, Japan, Indonesia, Guam. I was confident this would not be an option).

Allow me to graduate on time (I still needed approximately 60 credit hours, so this seemed impossible)."

I was confident that with such conditions, I would never have to go as a student missionary. I completed the necessary applications at the end of my junior year and was told that only one opening was available, on the island of Truk (now Chuuk) in Micronesia. Several months later that assignment was canceled.

Early during my senior year I called the General Conference to tell them that I would not serve if they did not have an opening to match my requirements. As I was about to hang up the telephone, the person on the other end of the line said, "Hold on a moment. An opening is coming in on the telex machine." I listened in disbelief as she read to me an opening for a bookkeeper to work in Belize. The primary language was English, and the secondary language was Spanish.

I accepted the assignment. I graduated on schedule in June and left in August for Belize, where I served for a year.

Stewardship is more than finances. It also involves management of your time for advancing the cause of God and agreeing, even if sometimes grudgingly, to serve anywhere He calls. I thank God for accepting my challenge and changing my life forever.

For with God nothing shall be impossible. Luke 1:37.

Denzle Harrison is a senior business consultant for Administaff in Atlanta, Georgia. He is a member of the Shiloh Seventh-day Adventist Church in Smyrna, Georgia.

A READING LESSON
By Marcia H. Singleton

VICTOR wasn't an eager reader, although I had read to him and encouraged him to read. When he was in the fifth grade he was given an extensive reading program to follow, with a challenging reading list. He decided that his first book from the reading list would be White Fang by Jack London. By the time we found an acceptable edition of the book, he had only thirteen days to read 240 pages. We figured out how many pages he would have to read each day, excluding Friday and Sabbath.

In the beginning, it was very difficult for both of us because Victor did not read fluently and I had very little patience. When he read through the periods between sentences, I would stop him and make him read the sentences again. If he mispronounced words I would immediately correct him. Of course, it didn't help that I was a type-A choleric mother who needed her son to read very well. After a few days of frustration, my poor son, with tears trickling down his eyes, said to me, "How will I learn to pronounce new words if you always correct me before I even get a chance to try. Please let me try first."

At that moment the Holy Spirit helped me realize how I had misunderstood my role in this reading assignment. It was my responsibility, as his mother, to support and guide Victor with love, respect, and affirmation. I needed to use this valuable time to nurture Victor and not criticize him. My son is a precious gift loaned from God.

It is sometimes easier to understand my responsibilities as God's steward of money or time. But do I remember that, in the most important sense, I am also God's steward of my son? I must remind myself that my Heavenly Father is observing whether I am following His will for loving and caring for Victor, as Jesus loves and cares for me.

Lo, children are an heritage of the Lord: and the fruit of the womb is his reward. Psalm 127:3.

Marcia H. Singleton is a medical technologist at John Peter Smith County Hospital in Fort Worth, Texas. She is a member of the City Temple Seventh-day Adventist Church in Dallas.

TIME WITH MY SAVIOR
By Joan Manzella

I WAITED to the last moment before deciding to go. It was yet another ministers' meeting for my pastor husband, and I was not enthusiastic about attending. I knew I needed spiritual renewal, but the prospects weren't promising. The schedule offered no programming for our children, so I would have to stay with them instead of attending the meetings for pastors. I had little hope of finding the spiritual enrichment I craved.

My spiritual life was in a drought, and nothing seemed to be helping. It wasn't the first year of the drought either. I didn't know what was going wrong. I had been a Christian for many years and a pastor's wife for more than ten. I now felt as if my prayers were not going above the ceiling. I was missing the spark that my relationship with my Savior once had.

As I fell into bed the first night, I silently prayed to the Lord to speak to my heart and show me how to fill the empty well in my life. I begged the Lord to give me a blessing from the few meetings that I would be able attend.

At one of the meetings Elder Morris Venden encouraged the practice of studying and contemplating the life of Christ, just as Ellen White encouraged us to do in *The Desire of Ages*, page 83. I committed myself to do this for one hour each morning.

Of course, I had been studying my Bible and praying during the drought. The difference was that now I was committing to an hour of meditation and contemplation of the life of Christ and prayer time every morning. I started doing this immediately because I wanted to have that dry spiritual well filled as soon as possible.

At first it seemed rather mundane and contrived to study this way every morning. I prayed that God would give me the desire to keep this commitment. Soon, driven by a new, inner encouragement, I found myself pushing forward, rising early in the morning for personal time with my Savior.

After several weeks of keeping this commitment, it became exciting! Miraculously I began to crave the early morning time with my Savior. The hour soon grew to sometimes two hours of morning worship and prayer time. Prayer time and worship had taken on a new excitement!

Looking back on the pastors' meeting from which I had expected so little, I saw that God had placed me in that time and place for a reason. It changed my life. Again I have begun seeing answered prayer, renewed spiritual vigor, and many areas of character development happening in my life.

Keeping a promise to my Lord and Savior has renewed my relationship with

Him. I probably still would be missing it had I not attended that pastors' meeting and made a commitment to meet with Him daily.

But we all, with open face beholding as in a glass the glory of the Lord, are changed into the same image from glory to glory, even as by the Spirit of the Lord. 2 Corinthians 3:18.

_____

Joan Manzella is a registered nurse and pastor's spouse in Bonnerdale, Arkansas. She is a member of the Bonnerdale Seventh-day Adventist Church.

GOD'S WATERWORKS
By Jeannette S. Baldwin

GIVE, GIVE, GIVE! The words resounded like a clanging bell in my ears as the conference stewardship director urged the congregation to make a greater commitment to support the Lord's work. I felt the Lord tugging at my heart, and we made a commitment to increase our giving.

For ten years we had struggled to make extra income from our farm for our daughter's Christian education. Each summer for those ten years the hand-dug shallow water well had gone dry, forcing us to haul water from the creek that flowed through our property. But as summer advanced, with temperatures soaring, the creek itself would dry up completely. With no running water for 1,500 laying hens, we had to lug water from my parents' well. Our very large vegetable garden from which we sold produce also suffered from lack of irrigation.

We had never borrowed money through the years when purchasing hundreds of baby chicks, farm equipment, or a new automobile. Our increased offering commitment meant that we would probably be hauling water the next summer instead of drilling a real well with borrowed money.

As time passed, we carefully budgeted funds for an automatic washer and dishwasher, certain that with the new water demands, the shallow well would surely go dry. But the well continued to supply an adequate amount of water, and the creek flowed plentifully as each week we laid the tithe and offering commitment in the plate.

Another careful round of saving netted us enough to build a long-planned dining room/family area onto our house, directly over the old and only well. A builder's failure to follow instructions resulted, three years later, in debris clogging the water system serviced by the shallow well. Believing that God would supply the necessary funds as we continued our giving commitment, we prayerfully secured a well driller as we shunned the temptation to go into debt.

The very day that the driller reached 78 feet, pumping eighteen gallons per minute, we received notice that my husband was one of the legatees of a distant relative's estate. As God would have it, we had the amount necessary for all the drilling expenses and a submersible pump.

To sum up God's goodness: The creek hasn't once gone dry in the 40 years since we have honored God with systematic giving. The creek flowed sufficiently to keep the irrigation pump running day and night, while other creeks in the area dried up. And the well put out an abundance of water. Our daughter never had a day of public schooling.

The water continues to flow. So do God's blessings!

The liberal soul shall be made fat: and he that watereth shall be watered also himself. Proverbs 11:25.

Jeannette S. Baldwin is a homemaker in Owego, New York. She is a member of the Tioga County Seventh-day Adventist Church in Candor, New York.

TAKING CARE OF A MYSTERY
By Raj Attiken

THEIR original flight had been canceled, and they had been rebooked on another flight. The way she stored her luggage and the manner in which she plopped herself in her seat were clues that she wasn't a happy passenger. I soon learned the reason for her frustration. Her husband had been "bumped" up to first class, while she got what they had paid for: an economy-class seat. She tried to elicit a reaction from me to the perceived injustice she felt. I remained non-committal, although I was tempted to remind her that they could have been stuck in this foreign country for a while longer, had the airlines not accommodated their need.

Eventually the conversation came around to introductions. Her husband was a prominent national sports personality whose name I quickly recognized from more than 30 years ago. She seemed well connected in society and even knew the families who lived in the neighborhood where I had grown up. She filled me in on the lives of several of my childhood neighbors.

When it was my turn to tell her about myself, I introduced myself first as a pastor, then as a Seventh-day Adventist Christian. I told her I was returning to the land of my birth for a visit.

She knew something about Adventists. "So, will you be going to church while you are here?" she asked, seemingly disinterested. "Will they ask you to preach?"

I responded that it was likely. She turned serious. "So what will you tell them in your preaching?"

I hadn't anticipated that question. "What does one say to a people who have endured years of civil strife, loss, betrayal, separation?" I responded, without pre-meditation. "The only message I have is that God, in Christ Jesus, comes to us in our brokenness, in the shipwreck of our lives, in the loss of all possible peace of mind, even in the very thick of our disasters. In Christ, God has embraced the world to Himself, and the final chapter of our story has already been written." We talked for a while about what that all meant.

She seemed contemplative and didn't say much for the next hour or so—until she introduced me to her husband, who had come back to share a snack with her. Almost as if our conversation of an hour ago had not ended, she abruptly announced, "That would be a good thing to say to our people."

It was my turn to be contemplative. What else could I preach about? I was, after all, a steward of the mystery of Christ.

Let a man regard us in this manner, as servants of Christ, and stewards of the mysteries of God. In this case, moreover, it is required of stewards that one be found trustworthy. 1 Corinthians 4:1, 2, NASB.

Raj Attiken is president of the Ohio Conference of Seventh-day Adventists in Mount Vernon, Ohio. He is a member of the Hill Seventh-day Adventist Church in Mount Vernon.

EIGHT DOLLARS OF TITHE AND 80 TONS OF HAY
By Curtis Thurber

MY WIFE and I had been married eleven years when we became Christians. The idea of attending church on Saturday instead of shopping was very new to us. Returning tithe was a new experience too.

I was farming and doing custom hay-baling. The economy was very tight for farmers in our area. They needed their hay baled but had no cash, so I often took hay for my pay. I ended the baling season with 120 tons of hay and no cash.

That winter, in February, the flu hit our area. The weather was bitterly cold, with a heavy snow on. All of my family were victims of the flu bug. We were down to our last $10.

Sabbath morning I was the only one able to attend church. As I started to leave for church, my good wife reminded me that we owed $8 in tithe.

"I'm not going to return tithe today," I said. "The Lord knows we need medicine and food."

"We should return our tithe first," she replied. "The Lord will provide if we are faithful."

Thank God for a faithful wife!

My wife's words kept haunting me during Sabbath school and worship. When the offering was received, I returned our $8 of tithe and $2 for church expense. Now I was broke, but I felt a deep, trusting satisfaction.

When I arrived home, everyone was much improved. My wife had prepared a huge bowl of the best potato soup I have ever tasted in my life.

Just after sundown that night the phone rang. A man wanted to buy 120 bales of hay! After I quoted the price, he said, "That's too cheap. Bring me 120 bales, and I will pay 25 cents per bale more than you asked."

Thank God for His goodness!

Early Sunday morning I delivered and collected my money, putting the tithe aside first. I stopped by the grocery store, bought food, and came home on cloud nine!

Sunday evening a neighbor who operated a large dairy farm stopped by. He asked if I had hay for sale, because he said he had seen me go out that morning with hay. He needed hay for his dairy cows. I didn't know he needed hay. Until that morning he didn't know I had hay. He bought 80 tons, hauled it himself, and paid top price for it.

The Lord really blessed my wife's faithfulness. The family recovered from their illness very quickly with no medicine, only the Great Physician's blessings. Needless to say, our tithe has come first ever since, regardless of the circumstances.

That experience occurred 50 years ago. We have been through many highs and lows in our walk with God, but thank God, if we remain faithful, He blesses and keeps His promises.

Bring ye all the tithes into the storehouse, that there may be meat in mine house, and prove me now herewith, saith the Lord of Hosts, if I will not open you the windows of heaven, and pour you out a blessing, that there shall not be room enough to receive it. Malachi 3:10.

Curtis Thurber is a retired rancher in Muskogee, Oklahoma. He is a member of the Muskogee Seventh-day Adventist Church.

You have a stewardship testimony you need to share and we need to read. See page 224 for details.

The SIXTH MEETING

Come and hear, all ye that fear God, and I will declare what he hath done for my soul.

Psalm 66:16

Dick Mackie

Wallace Boddy

Ray Hartwell

Newton Sinclair

Kandy Light

Dale A. Fleming

Robert L. Willis

Lily Dalupan

Wayne R. Vail

Elizabeth Boyd

OFF THE TOP
By Dick Mackie

I HAD NOT known of the tithing principle until I started attending the Seventh-day Adventist Church. The call to return one tenth of my income for tithe and to give additional freewill offerings was a major challenge to my thinking. After wrestling with the question, I compromised and began returning ten percent of my *after-tax* income. I rationalized that the taxes were automatic and were not really mine to administer. In reality, excluding taxes was just another way to keep more money for myself. To ease my conscience, I tithed any tax refund I received.

I did this for several years, but something (or Someone) kept nagging at me that this wasn't right. Then I was given a copy of the book *Over & Over Again!* Reading others' testimonies of their experiences with tithing convinced me that the tithe is to be ten percent of everything, before taxes or any other consideration. Now I had no excuse. I realized that tithe wasn't a subjective amount that could change according to my convenience. It was not a freewill offering that I could calculate as I chose. It was one tenth of whatever the Lord gave me, even if the bills were many and the money was tight.

I wanted to be at peace with God. I didn't want to wrestle over this issue anymore. I started to tithe the full ten percent off the top of my income. My wife tithed ten percent of her wages also. At about the same time we reduced our use of credit cards, buying only what we knew we could pay for. That year our income actually decreased, while our charitable contributions increased by almost 24 percent. Yet surprisingly (or maybe not so surprisingly), we seemed to have more cash available, and we accelerated payments on our student loans. It now appears those loans will be paid off in half the time that I had originally calculated.

For me, tithe is not a matter of giving God His due. It is an issue of trust: how much I believe God can and will take care of me. If I trust God with what I hold precious, whether my family or my finances, He will be a faithful partner with me.

And God is able to provide you with every blessing in abundance, so that you may always have enough of everything and may provide in abundance for every good work. 2 Corinthians 9:8, RSV.

Dick Mackie is the controller at Vail Rubber Works, Inc., in St. Joseph, Michigan. He is a member of Pioneer Memorial Church in Berrien Springs, Michigan.

ASK FOR HELP
By Wallace Boddy

I WAS BORN into a Seventh-day Adventist home and grew up hearing, studying, and reading the wonderful truths we cherish. I often was thrilled to hear stories from new converts relating their utter joy in discovering the truth. I was especially impressed with how their "first-love, on-fire" experience filled their lives.

I wondered how any person born a Seventh-day Adventist could ever experience that first-love joy. I wondered if I had missed out on something wonderful which never could be my experience.

I attended church every Sabbath, returned tithe, gave offerings, held offices, taught Sabbath-school classes, and did all the other good things we associate with being an active church member and Christian. Looking back, it is clear to me that I simply was not a converted man. I had a form of godliness but little of Christ's converting power in my life.

In 1972 I opened a business in the field I had pursued since college. Although, by God's grace, it was successful from the start, the business grew so fast that the stress level was very high. Personnel problems added to the strain and tension. But it was my business, and I going to run it.

I dutifully offered prayers at home every morning and evening. And when a financial crisis loomed, of course I prayed more often. But when the crises were over, it was back to routine prayers at the beginning and end of the day and "doing it my way" during working hours.

One Monday morning a frustrating personnel crisis suddenly erupted. Appointing myself chief arbitrator, expert prosecutor, and brilliant judge, I rushed out of my office and dived headlong into the matter, only to completely lose my cool, my dignity, and my Christian forbearance.

After the confrontation I returned to my office with guilt weighing heavily upon me. I realized with tears how costly to my Savior and to me personally that impetuous face-off had been. I felt that all the good from my efforts to help my employees, to pray with them, to give them literature, and to treat them with Christian kindness had been undermined by my outburst.

On my way back to my office I detoured to my private washroom and, on my knees, totally surrendered my heart to my Savior. Weeping bitterly, beginning with my shame in mishandling a problem, my failure in surrendering my entire days, my sinful life, and my selfish will to my Savior, I poured out my inner soul to God. The trauma of that occasion set forever a cherished benchmark in my life that I will never forget, a turning point to full faith and trust in my lovely Jesus.

As I rose from my knees, chastened, but with great peace, something inside said to me as clearly as anything I have ever heard, "Don't forget to *Ask For Help*. Now go and straighten out the harm you did." I returned to the scene and called the involved employees together. There I experienced just a small part of the humility that showed forth in the life of my Savior. I asked for their forgiveness. Then I prayed that God would give us wisdom to know how to handle the matter. The solution God gave us right there proved to be very simple. We repaired the breach and established a loving rapport. God was praised and exalted.

Ellen White often reminds us that we can ask God to help us to love Him more. So I pleaded for His help in becoming His fully trusting child. I made a covenant with God that I would trust and obey Him if He would give me the power and grace to do so. I knew this meant a moment-by-moment total surrender of my will. It meant placing every situation before my Savior in prayer. In keeping my covenant I had many battles with Satan. Often I had to order the enemy out of my mind and presence. I repeatedly claimed the promise, "Resist the devil, and he will flee from you" (James 4:7). The promise proved true.

Remembering that small voice that had told me to *Ask For Help*, I wrote the letters AFH on Post-It notes and put them discreetly in places where I would see them as I moved about the store. They were a constant reminder of the covenant I had made with my lovely Jesus.

Those three little letters, by the working of the Holy Spirit, helped me experience that "peace of God, which passeth all understanding" (Philippians 4:7) with Christ in my life. They represented to me the beginnings of a new love, an almost inexpressible joy in experiencing truly that first love, that rebirth, that victorious power from heaven, and the true assurance of salvation that comes from knowing that Christ, the Hope of glory, lives in me.

Thou wilt keep him in perfect peace, whose mind is stayed on thee: because he trusteth in thee. Isaiah 26:3.

Wallace Boddy is a retired businessman in Lineville, Alabama. He is a member of the Douglasville, Georgia, Seventh-day Adventist Church.

 # A COMMITMENT, A CAR, AND A CREDIT UNION
By Ray Hartwell

IN 1990 A GROUP of Adventist musicians from the Ukraine visited our church on their way to the General Conference Session. The way was just opening for evangelism to explode in the former Soviet Union. Our church family was deeply moved to hear their stories of struggle for their faith through the years. A few months later our congregation decided to sponsor the building of a house of worship for an Adventist congregation in the former Soviet Union.

My wife and I felt impressed to do all that we could to help. Since we had just finished paying for our only car and were debt-free, we pledged the amount equal to four car payments. Shortly thereafter my wife had unexpected major surgery that left us with serious medical bills. At almost the same, time our long-awaited adoptive infant arrived. This left our resources very tight, and we wondered how we would pay our pledge for the next four months.

We talked it over and decided that a promise is a promise. Over the next four months we would turn in an offering for the sister church in just the same amount as the car payment would have cost us.

As both of us were in ministry and often going different directions at the same time, we had an acute need for a second vehicle. Yet as we prayed, we felt that the need for us to help with churches in the former Soviet Union was greater than our need for another car.

Approximately a month into our four-month giving plan, I dropped my wife off at the grocery store. While we waited, my son and I wandered around the lot of an auto dealership nearby. When we were joined by the usual eager salesman, I explained that we were just idling some time away and would not be able to consider a purchase for a few months. After learning what type of vehicle and what price range we would be interested in, he took us to a vehicle a few months old with only 3,000 miles on it.

It was the right type of car and was affordable, but we wanted to keep our commitment for the church building project.

Then an announcement came in the mail from a credit union, offering the opportunity to purchase a new car with 100 percent financing. Calling the credit union, I found to my surprise that they treated any car with less than 5,000 miles as a new vehicle. Not only would they loan the full amount for the car; they would postpone the first payment-due date until well after we had finished paying our church pledge.

We still have that car. We paid it off early, and God has continued to bless us.

"For I know the plans I have for you," declares the Lord, "plans to prosper you and not to harm you, plans to give you hope and a future." Jeremiah 29:11, NIV.

Ray Hartwell is secretary of the Pennsylvania Conference of Seventh-day Adventists in Reading, Pennsylvania. He is a member of the Hamburg, Pennsylvania, Seventh-day Adventist Church.

TROUBLES WITH JOE
By Newton Sinclair

IF YOU can't work 24/7, you should seek employment elsewhere."
One Friday afternoon I was working with my group of analysts to fix a database file problem. The person who had the password needed to expand the file wasn't available, so there was little we could do. Since it was almost time for sunset, I went to see Joe, my new supervisor, and told him I was going to leave for the day. I knew then that I was in trouble.

Joe was new to the office. He didn't care much about my long years of distinguished service to the organization or for my Sabbath, and he told me so. In his view, if I couldn't make an around-the-clock commitment, I should leave. I went home feeling very upset. My former supervisors had always honored my request to have Saturday off for religious worship.

I requested special prayer from my local church and then appealed Joe's decision to the department director. The director scheduled a meeting to hear the appeal.

Those present at the appeal meeting were the department director, the department manager, my supervisor Joe, and I. I was asked to state my reasons for refusing to work on Sabbaths and also for not signing a 24/7 work pledge acknowledging my willingness to work all 24 hours in the seven-day workweek. After some discussion the director made the following rulings: My request to have Sabbaths off should be respected by both my manager and supervisor; I shouldn't be required to sign a 24/7 pledge; and more importantly, any future actions against me must first be approved by her!

Joe wasn't happy with the decision and became even more unhappy with me. My performance appraisals went from being positive to negative. Sometime later our department was given a new manager, and Joe wasted no time having me transferred to another section under a different supervisor within the department. I could no longer work on projects for which I had been trained.

Then, as suddenly as it started, it was over! First, I was asked to assist an analyst from my old section who was having trouble solving a systems problem. After I had resolved that problem in a successful and timely manner, I was given the responsibility to manage the entire system on which I assisted. In the following months other job responsibilities were added, to the extent that today I have more systems responsibilities in the department than any other analyst.

Joe's attitude toward me was also changing. Not only did he have me transferred back to where I was working before, but more importantly, on my most recent job-performance review, he started out with a blank sheet of paper and told me that he wanted to record only the statements with which we both agreed.

Not long ago Joe came to my office and inquired if I had read the past Sunday's local newspaper. I told him I hadn't. He then told me about an article in the paper that I would find amusing. "A pastor has written an article complaining about people desecrating the Sabbath day. This pastor doesn't seem to know that Sunday isn't the Sabbath that Saturday is." I was astonished.

What shall we then say to these things? If God be for us, who can be against us? Romans 8:31.

Newton Sinclair is a computer systems analyst in Dayton, Ohio. He is a member of the Hillcrest Seventh-day Adventist Church in Dayton.

....

A SADDLE FOR AMY
By Kandy Light

ON THE verge of turning fourteen, Amy needed a saddle for the gentle old mare she loved to ride. Her birthday was approaching, and we wanted very much to buy one for her.

Not long before that, my husband Rich and our three sons had started a lawn-and-garden landscape business. Family businesses take time to build up, and we definitely had no money for extras, especially expensive extras like saddles, in our family just then. Yet it seemed like such a critical time in Amy's emotional life that we asked the Lord what we should do.

Rich and I discussed the problem. Saddles typically cost in the hundreds, and we wondered where we could find even $50. Amy's birthday was three weeks away, and we didn't want to disappoint her. She needed a dream come true.

Unexpectedly, friends of ours who run a special children's camp called and asked if we would keep one of their campers for three days, offering us $75. Ah—saddle money! But where could we find a saddle for that impossibly low price?

My husband remembered that once or twice a year a local Amish auction included a "tack" sale. I phoned for information, and as it happened, the sale was scheduled for the next evening, a Friday evening. Sunset that summer evening would be at 9:05.

I managed to slip away early on Friday afternoon without Amy's noticing anything unusual. At the auction site I spied a beautiful shiny black saddle hanging over a fence rail. A voice seemed to say, "See that black saddle? That's the one." I argued with myself, refusing to believe that I could afford one that nice.

I focused instead on two beat-up saddles that looked as if someone had found them under a pile of rotten hay. "Probably more my price range," I reasoned. "Oh, well, at least they're saddles, and probably they can be cleaned up."

I took my auction number and found a place in front, feeling nervous and inexperienced. When I asked a couple behind me if they knew anything about the two beat-up saddles, they pointed out that one was a pony saddle and wouldn't fit a horse. That narrowed my odds even more. Now I had to get the one remaining tattered saddle. I was sure it was the only one I could possibly afford.

As the auction began, I was praying that the saddles would come up for sale before Sabbath arrived. I even considered explaining my beliefs to the auctioneer and asking him if he could please sell the saddles first, but I decided that the Lord could work it out if I was to have one. Still I looked at the nice couple near me. Maybe I could ask them to buy that saddle for me, and I could get it from them after Sabbath.

But no, that wouldn't be right. If I shouldn't buy it on Sabbath myself, then I shouldn't ask them to buy it for me.

"Okay, Lord," I surrendered. "I choose to leave here by 9:00, no matter what. I put You first."

Suddenly I remembered that I hadn't yet returned tithe on the $75 we had earned. I rationalized that perhaps I could return it later, out of some other funds. No, I finally decided. I'll return tithe on it first.

Gas and other necessary food purchases had already reduced the total to $62.50. Returning tithe would reduce the amount I had to purchase a saddle by another $7.50. In my upset state I didn't even try to calculate the balance. I knew only that I had 50-odd dollars for Amy's saddle. Prospects looked bleaker with every passing moment.

"Please, Lord, let them sell the saddles soon," I prayed as the clocked ticked toward Sabbath. Suddenly a Mennonite auction helper walked over and picked up the old saddle. My stomach lurched, my fists tightened. An impression came to me that I should bid on the shiny black saddle. But how could I know if the impression was coming from the Lord? What if I didn't bid on the old saddle and missed it, and then found the black one to be too expensive? "Lord, please work it out if I'm making a mistake," I prayed.

Finally the auctioneer opened bids on the old saddle. I hesitantly participated, my eyes wide as saucers. Then a miracle occurred: The bidding stopped with my bid of $25. The old saddle was mine.

But wait! What was the auctioneer saying to me? I've never heard an auctioneer do this before or since. "Lady," he was saying, "did you know that this saddle is broken? These men can fix it if they buy it. Do you still want it?"

"No," I said. I watched, close to tears, as the saddle—my saddle—went to the nearest bidder.

My hopes were dashed. But then the helper picked up the shiny black saddle. Before I knew what was happening, I was bidding on it. In what seemed like a flash, the bidding was over, and the saddle was being handed to me—for $55!

I joyfully lifted the saddle up, went to pay for it, and realized that $55 was the exact amount of money that I had left! A glance at the wall clock on my way out into the bright sunlight told me it was only 8:00–still an hour away from the start of Sabbath.

Tears filled my eyes as I realized that the Lord, the God of the universe, had been testing my commitment to Him. He cared enough to provide a saddle for Amy.

Them that honour me I will honour. 1 Samuel 2:30.

Kandy Light is a registered nurse and homemaker in Howard, Ohio. She is a member of the Mt. Vernon, Ohio, Hill Seventh-day Adventist Church.

PRAYING FOR A PRAYER MINISTRY
By Dale A. Fleming

ONE SABBATH morning the pastor and I discussed the need for a prayer ministry in the church. Over the next year and a half I periodically thought about the people who might be best suited to lead out. Looking back, I now know that God had a plan and was waiting for the right time to start this ministry.

In June 1998, at age 33, my wife was diagnosed with colon cancer. We prayed earnestly that her life would be spared. We began praying with our families and friends, who in turn prayed with their friends. The prayer chain reached all over America. God didn't seem to be hearing us. After some time of agonizing over God's apparent silence, my wife and I finally asked Him to take full control. We simply prayed that He would give us the faith we needed to get through the difficult time ahead, whatever it might be.

Over the next eight months God was able to help us as we made numerous trips to the Mayo Clinic for treatments. There we would see people, including small children, who were suffering far worse than we were. In silence we prayed for those around us, that they too would find peace.

During this time I realized it was *I* God was calling to develop that prayer ministry in our church. I began to pray more and more with and for others—at church, at work, and in my family. As I walked closer with my Savior, my faith grew stronger. Soon I stepped out in faith and started the Wednesday-night prayer meeting, asking that God would send people my way who needed a message of hope and encouragement.

Our first meeting was in March 1999. Fifteen people came out. Our pastor was excited. In the past, prayer meeting had usually drawn only two or three. I began to pray earnestly for bigger things, and I asked God for a larger attendance.

By the fourth meeting, we had 38 people. God was answering our prayers. We started a prayer journal with our petitions, thankfulness, and praise to watch how our loving Father answered our requests.

With daily study and prayer God has developed in me a greater faith. He has been leading me to former Adventists in our area, often through work-related co-incidences. My wife has had no recurrence of her cancer since her original treatments. Thus, in the end, God did answer my original prayer for sparing my wife. But first He needed to develop my *faith* and my *faithfulness* in answering His call and doing His biddings.

[God] comforts us in all our tribulation, that we may be able to comfort those who are in any trouble, with the comfort with which we ourselves are comforted by God. 2 Corinthians 1:4 NKJV.

Dale A. Fleming is a partner in Fleming Bros. Construction, in Rochester, Minnesota. He is a member of the Rochester Seventh-day Adventist Church.

....

OUT OF THE WAY
By Robert L. Willis

YOU AREN'T going to do it, are you?" my wife asked me as I hung up the telephone.

I had spent more than 30 years teaching church school, but never had I received a more heart-rending telephone call. One of my sixth-grade girls called late in the evening. She was in tears.

"Mr. Willis, could you come over every morning and pick up my brother and me and take us to school? My mother is mad at Mrs. Jones and won't let us ride with her any more. And my mother won't take us herself because it's too early to get up. She says if I can't find a ride, she's going to put us in public school. Please take us!"

I heard myself telling her to be ready at 7:30.

My head was buzzing as I hung up the phone. "Are you really going to drive way over there and take them to school?"

I heard my voice saying, "Yes, I am."

I spent a restless night. My heart ached for those children.

When I picked them up the next day my good deed wasn't rewarded with pleasantness. The mother was surly, the children sullen, and the trip to school was not a joyful occasion. About the time we arrived at school the children told me I needed to take them home as well.

At staff meeting I told the other teacher of the call, and her response was predictable. "You aren't going to do it, are you? You know how much trouble the boy is in my classroom. And they won't appreciate what you're doing for them."

I looked across the table and replied, "I brought them here this morning, I'll take them home tonight, and I intend to keep doing it as long as they are willing to come. I'm not doing it to be appreciated. I'm doing it for God, because He loves these children, and so do I." How could I do otherwise than go out of my way for these children in my charge? After all, my Savior went out of His way for me.

By this all will know you are my disciples, if you have love for one another. John 13:35, NKJV.

Robert L. Willis teaches Adventist elementary school in Minocqua, Wisconsin. He is a member of the Lakeland Seventh-day Adventist Church in Minocqua.

A BED TO MAKE
By Lily Dalupan

AS A CHILD and teenager, I slept on bamboo floors. When I turned eighteen, I started work as a maid, moved away from my village, and lived my dream of sleeping in a real bed that I could make. I got married, had children, moved to Canada, and began learning about God and His works. My family settled in Québec, where my life was blessed with many challenges.

I had become the sole provider for my family and was able to buy a house. I was diligent in returning my tithe and offerings. The Lord established me in my house, helping me to turn it into a safe home to raise our four children, as well as a foster home business and a shelter for me during the biggest storm of my life.

After 20 years of marriage, my husband took his own direction. Our marriage ended. Since then my devotion to the Lord has become my life goal.

God fulfilled my wishes and dreams. Blessing my simple high school education, He gave me the ability to run a prosperous business. My home has become my means to witness to all who have set foot in it—those who are ill, student boarders, strangers in need of rest, evangelists, church prayer groups, and many others. My children and grandchildren have grown to know the Lord here, along with their friends, who call me "Mom." No one has ever gone hungry or poor in this home. The Lord has never left me alone.

As adults, my children have wondered why I have often asked, "Did you make your bed?" It's simply because I know that if we are wholehearted in handling the small things, God will see our works and allow us to handle bigger things for

His glory. All I ever really wanted was one bed to make, and now I am handling more than ten beds. Even through my worldly struggles, God has rewarded my simple faith beyond my needs, because in times of economic drought these beds are always occupied.

I hold the thoughts of Joshua 24:15 dear to my heart. The Lord has been my business card of happiness and success for my family, friends, and the strangers that I welcome into my home.

But as for me and my house, we will serve the Lord. Joshua 24:15.

Lily Dalupan owns and operates a foster home in Val d'Or, Québec. She is a member of the Seventh-day Adventist Abitibi Company in Val d'Or.

AN ACCOUNTANT'S ACCOUNTABILITY
By Wayne R. Vail

WHEN my wife and I returned from mission service in Africa in 1966, circumstances made it advisable for me to leave denominational work. I decided to take advantage of the break in service and advance myself professionally. I looked for work that would qualify me as a certified public accountant. Since my parents were working in San Francisco for the General Conference, we went there.

Because tax preparation is a significant part of most accounting practices, the months prior to April 15 were hectic. Many practitioners worked seven days a week, and the workdays were well in excess of twelve hours each. Because I wouldn't work on Sabbaths, the placement agencies wouldn't recommend me to any of the accounting firms. As they saw it, it wasn't reasonable to ask for Sabbath privileges. I followed up every advertisement I found for openings with certified public accounting firms, but without success.

The local office of the California CPA Association had a little card file where firms sometimes announced openings. The clerk at the association office pulled out an announcement for a firm down in the financial district of San Francisco and gave it to me.

"Here, this may be just the firm for you," she said. "I know the people there. It's a small firm, but it's congenial to work with."

This firm accepted me, and I began working almost immediately.

I had worked for the firm about two months when the clocks were changed back from daylight-saving time to standard time. Having grown up and served in southern Africa, where there was no daylight-saving time and no significant fluctuation in sunset times, I was shocked to realize the Sabbath would begin before normal office closing time on Fridays. I asked the senior partner for the privilege of leaving the office one hour before sunset.

"Wayne," he said, "my grandmother was a Seventh-day Adventist. She was the most wonderful person I ever knew. You will never have a problem in this office regarding Sabbath observance. Arrange with my partner how you will make the time up."

During my two-year internship I never had any conflict over Sabbath observance. In fact, my Sabbath observance was never challenged in any office I worked in from then on.

Let thy tender mercies come unto me, that I may live: for thy law is my delight. Psalm 119:77.

Wayne R. Vail is retired from church treasury work. He lives in Vancouver, Washington and is a member of the Vancouver Seventh-day Adventist Church.

"YOU MEAN YOU GIVE IT AWAY!"
By Elizabeth Boyd

I WAS pushing full speed ahead in my career of owning and operating my own traveling physical therapy company when I fell in love with a wealthy man.

One evening we were snuggled up on the couch talking about the possibility of getting married.

"Tom," I said, "I think you need to know how I spend my money. You may just want to send me home when I tell you. I give ten percent of my income for the use of the church."

His eyes widened.

"Yes, and I have dedicated another ten percent of my income to benevolent projects as they come along, like keeping my sister's kids in a Christian school."

Tom gasped.

"Besides that, the Bible says if your brother is in need, open your hand wide. So I don't want to limit myself to twenty percent if the need becomes evident."

Tom got up from the couch. "You mean you give away your money?"

He was shouting as he stomped to the fireplace and back, then to the kitchen door. "You mean you give it away! That's irresponsible! That's just irresponsible!"

"Well," I said calmly. "That's the way it is."

Tom came back to the couch and looked me full in the face. "I'll have to think about this!"

Sunday morning Tom took me to the airport for my flight back home. I wondered if he had decided that I was too expensive for him.

"I've been thinking about what you said the other day about the way you handle your money. I've decided that as long as it's your money, I shouldn't worry about it. If we should get married, I'll just set up a trust for my money if I should die."

I suppose it would be interesting to end the story by saying that we got married and I doubled my income. Of course, that's not the way it worked out. I knew that no woman would get ahead in life by marrying a man who thinks it's irresponsible to open your hand wide when you see your brother is in need. So, sadly, I ended my relationship with Tom.

Two months later my brother called. "Elizabeth," he said, "my ex-wife is suing me for custody of the kids. If she wins, the kids will have no religious training at all. I think God wants them where they will have Bible stories and songs and some positive direction for their little lives. But I just can't afford the $10,000 it will cost to fight this thing!"

"DeWitte," I answered, "we are in luck. The business is doing well, and I have set aside a special fund above my regular tithe and offerings to use just in case God should need it for something special like this."

The litigation was successful, and two of DeWitte's three children chose the Christian home.

If there is a poor man among your brothers in any of the towns of the land that the Lord your God is giving you, do not be hardhearted or tightfisted toward your poor brother. Rather be openhanded and freely lend him whatever he needs. Deuteronomy 15:7, 8, NIV.

Elizabeth Boyd is a writer in South Harpswell, Maine. She is a member of the Brunswick, Maine, Seventh-day Adventist Church.

You have a stewardship testimony you need to share and we need to read. See page 224 for details.

The
SEVENTH
MEETING

Come and hear, all ye that fear God, and I will declare what he hath done for my soul.

Psalm 66:16

Myrtle Brown

Linda Basquez

Edward Atwood

M. Kay Cote

Olga Speer

Jere Patzer

Dan Jackson

Jack McNeilus

Jim Ashlock

Gordon Bietz

MOUNTAINS OF BLESSINGS
By Myrtle Brown

ABOUT 30 years ago we had just built the little Columbia, Mississippi, Adventist Church. All we had were four walls, a roof, and one restroom. The local conference was letting us use some folding chairs. We had about 30 members.

I wanted us to have nice pews. I decided to start a pew fund. But what could I do to raise money? I began to think, pray, and wonder.

One day a friend of mine showed me a book with the picture of a quilt in it. She said, "Myrtle, I will give you $100 to make me a quilt like this."

Well, I made that quilt and fixed me a little box and marked it "Pew Funds." I returned my tithe and put $90 in the box. This was my secret project.

It seemed that everyone who saw that quilt wanted one. Soon I had orders for 36 quilts, and it took me about three weeks to make one. I really felt I might have taken on more than I could do. But all those people said they would wait as long as it took to get their quilt. So each night I had a long talk with my Father, and He gave me faith to go on.

Pretty soon I had to get a bigger box.

When I thought I had enough money to get the pews, I traveled to north Mississippi and visited a factory that made church furniture. I ordered a pulpit, a communion table and all the pews we needed. Soon we had padded pews that those quilts bought. I had sewed day and night for three years to get those pews.

I give God all the glory, and now I know faith can move mountains.

If ye have faith as a grain of mustard seed, ye shall say unto this mountain, Remove hence to yonder place; and it shall remove; and nothing shall be impossible unto you. Matthew 17:20.

Myrtle Brown is a retired practical nurse in Columbia, Mississippi. She is a member of the Bass Memorial Academy Seventh-day Adventist Church in Lumberton, Mississippi.

LORD OF THE MAIL
By Linda Basquez

SHORTLY AFTER moving our family from California to Florida, my husband Don had to return to California to care for some property we had rented out. Our renters had quit paying and were now tearing the place apart. With our family living on two coasts, money was tight. Don found a temporary job in California, while my adult daughter, Dawn, and three grandchildren moved in with me.

Dawn's monthly paycheck covered the Florida house payment and most of the other bills, but still we looked at it with wonder. How could it ever stretch far enough to cover all the needs? Often I was tempted not to return our tithe, calculating that the extra money might help us through the month. By God's grace I resisted the thought.

Being new to Florida, I knew we needed air conditioning during the summer, but I didn't know how expensive it was. When the first bill came, it was more than $300. Where was that amount of money ever to come from?

I called my husband in California to see if he could send us the money to pay this whopper of a bill.

"No," he said. "I'm having trouble paying my own bills." And he hadn't been working long enough at his job to get an advance. Time was running out. I called the electric company to see if they would accept partial payment on the bill.

"No," the agent told me, "you need to pay it in full."

With only six days left to pay, my back was against the wall. I even asked the pastor if the church could possibly help. "Your request will have to go to the church board," he said. I waited, hoping for a quick reply, but no answer came. Each night I asked the Lord for help.

With just three days left to pay the bill, I went to the mailbox to see if a letter from Don was there. I needed cheering up. What I found instead was a letter from a California real estate office. They had been collecting rent on a house we owned in Mojave, California, but had misplaced our Florida address. Enclosed with the letter were two six-month-old money orders that totaled $900.

Who cared about my pride? With tears running down my cheeks, I thanked the Lord right there in the post-office parking lot.

"So do not worry, saying, 'What shall we eat?' or 'What shall we drink?' or 'What shall we wear?' For the pagans run after all these things, and your heavenly Father knows that you need them." Matthew 6:31, 32, NIV.

Linda Basquez is a food-service worker for Blountstown High School in Blountstown, Florida. She is a member of the Marianna, Florida, Seventh-day Adventist Church.

BLESSED ASSURANCE
By Edward Atwood

My WIFE Marice works in a home for special care. One day she received an unusual request from Marjorie, a member of our church. At 91 years old and twice widowed she asked, "Would you be willing to take me into your home and care for me in the time I have left?" When she said "home," she didn't mean the place where my wife worked. She didn't want to be put in a home for the aged. She wanted to live in a real home with a real family. She had chosen ours.

Marice and I thought of many reasons why we would not be able to accommodate Marjorie's request. Our house just wasn't big enough. Our plans to build an addition had never materialized, and with six in the family, our house was constantly the center of bustling, high-density activity.

We talked and prayed about the situation. Did God want us to take this aged child of His into our home? We believed He did. Marjorie was overjoyed when we finally invited her to be part of our home. We moved one of our sons into the cluttered basement by a noisy furnace and gave his room to her.

Marjorie went to church almost every week, but as time passed, she became more frail and could no longer attend. However, she was still able to manage alone for several hours while the family went to church.

She would often ask to talk with me about some Bible text that was unclear to her. I was troubled when, on one occasion, she confided that she did not have the assurance of salvation. My study time with her seemed to be of little help. We continued to ask God to bless her. I did not realize to what lengths the Lord would go to answer our prayers and care for His frail child.

One Sabbath afternoon as we arrived home from church, I heard voices inside as I approached the door. Our collie dog would never let anyone near Marjorie unless we were home. I entered the house just in time to hear the ending of beautiful voices in song. Marice and I expected to find people there, and we were surprised to see that no one was in the house except Marjorie. "Who has been singing to me all this time?" she asked. "It was the most beautiful music I've ever heard."

As I think back on that day when God sent a delegation from heaven to our home for such a purpose, I feel honored. Marjorie spent her last two and a half years with us, and I am happy to report that somewhere in that time she gained the assurance of salvation.

We did build an addition to the house, and although it wasn't completed in time for Marjorie to enjoy, we were able to provide a home for my elderly parents. My father passed away here at home in 1997. My mother is still with us.

Even to your old age, I am He, and even to gray hairs I will carry you! I have made, and I will bear; Even I will carry, and will deliver you. Isaiah 46:4, NKJV.

Edward Atwood is a sawmill owner and operator in Oak Park, Nova Scotia. He is a member of the Oak Park Seventh-day Adventist Church.

THE BLESSINGS OF FAITHFULNESS
By M. Kay Cote

I DON'T REMEMBER a time during my working years when I didn't return tithe to the Lord, along with some offerings. There were times when it wasn't easy. For years I didn't recognize all the principles of stewardship, and I married out of the church, not taking into account God's counsel not to be "unequally yoked." This sometimes caused difficulties.

In the early 1970s I returned to work because I wanted my daughters to receive a Christian education. When it came time for the eldest to attend academy, a representative from the school visited my husband and me. We talked about finances. My husband isn't a Christian, and he wanted our children to attend the local public school. I was determined that our daughter attend the academy, so he agreed to send $50 a month for her education. Later he withdrew the offer, which meant that the total responsibility for our daughter's school bills fell on me.

The Lord is good. I faithfully returned His tithe on my salary, and He provided the money needed. The school gave her help from the needy-student fund, and she worked on campus in different jobs to help with her tuition.

At camp meeting one summer, while our daughter was still in academy, the conference began promoting the 10+10 plan. We were encouraged to give another full ten percent in offering above tithe. I was impressed that this was something I needed to do, and frankly, I wanted to see how God would work. As soon as my next paycheck arrived, I instituted the new giving plan, and my daughter graduated, diploma in hand, with all her bills paid!

For the next two years she attended Walla Walla College, and she received her associate degree in early childhood education. Then she went on a Task Force assignment to Arizona for a year. She enjoyed teaching so much that she decided to go on for a full teaching degree. She returned to Walla Walla, and again graduated with her school bills all paid, except for a couple of small student loans that she was able to repay shortly. God never failed us.

Faithfulness in returning tithe and offerings from my salary has blessed our entire family. We are retired now, and daily we have evidence of His care in providing money to live on through some savings and retirement income. We are never short of funds to cover expenses and to help others, including our church, locally and worldwide.

I praise God for His goodness and care for us over the years. One of the best rewards is the change I see in my husband's attitude toward God.

For the unbelieving husband is sanctified by the wife, and the unbelieving wife is sanctified by the husband; else were your children unclean; but now are they holy. 1 Corinthians 7:14.

M. Kay Cote is a homemaker and retired secretary in Dillon, Montana. She is a member of the Dillon Seventh-day Adventist Church.

OPENING DAY
By Olga Speer

WHEN my late husband and I got acquainted, he operated a seasonal business, which was open seven days a week during the summer and closed during the winter months.

During the winter that Ralph and I got acquainted, he started to keep the Sabbath and to return tithe. When summer came, he decided to keep the business closed on Sabbath. His father said, "There is more business on Saturday than on any other day of the week. If you close on Saturday, you will starve."

Ralph kept his business closed on the Sabbath that normally would have been the opening day of the season. He held his opening day the next day—on Sunday. He had more business on that one day than in any entire *week* before, when the business was open seven days a week.

Ralph and I were married a short time after this. We always found that God blesses those who love Him and keep His commandments.

Who is the man who fears the Lord? He will instruct him in the way he should choose. His soul will abide in prosperity, and his descendants will inherit the land. Psalm 25:12, 13, NASB.

Olga Speer is a retired Bible instructor in Ardmore, Oklahoma. She is a member of the Summit Ridge Seventh-day Adventist Church in Harrah, Oklahoma.

A COMMENTARY ON ASSURANCE
By Jere Patzer

MY WIFE and I were newlyweds at Andrews University in Michigan, where I attended graduate school. Each month we had just enough money to return our tithe, give a little offering, and pay our bills.

Once a year various publishers came on campus with a special one-week book sale just for students. As I browsed through the sale, my eye caught a set of Bible commentaries. The more I thought about that set, the more I wanted it. Certainly those books would be a practical addition to a would-be minister's library. But the price, though significantly reduced, was still $63. That's not much in today's economy, but it was a lot to a young seminarian at that time. I decided to make it a matter of prayer.

At that time in my life I needed some special assurance that God was with me and that I was doing His will. I decided to give God the opportunity to show me His presence in some meaningful way, such as getting that set of Bible commentaries.

A few evenings later the phone in our campus apartment rang. "Hey, Jere," the caller said, "I just realized I still owe you some money for that painting you did for me last summer. I'll put a check in the mail."

"Okay, God, it's looking better," I prayed. "But I need to get at least $63, and it has to be here before the sale ends on Friday." More prayer, anticipation, and then some doubts. The man hadn't paid me for weeks. What would make me think he'd rush a check off to me in time? Furthermore, I didn't even know how much he owed me. More prayer. "Please, God, this is not a life-or-death situation, but . . . it certainly would strengthen my faith."

I went to the mailbox on Friday, the last day of that book sale. Yes, there was an envelope from the paint contractor. I took it back to the apartment. One more prayer. Now my hands were almost shaking with anticipation as I opened the envelope. There was the check, and it was for $70. Wow! Praise the Lord. The $70 minus $7 for tithe left $63—the exact amount I needed.

Still praising the Lord, I rushed off to get my books. And then came a worry. What about Michigan sales tax? I got to the sale before closing, grabbed my set of commentaries, and asked the cashier, "What's the total with tax?"

"Oh," she replied, "There is no tax, because this is an out-of-state sale."

I was one excited seminarian that Sabbath. And today, as I write this testimony, I can look over at my shelves and see the books that God gave a young seminary student just to increase his faith.

Does God always respond to me like that? Of course not. In fact, that may be a once-in-a-lifetime experience. But it was enough to give me confidence today, so many years later, that God does care about us.

If ye then, being evil, know how to give good gifts unto your children, how much more shall your Father which is in heaven give good things to them that ask him. Matthew 7:11.

Jere Patzer is president of the North Pacific Union Conference of Seventh-day Adventists in Portland, Oregon. He is a member of the Hood View Seventh-day Adventist Church in Boring, Oregon.

OUR WAYS, HIS WAYS
Dan Jackson

IN DECEMBER 1980 I was invited by the General Conference to serve as a pastor and district leader in Colombo, Sri Lanka. After agonizing over the decision, our little family, so happily situated in the beautiful Okanagan Valley of British Columbia, decided that no place in the world is better than the place where God wants us to be. For us, Colombo, Sri Lanka, was that place. Our experience over the next five years in Sri Lanka and India provided us with great blessings and taught us many needed spiritual lessons. However, one of the greatest lessons came in the area of stewardship.

After we accepted the call, the basic pre-move arrangements needed to be made. Among many other things, we needed to sell our house. We had owned it for only eleven months. By the grace of God we sold it the same day we put it on the market, and we made a very handsome profit. After returning our tithe, we were able to pay off all of our debts. Even then, we still had $20,000 to invest. We decided to purchase a piece of property that we believed would appreciate in value. We planned to use the proceeds from the sale of that land to provide for our children's academy and college education when we returned from Sri Lanka. This seemed like a great idea. We left the matter in the Lord's hands and moved to southern Asia.

Five years later we returned to Canada. We enrolled our children in church school and academy and, according to our plan, we put our land up for sale. Within two years we had two children in two different academies. Monthly tuition costs were far greater than we could afford. And the land did not sell.

Because we had trustingly placed the matter of our children's education in God's hands, we determined to leave the matter right there.

Over the next several years we saw the intervention of God time and time again. On one occasion my conference president told me that an individual had given him a donation to be applied to my eldest daughter's school bill. Another time we discovered we qualified for a benefit that we had not expected, so our youngest daughter was enabled to attend Upper Columbia Academy. While we were often challenged, the Lord provided all our immediate needs, and our children finished their education in our schools.

Sometime after our youngest child had finished academy, we finally sold that land. As it turned out, our investment had been a very poor one. We received only $7,000 from the sale. We used it to pay off a few debts, but by that time, praise the Lord, none of it was needed for school bills.

Our heavenly Father, who knows the end from beginning, provided for the

Christian education of our children without having to rely on our plans. Our well-intentioned ways are not necessarily His ways. We learned the lesson of trust.

For my thoughts are not your thoughts, neither are your ways my way, saith the Lord. For as the heavens are higher than the earth, so are my ways higher than your ways, and my thoughts than your thoughts. Isaiah 55:8, 9.

Dan Jackson is president of the Manitoba-Saskatchewan Conference of Seventh-day Adventists. He is a member of the Saskatoon Central Seventh-day Adventist Church in Saskatoon, Saskatchewan.

MONEY BACK–OR AHEAD?
By Jack McNeilus

As A businessman who believes in Bible principles of stewardship, I've been used to returning what I thought was a faithful tithe. Each year, after the accounting is done, I've corrected the amount of tithe that I had contributed and was happy in the thought that I was faithful.

But a sermon by our pastor changed my thinking. In essence, the pastor described a money-back offer: If we had returned our tithe in faith and found that we couldn't do without that tithe money in our budget, he would see to it that we got it back after a period of time. That offer really got me thinking.

Was I really living on faith, trusting my needs to God, or was I just returning a dividend on what God had given me? That month I decided to find out.

I decided to return my anticipated next year's tithe for the whole year in advance and see what God would choose for my income. I added a fourteen percent increase over the previous year's tithe and put the check in the tithe envelope. In April I changed my business from a sole proprietor to a corporation and started receiving a monthly salary. On this income I returned tithe also.

A year went by; my business gross sales for that year were up fourteen percent, and so was my faith. My warehouse is now full to overflowing.

But rather seek ye the kingdom of God; and all these things shall be added unto you. Luke 12:31.

Jack McNeilus is the owner of Baraboo Steel in Baraboo, Wisconsin. He is a member of the Baraboo Seventh-day Adventist Church.

ONLY A DREAM
By Jim Ashlock

I GREW up in an Adventist home and generally tried to follow the basic beliefs of the church. There were times when I was doing many things I knew were not right, and during those times I'd try to convince myself that my life was nobody else's business—not even God's. During these low periods in my relationship with the Lord, when I really wasn't even trying, I would stay up late at night so that I would fall asleep quickly and not have to think when the lights were out. I didn't want to think about where I knew I was going to end up.

On one of these nights, when I fell into bed exhausted, I had a memorable dream. It was in "living color," and it's as clear to my memory now as it was to my dreaming consciousness on that night more than twenty years ago.

I saw the second coming of Christ, portrayed exactly like some of the paintings in Adventist publications. Men, women, and children of every race were standing in their graves looking up to Christ. They had crowns on their heads, and some of the older ones had many stars in their crowns.

Suddenly someone I knew appeared and said, "Well, Jim, I see that you not only didn't make it but that you also kept a number of others from making it."

What could he mean? Then I realized I was wearing a crown, but when I took it off, I saw that it was a black crown with a number of stars in it. But the stars represented people who would *not* be in heaven *because of me.* While I was looking at my crown, the stars turned into faces that I recognized from my past—people who were lost forever because of me.

I woke from my dream in a cold sweat. I got down on my knees and asked God to forgive me. For the first time in my life I surrendered completely to Him. I realized forcefully that my life is not my own; it's His. I have a responsibility, not only for myself but for others whose prospect for eternal life I may help or hinder.

In the years since, with the Lord's help, I've done everything I can to undo the wrongs of my past. In many cases those concerned are no longer living. But since Jesus is the Lord of my life, I gladly put all my trust in Him. He knows my heart.

Create in me a clean heart, O God, and renew a steadfast spirit within me. . . . Then I will teach transgressors Your ways, and sinners shall be converted to You. Psalm 51:10, 13, NKJV.

Jim Ashlock is a retired educational administrator in Collegedale, Tennessee. He is a member of the Collegedale Seventh-day Adventist Church.

SPIRITUAL DOING AND SPIRITUAL BEING

By Gordon Bietz

IN ONE OF my favorite cartoon strips the first panel shows Garfield the cat standing in the shadows on one side of bright sunlight that is beaming through the window. He contemplates the warmth of the sunlight. The balloon above his head contains the words, "I wonder if I can get across this time."

The second panel shows Garfield making a tremendous leap, trying to get through the warmth of the light to the other side. The final panel shows him collapsed in a heap in the midst of the warm sunbeam. He had fallen totally asleep in the warmth and comfort of the sun.

That cartoon is a picture of my journey into my office each morning.

On the far side of my office is a chair where I am committed to having my personal devotions. My Bible is there. But on the way to that chair I must pass the irresistible draw of my desk and computer. The desk is piled high with work, and the computer beckons with the siren song of e-mail. It is as if there is a black hole that irresistibly draws me. From pastor, to conference president, to university president, the ongoing nemesis of my life is my activist personality—the desire to do things and please people instead of taking time to be with God.

I have stood when calls were made to spend one hour a day in prayer. I have stood when appeals were made to spend fifteen minutes a day in Bible study and prayer. I have made appeals to others at the close of sermons and then had to live with the guilt of personal lack of performance.

With Paul I say, "For I have the desire to do what is good, but I cannot carry it out." (Romans 7:18, NIV.) I have rationalized my weakness, but my human nature goads me to please man, not God. When I answer mail, write letters, organize events, and send thank-you notes, I receive many rewards. The rewards of spending quiet time with God are not as immediate; God doesn't send me thank-you notes.

Unfortunately, I am prone to measure my worth by the things I do rather than the person I am. I would rather do a spiritual task than be a spiritual person, not realizing that I can do nothing spiritual until I am spiritual. I have come to the realization that, for me, I must not wait until the day is in gear before my spiritual life is in gear. Rather, I must take time for my highest priorities before I get there. So now, before I get to the office, I have a time of exercise and prayer. I may not finish as many tasks, but no one seems to miss my doing what I thought was so crucial.

OVER AND OVER AGAIN!

Be still, and know that I am God. Psalm 46:10.

Gordon Bietz is president of Southern Adventist University in Collegedale, Tennessee. He is a member of the Collegedale Seventh-day Adventist Church.

You have a stewardship testimony you need to share and we need to read. See page 224 for details.

The
EIGHTH
MEETING

James Brauer

Raymond O. West

Evelyn Johnson

D. G. Gordon

Eugene F. Durand

Sherian Atkins Wills

Mary Ann Conrad

Sandra A. Smith

Roscoe J. Howard III

Robert L. Davidson

A BALM FOR BITTERNESS
By James Brauer

I DIDN'T WANT to believe what I was reading. Chapter 11 . . . filing for bankruptcy. . . . How could he? He owed me $14,000! I had my own lawyer. I had promissory notes. I was angry!

Then I remembered what a preacher had recently said: "When the Lord allows you to be placed in a difficult situation, don't focus on yourself and your loss. Focus on others and minister to the one who is hurting you. Maybe he is hurting worse."

Hmmm. . . . How could he be hurting worse than I was? But I decided to try it. I bought a copy of that famous "footprints" poem, gift-wrapped it, and went to his house.

When he came to the door, he was wary. Maybe he thought I was going to hit him. Maybe other people had already tried. As I offered him the gift and said I was praying for him, I suddenly realized stewardship wasn't about money. It was all about how I managed my relationships, even with people who took things from me. After all, the only thing I can take with me to heaven is . . . other people!

There is no huge miracle in this story. The man didn't get baptized the next week. And he didn't give me back my money. But I simply learned that through giving, my anger and my bitterness disappeared.

If your enemy is hungry, give him bread to eat; And if he is thirsty, give him water to drink; For so you will heap coals of fire on his head, and the Lord will reward you. Proverbs 25:21, 22, NKJV.

James Brauer is president of the Rocky Mountain Conference of Seventh-day Adventists in Denver, Colorado. He is a member of the Arvada, Colorado, Seventh-day Adventist Church.

A CORRELATION OF ONE
By Raymond O. West

I WAS ABOUT ten years old when I got my first vivid lesson on stewardship. On the way to school I spotted on the sidewalk a glasses case, with the address of the owner crudely inked on the inside lining. After school I showed my find to my mother. She suggested that the owner might give me a reward for its return. I practically ran to the address, three blocks from my home, carrying the glasses case intact. The owner, a myopic teenager, wasn't home yet, but her mother opened the door to my insistent knock and accepted the case with barely a word of thanks. Disappointed, I turned away. When I was halfway down the walk, she called me back. In triumph I ran back home with my reward, a dime safely tucked in my pocket.

In those days ten cents could buy a double-scoop ice-cream cone or two packs of Wrigley's double-mint gum. For a grand minute or so I had purchasing power. That is, until my reward-oriented mother reminded me of my tithe obligation. No longer could I purchase two candy bars or a frosty milkshake. My coveted silver dime had suddenly shrunk by one tenth. But wait! She wasn't finished yet. A dart pierced my heart when she suggested that maybe I could drop in my own offering this coming Sabbath. That would leave me with four copper pennies.

So it was one cent in the tithe envelope and one shiny nickel in the offering plate. Joyful stewardship was not my disposition, before, during, or following Sabbath school on that particular day. Nonetheless, it was a courageous, if lip-quivering, beginning.

A few years later, my academy sweetheart and I were newly married, we agreed that we would return to God a first and second tithe on all our income. Heaven was quick to respond.

In the fall of 1945 I was discharged from the Canadian Navy just in time for college to begin. Did we dare register for classes, possessing neither work skills nor checking accounts? Our single asset was the Canadian GI Bill of Rights—one month's tuition and a monthly cost-of-living check ($80 Canadian) for each month served, and even more for good grades.

But now a new obstacle intruded. We had set our hearts on the study of medicine at what was then the College of Medical Evangelists, in Loma Linda, California. But the beneficent bureaucracy declared that my veteran's benefits were effective only in Canada. It would have to be an M.D. degree from the University of Toronto or Montreal's famed McGill University.

Or would Heaven intervene and give us those coveted veteran's benefits at Loma Linda University?

Perhaps one day we will know how it was that those government officials granted us six years of GI bounties at Loma Linda. But if not, it's okay, for over several decades we have enjoyed heaven's benevolences in abundance. Never have we had a serious want. We've even had some luxuries and been blessed with superb health and happiness.

Good stewardship and blessings in abundance—a correlation of one.

And God is able to make all grace abound toward you, that you, always having all sufficiency in all things, may have an abundance for every good work. 2 Corinthians 9:8, NKJV.

Raymond O. West is a retired physician and professor in Belfair, Washington. He is a member of the Belfair Seventh-day Adventist Church.

THE JOY OF LIBERAL FRUGALITY
By Evelyn Johnson

ABOUT nine years ago I resolved to return to God 100 percent of the income He entrusted directly to me. I've been blessed with a monthly Social Security check plus annual farm shares and inheritance incomes, as well as unexpected money gifts.

We operate our household with my husband's Social Security check. This pays for the taxes on my income, various insurances, transportation, medical expenses, clothing, food, and the other usual home expenses. God's blessings and my contentment, and even joy, with frugality enable me to return to God about 25 percent of this income also.

All of my needs (not greeds) are met by our awesome God, who multiplies my bank account as He did the widow's oil and meal in 1 Kings 17:8-16.

To God be the glory, thanks, and praise! I appreciate and thank my unselfish husband also.

Cast thy bread upon the waters: for thou shalt find it after many days [with peanut butter and jelly (as amended by me)]. Ecclesiastes 11:1.

Evelyn Johnson is a retired schoolteacher in Shelby, Montana. She is a member of the Shelby Seventh-day Adventist Church.

I LOVE MY JOB, BUT THE LORD COMES FIRST
By D. G. Gordon

I WORK for one of the largest car-parts manufacturing companies in North America. I wasn't a Christian when I began work there, and things seemed to be going very well. I worked a lot of overtime, sometimes six days a week, and the pay was not bad.

The company began to expand rapidly. Its reputation is based on production efficiency and quality, so they brought in new and more efficient machines. The nature of my job is multipurpose. I am a punch press operator, setup man, and material handler. My supervisors told me they wanted to train me to operate these new machines.

While this company expansion was going on, the Lord found me sinking deeper and deeper in sin, and He rescued me. I accepted Jesus as my Savior and purposed in my heart to follow Him all the way. This was a big change in my life. As a Sabbathkeeper, I could not work on the Sabbath anymore. This was a concern to my employers, who wanted me to continue working on Saturday. When they continued to ask me to work on Sabbath, I told them I could work any time *except* on Saturday. However, my supervisor insisted on training me to operate these new machines. This was fine with me, as long as it didn't mean I had to work on Sabbath.

A few months later, after I was trained on the new machines, my supervisor asked me to work on the afternoon shift, which would break the Lord's Sabbath. I told him I could not work that shift. He informed the general manager, who came to me and told me he would like me to work on the afternoon shift because he would like me to be in charge of these new machines. He said I would also receive a raise of $4 per hour, which I must say was very attractive. But how could I accept that offer and disobey the Lord? With the Lord's help I was able to say no to the temptation. After all that, the Lord made a way for me so that I do not have to work on the Sabbath, and I have worked for that company for nearly 25 years. I am now on the safety committee and the fairness committee. But I have to decline any promotion that would infringe on the Lord's Sabbath. Even though the company policy says, "No solicitation," my coworkers are my best supporters in my Ingathering. I love my job, but the Lord comes first. So I just want to say, "Thank You, Lord, for always coming through for me."

Then Peter and the other apostles answered and said, We ought to obey God rather than men. Acts 5:29.

D. G. Gordon is a punch press operator for a car-parts manufacturing company in Concord, Ontario. He is a member of the Perth Avenue Seventh-day Adventist Church in Toronto, Ontario.

....

ALL GREEK TO ME
By Eugene F. Durand

AFTER fourteen years of pastoring and another four of teaching language, earning the Ph.D. seemed like the logical preparation for securing a position as a religion teacher at an Adventist college. But I had a family to support and no job at the moment. Should I go back into pastoral work?

By God's grace my wife found employment in the county public health department at a better salary than I had earned as a pastor and teacher. At the same time, I was able to secure a government-backed student loan to cover expenses at the university. I devoted full time to my study.

But nagging questions persisted. Was this the right thing to do? What kind of husband and father was I, letting my wife support the family completely for several years? Was it right to make my girls work to earn their academy tuition? Would I find the position I was studying for? Could I pay off the thousands of dollars in student loans? I had no one to sponsor me and no promise of a job when I graduated. In sum, was I being a good steward of my time, talents, and finances?

After two years of classwork under these circumstances, the time came to take my exam for the second language requirement. The first, Spanish, had been a breeze. But for the second language I had chosen New Testament Greek, which I had studied for two years in college but forgotten during the intervening 22 years. After a summer of diligently reviewing that ancient language on my own, the test loomed.

For three months I had read exclusively from the Gospels in my Greek Bible. But the morning of the exam I decided it might be wise to practice reading from some other New Testament book. At random my eyes fell upon Acts 17:16-34, the story of Paul preaching on Mars Hill, in Athens. After studying that passage and praying earnestly for Heaven's help, it was time to leave for the university.

Upon entering the office of the Greek professor, I was handed a Greek New Testament and asked to translate a passage. Out of the 260 chapters and 7,957 verses in the New Testament, he asked me to translate the story of Paul preaching on Mars Hill.

You can imagine the emotions that swept over me! I felt almost too stunned to do the assignment. Needless to say, when I recovered from my amazement (I could hardly refrain from telling the professor what was happening, but I thought it best not to, lest he change the assignment), I was able to complete the translation that was so fresh in my mind.

Given my uncertainty about the course I was pursuing, this experience came to me as the Lord's assurance that I was doing His will and that He would see me through. I can't tell you how it lifted my spirits!

And see me through He did. Two years before I graduated, I received an invitation to join the editorial staff of the *Adventist Review,* where I remained until retirement eighteen years later. It turned out that my previous experience and humble talents were far better suited to that position than to the teaching position toward which I had been working. Even though I had never dreamed of becoming an editor, the Lord put me where I could give the best account of my stewardship.

Oh, by the way: The Review and Herald Publishing Association paid off the entire $6,000 of my student loan.

How can I repay the Lord for all his goodness to me? . . . I will fulfill my vows to the Lord in the presence of all His people. Psalm 116:12-14, NIV.

Eugene F. Durand was an assistant editor of the Adventist Review in Silver Spring, Maryland, before his retirement. He is a member of the Frederick, Maryland, Seventh-day Adventist Church.

A TAX ON TRUST
By Sherian Atkins Wills

WITH two sons in an Adventist academy, my husband and I were struggling to make ends meet. Convinced of the merits of Christian education, we had sold practically everything of value to keep our sons in school. Then came tax time.

With trepidation, my husband and I filled out the tax forms. We had a small federal tax refund coming, but Virginia state taxes hadn't been withheld from our military-retirement check. We owed $300! That might as well have been three million. We had no money in reserve.

"What shall we do?" my husband worried. "Perhaps we can borrow it from your mom."

"Not this time!" I exclaimed. My parents were always bailing us out. They were even helping with the kids' tuition. I was determined not to ask for another penny. Instead, I decided to claim God's promises.

Every morning I knelt in prayer and presented our need to God. Every night when my husband came home from work, he would ask, "Did you get the money from your Mom yet?"

"No, the Lord will provide," I would answer. But as the April 15th deadline approached, even I began to worry. Then, feeling ashamed, I'd push my worries aside and renew my fervent prayer.

D-day arrived. The moment I opened my eyes in the morning, my husband's barrage began. "You have to get that money from your Mom today and mail in that check," he said. In fact, he said, he had already discussed the matter with her.

I might as well admit it: God has let me down, I thought. As I drove to my parents' house I began to cry, *God, I just don't understand!* I sobbed. *We're trying to do everything You ask. We return tithe and give offerings. We sacrifice to give our kids a Christian education, and my parents have to pay our bills. It isn't right!*

Mom gave me cash, so I deposited it in the bank, wrote out a check, and stuffed it into the tax envelope. Still I couldn't bring myself to mail it. Instead, I felt impressed to pay our taxes in person at the courthouse. As I handed the clerk the forms, she said, "Just let me check your figures."

In a moment she was back with a smile. "Well, it appears as if somebody made a mistake. You don't owe $300. You'll get a refund."

I was suddenly speechless. A refund? That was impossible, for we had gone over those figures a dozen times! She took the forms, signed her name to them, and sent them off. I praised God all the way back to return my parents' money.

As it turned out, our figures actually had been correct; we did owe that money. Because the clerk at the courthouse had made the mistake, no penalty was added. By the time we received a payment notice, the funds were available, and we didn't have to borrow anything.

But my God shall supply all your need according to his riches in glory by Christ Jesus. Philippians 4:19.

Sherian Atkins Wills is a free-lance writer living in Bedford, Virginia. She is a member of the North Valley Seventh-day Adventist Church in Roanoke, Virginia.

AFFIRMATION AT A RUMMAGE SALE
By Mary Ann Conrad

WE WERE hard-pressed for funds again. Our son's tenth birthday was in two days, and I had hoped to get him a good, heavy sleeping bag. I knew that the next few years would bring many opportunities for Steve to go on camping trips. I also knew that sleeping in a tent in New England weather requires warmth. But we didn't have the extra cash to go out and purchase something new. We just couldn't afford it.

My husband Bruce and I had come under the conviction that once we started our family, I needed to be at home during the children's formative years. As much as we wanted this, we both knew it would be an act of faith, because up until now we had depended on my income as a nurse for home expenses. Bruce would have to take on this load plus that of building his business.

I didn't mind learning to scrimp and save to stretch our resources if it meant that I could be with the children. So I soon learned where the best thrift shops and rummage sales were held and how to judge the quality of an item quickly. I purchased much of our clothing and home accessories secondhand. But still I found it very hard to go to Bruce with my hand out asking for money each time we needed something extra.

Bruce is a self-employed auto repairman, and at that time our income was anything but steady. Some weeks we had enough money to meet our needs, but other weeks were difficult. We often marveled at how an outstanding payment would come in just when we needed it. Or at just the right moment Bruce would be able to sell a car or other piece of equipment he had bought to fix up. In fact, we would often wonder out loud how the Lord would help us meet our obligations "this time."

I had been watching for sales on camping equipment and scanned the classified ads regularly for a month, but I didn't see any sleeping bags for sale.

There was to be a rummage sale in a neighboring village the next day. I had never seen a sleeping bag at a sale like this before, but I prayed that God would have one there for Steve. Otherwise, I knew I'd have to go to the discount stores for a cheap sleeping bag that wouldn't hold up to the use it would get. And I would have to draw from the grocery money to buy it. It was against my better judgment to throw money away on something that wouldn't last, but time was an issue.

I was at the sale when the doors opened. Scanning the room, I approached a display area for the outdoor items. I saw the usual old lawn mowers and bikes, some sleds, and various sizes of skates in various states of repair. I sighed and kept looking: a tennis racket and exercise equipment, odds and ends of gardening supplies, and some tools. And there on the corner of the stage was what looked like some lightweight canvas rolled up and tied.

Investigating further I found exactly what I had hoped for, an extra-thick sleeping bag. Wow! And it was marked $3. I looked it over and found it was in great shape and much, much nicer than what I had seen in the discount stores. I didn't hesitate to pay the price as marked, and with tears in my eyes I drove home rejoicing in a heavenly Father who not only honors us for our home and family commitments, but who also cares about a little boy's birthday gift.

If you, then, though you are evil, know how to give good gifts to your children, how much more will your Father in heaven give good gifts to those who ask Him! Matthew 7:11, NIV.

Mary Ann Conrad is a homemaker and registered nurse in West Hartford, Vermont. She is a member of the West Lebanon, New Hampshire Seventh-day Adventist Church.

....

HIS EYE IS ON THE SPARROW
By Sandra A. Smith

THE sparrow landed on the ledge just outside my office window. The view was perfect as I watched this little ledge-dweller go about its business of the day. I was reminded of God's care for the "fowls of the air" and my own experience as a "sparrow."

Some time ago I was between jobs. With a rewarding job of almost seven years behind me and a new, exciting one on the horizon, I eagerly waited to start my new career. There was one hitch; I would not be able to start right away. Circumstances beyond my control did not allow me to start in this new position for four months.

Finances diminished as the bills grew. More so, worrying (a slow killer of the human spirit) festered and grew in my soul. Doubt was slowly replacing the faith that I was given to trust that God would take care of my needs. I constantly was discouraged and depressed. I didn't sleep well.

As I watched the little bird and reflected on my "dark" hour, I realized these trying times made up one of the greatest experiences in my life. I was the steward of faith the size of a mustard seed. God had entrusted to me a measure of faith that I was to develop. No matter what I was going through, God still expected me to trust Him and to carry out the duties that He had called me to do.

One of the responsibilities that I had was that of co-director of the hospitality ministry at my church. This job involved buying supplies to be used by all of the teams that offered the weekly lunch. It also involved buying food to contribute to the once-a-month churchwide potluck. With the start date for my new job some time yet in the future and with limited finances, I had to decide what to do. I could give up the church position or trust and obey. I decided on the latter.

Although worried at times about how much money I had left in the bank, I used my scarce resources to buy what was needed. I was faithful in carrying out well the duties that the Lord had asked me to do. I wanted to give Him my very best, even when it came down to simple things like having enough utensils and food for our church family and guests.

The wonderful thing about trusting in God was the assurance that He would take care of me. My faith, although tiny, was the only thing that I had to cling to. Even though I wavered at times, I did not give in to the temptation of letting go of His caring hand. During my time of financial crisis I never went hungry or homeless. In my darkest hours God constantly reminded me through family and friends that He loved and cared about my well-being and survival.

Four months later I was blessed to start my new job, and shortly thereafter I happily deposited my first paycheck in the bank. Throughout this trying experience I realized that God's eye *is* "on the sparrow" and that He *is* faithful.

Are not two sparrows sold for a copper coin? And not one of them falls to the ground apart from your Father's will. . . . Do not fear therefore; you are more value than many sparrows. Matthew 10:29-31, NKJV.

Sandra A. Smith is assistant professor of social work at Atlantic Union College in South Lancaster, Massachusetts. She is a member of the Boston Temple Seventh-day Adventist Church in Boston, Massachusetts.

RIGHT ON TIME
By Roscoe J. Howard III

IT WAS OUR first month of marriage, and we were filled with wide-eyed zeal and love for the church. I was not yet employed, and my wife was also looking for a job. In two weeks I had an interview with the conference president—perhaps to be hired as a ministerial intern. We were living off our wedding-present money.

That money was running out, and we still had a week and three days until the interview. In fact, all the money we had left was our tithe and offerings. On Friday afternoon, with our food supply almost exhausted and our rent due the day after the interview, I found it very tempting to use that tithe money for more tangible needs. I tried to reason with my wife that God would understand and that He didn't want us to starve or be street people. And who knew if we would even get a job? We could pay back the tithe when we got hired.

In her quiet and unassuming way, she looked at me and said, "We must trust God and return to Him what is His." I remembered how I had spent my tithe when I was in college and how I had regretted it. Somehow I never got around to paying it back because another emergency would always seem to pop up.

Sabbath morning I finally resolved that I didn't want to repeat the mistakes of the past. But I watched with longing eyes as our tithe envelope traveled to the front of the church, to be sung and prayed over, and then consigned to the church treasurer's office.

On the way home from church I couldn't stop worrying about what we would do that week without money, food, or a job.

While entering our little apartment, I noticed a large brown envelope stuffed into our mailbox. We assumed it was some belated wedding pictures. We opened the envelope and poured the contents onto the bed. A heap of dead presidents' pictures stared up at us. My wife's mother had sent us 25 belated wedding cards filled with cash.

Hallelujah! We paid our rent, bought food, returned our tithe and a thank offering, and got hired two weeks later.

And it shall come to pass, that before they call, I will answer; and while they are yet speaking, I will hear. Isaiah 65:24.

Roscoe J. Howard III is executive secretary of the Mid-America Union Conference of Seventh-day Adventists in Lincoln, Nebraska. He is a member of the Allon Chapel Seventh-day Adventist Church in Lincoln, Nebraska.

THE PROMISE DID NOT SAY "MAYBE"

By Robert L. Davidson

SEVEN years and three children after Lenna Lee and I were married, our church in Tulsa decided it was time to build a new church. It is well known that young couples seldom have extra funds lying around for philanthropic projects. We were no exception. Our family budget was very tight. However, we wanted to do our part to contribute to the new building.

After much prayer we made a covenant with God and made a three-year pledge to help fund the building. We claimed the promise in Philipians 4:19 that God would supply all our needs. We noted that the promise did not say "maybe." In our reasoning we planned to raise the money through my work, because we were committed that Lenna Lee, a nurse, should be home with the children. However, we were prepared, if necessary, for Lenna Lee to go back to her nursing work just long enough to pay our pledge. Yet we trusted that God would honor our commitment to our children just as we were determined to honor our pledge to the church.

Not long after this my brother-in-law suggested that I apply for work at Douglas Aircraft Company. I was not sure I wanted to be employed by Douglas. They were highly dependent on government contracts, which meant that work was here today and gone tomorrow.

After worship one evening I told Lenna Lee about Douglas, and we decided that maybe this was God's plan to meet our pledge. I applied. In filling out the form, I was to sign a statement saying that I would work any day or hour assigned. I could not sign it and honor God's Sabbath. I left it blank.

The next day I completed the required physical examination and turned in the application form to work at Douglas. The man in charge told me that I needed to sign the statement I had left blank. When I told him I couldn't because of God's Sabbath, he became angry. After much discussion, I told him I was sorry I had wasted his time and that he had wasted my time. Suddenly his attitude changed, and he asked me to sit in the waiting room.

A short time later I was called in and asked to approve my application form. Stapled over the statement about working any day was another typed statement that read, "Due to religious convictions, this employee will not be required to work from Friday sundown until Saturday sundown." I signed on to work at Douglas. The increase in salary would be just enough to keep up with our church pledge and return the extra tithe.

I had worked only a few months when Douglas lost a major contract and began laying off workers. There were 23 in my department of math and engineering, and I was "low man." Every time the pink slips arrived, I expected to be laid off; but each time someone would either quit or move to another department. I continued to work, even with some overtime, for more than three years. When my pink slip finally came, only two of us were left—my boss and myself. By that time we had finished paying our church pledge, I had finished my teaching degree, and was I able to start teaching at Tulsa Junior Academy.

Honour the LORD with thy substance, and with the firstfruits of all thine increase: So shall thy barns be filled with plenty, and thy presses shall burst out with new wine. Proverbs 3:9, 10.

Robert L. Davidson is a retired math and science teacher in Claremore, Oklahoma. He is a member of the Claremore Seventh-day Adventist Church.

You have a stewardship testimony you need to share and we need to read. See page 224 for details.

OVER AND OVER AGAIN!

The NINTH MEETING

Ofelia A. Pangan

Liz Sunbeam Robert

Gloria Ann DePalma

LeRoy Finck

James Gilley

Larry D. Word

Gary and Don Emelander

Charlene VanVliet

Ronald J. Goss

Sylvia Davidson

THE SABBATH AND SECURITY
By Ofelia A. Pangan

WHEN MY husband resigned from teaching in a small church school in 1984, we decided to go back to Toronto, where we hoped he could find another job. Though he was drawing a small unemployment benefit, just enough to help us survive, our biggest concern was how we could support our three children in college—one at Canadian Union College and two at Pacific Union College.

I had a part-time job at a nursing home, working in the kitchen for an hourly wage. Initially, my fellow workers gladly exchanged hours on Friday nights or Saturdays whenever I was assigned to work those shifts. But when they discovered I was exchanging my shifts because of religion, nobody would accommodate my request. Suddenly they wouldn't tolerate my not working on Saturdays.

As a last recourse, I approached my supervisor and appealed to her to let me keep my Sabbath. I told her I was willing to work the whole Sunday or put in more hours, but my plea fell on deaf ears. She thought I was very foolish: Not only were jobs scarce, but I had just gotten a raise, which she knew I needed to keep three children in college. The only thing I could do was to resign from my job.

Our family doctor learned of our plight and offered me three to four hours each day at her office as a receptionist. Though I wasn't trained as a secretary, in a few days God helped me learn how to use the multifunction telephone, how to bill the patients, how to make patient appointments with specialists, and many other things. I did my best, and the doctor was pleased with my progress in helping at her office.

One day I saw an ad in the newspaper, seeking a teacher of English as a second language in a factory where courses were offered before the night shift and after the day shift. I had trained to teach English as a second language, and I began to pray earnestly about the job. Though the position offered only twelve hours of work each week from Monday to Thursday, I was convinced that God was leading me to do that kind of work.

I applied for the teaching job, convinced more than ever that God wanted me to use my expertise in teaching to help us financially and to reach out to others. The Lord helped me get that job, and it paid almost four times as much as the receptionist job and three times the pay of the nursing home. Within a few months, I transferred to a school setting, which helped secure our financial position until my husband found employment again.

If you turn back your foot from the sabbath, from doing your pleasure on my holy day...; then you shall take delight in the Lord, and I will make you ride

upon the heights of the earth; I will feed you with the heritage of Jacob your father, for the mouth of the Lord has spoken. Isaiah 58:13, 14, RSV.

Ofelia A. Pangan is a retired teacher in Clovis, California. She is a member of the Central Valley Fil-Am Seventh-day Adventist Church in Fresno, California.

A PRICELESS THREE-DOLLAR ANSWER
By Liz Sunbeam Robert

WHILE living at the Onondaga Indian Reservation in upstate New York, I gave my heart to the Lord and was baptized into the Seventh-day Adventist Church. Although my little family and I were very poor, I always knew that everything I had was precious and a gift from God. The Native American traditions teach us that the Creator made all things and that we are only stewards of the land and its bounties. But after my baptism I soon learned that God requires us to acknowledge these gifts through our tithe and offerings. Never having tithed before, I was unsure whether I could possibly do this.

The first time that I resolved to return tithe, I figured out my tithe amount and our bills. I was dismayed to find that I lacked $3 to meet both needs. That first day—all day—I agonized over what I should do. If I returned tithe, I would likely have my electricity turned off. If I paid my bills, then I would be taking what did not belong to me. I finally decided to ask the Lord what to do. I knelt and prayed, "Lord Jesus, I want to do Your will. I love You, and I trust You to show me what to do."

I immediately had my answer. I arose from my knees, took God's money, and put it into an envelope. My heart felt light, and I was no longer worried about how God would supply my needs. I just knew He would.

Shortly after this, I went upstairs to our little Indian library, and in the first book I opened—I couldn't believe my eyes—were three one-dollar bills tucked away inside! I knelt down right then on that hardwood floor, thanking God for fulfilling His promise to take care of my every need if I returned my tithe faithfully. I've seen many blessings ever since that time as I continue to honor God through my tithe and offerings. Thank God for His great love and His faithfulness!

Your Father knoweth what things ye have need of, before ye ask Him. Matthew 6:8.

Liz Sunbeam Robert is a retired nurse in Oneida, New York. She is a member of the Oneida Native American Seventh-day Adventist Church.

EXACTLY THREE HUNDRED AND FIFTY DOLLARS
By Gloria Ann DePalma

WE NEED a new car. We can't postpone it any longer. I need dependable transportation."

My husband, John, gave me the grim news after arriving home from work late one evening. He had recently joined our conference office as trust services director, a job that required extensive travel to meet the members' needs. Reluctantly I agreed to the purchase because I realized the urgency of our predicament. In leaving a prestigious position in local city government to work for the conference, he had taken a sizeable salary cut. This resulted in family finances that often were tight.

A friend recommended we buy a car from an Adventist Subaru dealer in Pennsylvania, so my husband called and ordered one. When he went to pick it up, the dealer informed him that the new cars had not yet arrived. He would sell John a used one and take it back in trade when he took delivery of the new car. My husband agreed to the arrangement.

One evening John's brother, sensing our financial need, gave him $500. The next morning, during worship at the office, the publishing director related the experience of a struggling literature evangelist who was facing great financial difficulties. The story tugged at John's heartstrings, prompting him to give $100 to help the man. After tithing on the $500 he was left with $350.

Two months later we began to have problems with the used vehicle. A mechanic told my husband that a protective boot on the front axle was torn and would cost $350 to repair. We decided to postpone the repairs, but soon the engine began burning oil because of a burnt valve. The same mechanic told us this work would cost an additional $350. Again we decided to wait on repairs.

We soon received word that our new car had arrived and that we could pick it up. My husband told the dealer about the used vehicle's need for repairs, which now totaled $700, and asked if we should have the work done or wait for the dealer to do it. The dealer told John to drive the car to Pennsylvania, where he would repair it and charge accordingly.

When my husband arrived at the Subaru dealership to pick up the new car and trade in the used one, he received an estimate on all the repair work for only $350! This was the exact amount he had left from his brother's $500 gift after he tithed it and used some of it to help someone else in need.

The liberal soul shall be made fat: and he that watereth shall be watered also himself. Proverbs 11:25.

Gloria Ann DePalma is a secretary at the Northern New England Conference of Seventh-day Adventists in Portland, Maine. She is a member of the James White Memorial Seventh-day Adventist Church in Portland.

BLESSINGS BEYOND UNDERSTANDING
By LeRoy Finck

AS EARLY as my days in boarding academy I had often sensed that God was calling me into the ministry. So I started college with that goal in mind. But then the finance department of the college I was attending told me I would have to take out a loan to continue in school. I left college and got a job to save some money for the next year.

Saving began as planned, but a car entered the picture and took a sizeable share of my income. Then a lovely lady became my wife, and a family came along. All of these demanded more and more of my income. Before long there wasn't anything going into savings to continue college, and we were living from one paycheck to another just to meet the bills of sustaining a family.

In the meantime I had convinced myself that the Lord would settle for my working as an active layperson in the local church to keep it running effectively for Him. I tried for years to keep up the facade that I was answering the call to enter the ministry by the many things my wife and I were doing in leadership within the local church. However, every time we had an evangelistic meeting, I felt the strong conviction that the Lord wanted my full attention; He did not want my "leftovers." He wanted all my energy to be focused on ministry instead of just something I did after earning a living for my family.

The Lord allowed me little peace. Whenever I had these impressions from the Lord, my argument was that I never had enough money to reach from one paycheck to the next, so how could I possibly add the expense of tuition and books on top of that? But as my wife and I continued to pray about it, we decided to put God to the test and follow His leading. I soon was experiencing the "peace . . . which passeth understanding."

And what happened in our lives is beyond understanding too. Without any financial help from family or friends, we got me through college, my master of divinity degree, and into full-time ministry in our first church. We did all that without owing anyone anything, and we started with nothing.

My testimony is that when you return to the Lord what He claims as His (not just your means, but your life) and trust Him when He says all of His biddings are accompanied by His enablings, He will bless you beyond human understanding.

If anyone serves Me, let him follow Me; and where I am, there My servant will be also. If anyone serves Me, him My Father will honor. John 12:26, NKJV.

LeRoy Finck is secretary of the New Jersey Conference of Seventh-day Adventists in Trenton, New Jersey. He is a member of the Princeton, New Jersey, Seventh-day Adventist Church.

....

NOT FORSAKEN
By James Gilley

YOUNG MINISTERS don't make a lot of money, but I wasn't prepared for making less money than I had made as a student. Yet that was the case as we went to pastor our first district after finishing the seminary.

Camille and I were the proud parents of a baby boy. As we sat down at the kitchen table to pay our bills, we wrote the tithe check first. Then we paid the bills. When we finished, we had only $8 left and a whole month before another check. How would we put gas in the car, buy formula for the baby, or feed ourselves? We had no other income except our salary, and the cupboard was empty.

Of course, we considered holding the tithe check for a week or so. It wasn't our bread we were so worried about, but our baby's, and I was supposed to be the breadwinner of the family. After a heart-searching discussion and a little time of prayer, we decided that by faith we would return the tithe, pay all of the other bills that we owed, and trust God to open the doors. We promptly got into the car and went for a ride, which was very poor economy when we needed to save gas!

Upon returning, we found a car parked in front of our home. It was Howard Lee, the local Worthington Food representative. After we had visited for a few minutes, Howard asked, "Could you folks use some health food?"

"Could we!" Camille and I cried in unison. Then Howard went to his car and brought back some fantastic Worthington Foods (I've had a soft spot for Worthington ever since), including some frozen foods! I knew right then that we wouldn't starve.

Throughout that month little miracles like that happened! Someone left some fresh vegetables on our front porch (we never knew who); a lady in our church who raised hens and sold eggs brought us a couple dozen as a gift; a refund check from a utility company where we had lived in another state arrived when we needed it most! There were always plenty for the baby and plenty for us! And at the end of the month we had $34 left over, after starting with only $8.

I have been young, and now am old; yet have I not seen the righteous forsaken, nor his seed begging bread. Psalm 37:25.

James Gilley is president of the Arkansas-Louisiana Conference of Seventh-day Adventists in Shreveport, Louisiana. He is a member of the Shreveport South Seventh-day Adventist Church.

PRINCIPLES SET IN CEMENT
By Larry D. Word

IN THE summer of 1959 a team of evangelists conducted a crusade in Roanoke, Virginia, in which more than 280 precious souls were baptized. Among them were my mother, father, grandmother, several aunts, uncles, cousins, and three of my brothers. I was very young at the time, but I do remember going to the tent meetings.

Before his baptism my father used to gamble on cardplaying every weekend to make ends meet. His weekly salary was $55 a week digging ditches. At home were six hungry boys, ages four to fourteen, and one daughter, age two. My father says he never lost while gambling, because he always had a jug of moonshine on the table for his fellow gamblers to drink, which impaired their judgment.

However, after my father joined the Seventh-day Adventist Church, he and my mother stopped smoking and drinking, and my father immediately stopped gambling. But he still had the problem of not making enough money to feed, house, and clothe his seven children.

As he prayed about the situation, God heard his prayer. My father took up cement masonry. He worked hard at his new trade and learned fast. The harder he worked, the faster he learned his new job.

The two principles he taught his children were to return an honest tithe and liberal offering and to keep the Sabbath holy. Every evening at the dinner table the whole family would gather for family prayer, and my father taught these principles with everyday lessons.

Soon the jobs began to pay more money, and my father always returned an honest tithe and offering. He became so good at his job that he was promoted to supervisor at the place where he worked. Eventually, with some encouragement from his fellow workers, he started his own cement-finishing business.

That's when the blessings really began to flow. We bought our first new car and our first home. My father had two trucks, a car, and all the tools and equipment needed to run his business. He was able to send his last three children to college, and my mother didn't have to work so hard anymore just to make ends meet. He was able to buy his daughters (he had another daughter by now) pretty clothes. Yet he never forsook the church. He gave even more to the church. He became a deacon, and he took care of the grass and maintenance of the church, never charging a dime for his labor.

So the Lord blessed the Word family tremendously from the meager $55 per week. The Lord has blessed all my father's children to reach maturity. One of his sons has a real-estate company, and his properties are worth more than $2 million. One is a firefighter for the city. Another is a nursing assistant at a Veterans Administration hospital and an elder in the church. Two sons learned the cement business from him. A daughter graduated from Oakwood College, has a master's degree in education, and was voted Teacher of the Year in Florida. The other daughter is in school pursuing a master's degree in physical therapy. The principles my father taught me served me well through a bachelor's degree from Oakwood College and a master's degree from Mercy University. I am also a certified public accountant.

My father's $55 per week has multiplied to more than $1 million a year only by the blessings of the Lord, all because he and his family chose to serve God and to be faithful stewards of blessings.

Above all, the Lord has blessed us to have a stable family. Mom and Dad, as of January 13, 2000, had been married for 55 years. "To God be the glory, great things He hath done."

So then neither is he that planteth any thing, neither he that watereth; but God that giveth the increase. Now he that planteth and he that watereth are one: and every man shall receive his own reward according to his own labour. 1 Corinthians 3:7, 8.

Larry D. Word is treasurer of the Northeastern Conference of Seventh-day Adventists in St. Albans, New York. He is a member of the Bethesda Seventh-day Adventist Church in Amityville, New York.

THE LORD MAKES THE HARVEST
By Gary and Don Emelander

IT WAS spring, and the wheat needed to be sprayed. When the contractor got to the last field, he sprayed only part of it. He told us it was so poor that we should plow it up and plant corn or beans instead. That would mean a total crop loss. We decided that it sounded more like an Investment project.

We figured that if we got 40 bushels per acre, we would break even. So we would give everything over 40 bushels an acre to Investment. We didn't even bother to spray the rest of the 65-acre field.

At harvest the field produced an average of 57 bushels per acre (our best field was 59 bushels an acre). That meant the yield was seventeen bushels per acre beyond our break-even point. On 65 acres, that meant 1,105 bushels for God— this from a supposedly worthless crop.

A few years earlier our wheat harvest was almost done when rains came and caused it to sprout in the field. We took three samples while we loaded the truck. The last 1,200 bushels showed 100-percent sprout. That meant those 1,200 bushels were good only for feed and worth less than half the price.

The standard for acceptance as good wheat is anything less than a sprout rate of 50 percent. We offered half the load to God if it could pass the inspection standard of less than 50 percent sprout, even though our tests already showed 100 percent sprout. Later we felt guilty for giving God half of something worthless, so we gave it all to Him. The next day the results came back showing seven percent sprout, the best load of the season.

God can make anything bad, good.

Give, and it shall be given unto you; good measure, pressed down, and shaken together, and running over, shall men give into your bosom. For with the same measure that ye mete withal it shall be measured to you again. Luke 6:38.

Gary and Don Emelander are farmers in Belding, Michigan. They are members of the Ionia, Michigan, Seventh-day Adventist Church.

A PUZZLE FOR THE NIH
By Charlene VanVliet

IN THE summer and fall of 1996 I began to feel ill. A feeling of depression and fatigue grew steadily worse until it was all I could do to drag myself to work, help out at church, or do anything active. We went from doctor to doctor trying to identify the problem. Finally, I believe God led me to a Seventh-day Adventist doctor, who at that time practiced in Chattanooga, Tennessee. After he had examined me and run some tests, he asked if I would allow him to call the National Institutes of Health (NIH) about my case. I consented.

About this time I felt impressed to be a better steward of my health. I began by trying to be in bed no later than nine o'clock each evening so that I would be able to get up early enough to spend time alone with the Lord. I developed the habits of drinking more water, watching my diet more carefully, and exercising regularly.

Soon NIH called and asked if I would allow them to examine me in Bethesda, Maryland. I declined, but after my local doctors soundly scolded me for turning down the opportunity, I finally agreed. In October 1996 I made my first trip to NIH.

As they examined and tested me, they discovered that I had hypogamma-globulinemia. This big word meant, in essence, that I had no immune system. On one of my trips I roomed with a young lady with the same ailment. She had been in the hospital seventeen times in four months with different kinds of infections. The specialists at NIH couldn't understand why I wasn't sick all the time with colds or infections, as was every other patient with this disease. I rarely have a cold or infection. They prescribed a gamma globulin infusion every month, and I now feel better than I have in many years.

Not long ago my seventeen-year-old granddaughter, pen and paper in hand, asked me to tell her all my health problems. The list included arthritis, fibromyalgia, osteoporosis, and hypogammaglobulinemia. But in spite of all these problems, I am able now to serve my church as treasurer and hold down a full-time, stress-filled job as administrative director for a large government agency.

I give God all the praise and firmly believe that He has honored my faith in Him and my stewardship of the health He has given me. He has strengthened me to work for Him.

Beloved, I pray that you may prosper in all things and be in health; just as your soul prospers. 3 John 2, NKJV.

Charlene VanVliet is administrative director of Monroe Housing Authority, in Monroe, Louisiana. She is a member of the Westlakes Seventh-day Adventist Church in West Monroe.

TESTED AND PROVEN FAITHFUL
By Ronald J. Goss

IN 1961 I was honorably discharged from the United States Army. After paying my bar and gambling debts, I had $22 to my name. I had no job, no car, and no other place to go, so I went home to my mother. I was a prodigal son. I had grown up knowing the truth, and I had attended Adventist elementary schools and academy. Sadly, like many others, I had decided to serve the world.

Faithful and loving Christian that she was, my mother invited me to church on my first Sabbath home. To please her, I went. The sermon was on stewardship. As I listened, I had a strong impression that I must put $20 into the offering plate before leaving church that day.

"This is crazy," I thought to myself. "Remember, you have only $22, and no job and no transportation." But the thought kept coming: "'Prove me,' says the Lord."

Before I left the church that day, I put $20 into the offering plate. On the way home I wondered if I was losing my mind. That evening, while I was unpacking my army-issue travel bag, I came across my address book. Tucked away inside in a place long-forgotten, was a twenty-dollar bill. That made quite an impression on me. A short time later the Lord provided me a job with the State of Maryland, where I soon became head of my department.

Even though I didn't rejoin the church until several years later (during which time I got married), God blessed me, just as Malachi 3:10 promises He will. From a trust relationship with God that began in faithful tithing, I grew in grace until I became a faithful and active member of the Seventh-day Adventist Church.

My wife had no use for my renewed faith, and she divorced me. She had a well-paying job. Now, with only half the income, I couldn't make the payments on our small farm.

A tough, frugal man held the mortgage. The only possible way for me to make the payment would be to use tithe money. But I made a firm decision that I wasn't going to borrow on the Lord's tithe.

One day the mortgage holder called me. He said, "I understand you have a birthday coming up soon." I confirmed that it was so. To my utter amazement, the man told me to skip the next month's payment as a birthday gift! Every month after that God saw to it that I could make the payment, often at the last moment. As C. D. Brooks says, "When you're down to your last dime, the Lord steps in just in time."

Throughout the years God has proved to me over and over again that He keeps His word. He gave me a Christian wife, and for many years now we have returned a double tithe to the Lord. He has always taken care of the necessities of life as He promised. He has proved to us that what we couldn't do with 100 percent of our income, He can do with 80 percent. God has a thousand ways of which we know not.

The Lord will give grace and glory: no good thing will he withhold from them that walk uprightly. Psalm 84:11.

Ronald J. Goss is president of Project Restore in Locust Dale, Virginia. He is a member of the Amicus Seventh-day Adventist Church in Ruckersville, Virginia.

....

THE POTATO FIELD
By Sylvia Davidson

IT STARTED out as an ordinary fall day, crisp and beautiful. A friend called and asked if I would like to dig potatoes. She explained that a family from church, who operated a large market garden, was going to plow under a field of potatoes because they had no time to harvest them. They gave permission for us to take whatever we wanted before the plow arrived.

I couldn't use many potatoes for myself, but my children's families could make use of some. So could my brother. Soon a list formed in my mind.

My friend called the church registry, and families came from all directions to meet at the market garden in Watino. We had a fun time of shared work and comradery, but when the morning was old and all of us had what we wanted, it still appeared that the field of potatoes had barely been touched. What a shame that it should all go to waste! But someone else would have to do the digging. My back was breaking from the unaccustomed hard work.

My little Dakota pickup groaned under a full load of potatoes, so I decided to take the secondary highway home through Girouxville. That's when I heard that still small voice I've come to know as the Holy Spirit. He said, "Take some potatoes to Cathy."

As I passed the street leading to Cathy's house, I grit my teeth, hardened my heart, and pressed the gas pedal. No! Cathy had hurt me by spreading a false story about me, and I would not give her anything. No. Never. So what if she was a single parent of three little ones and was on social assistance; she had wronged me.

Putting that bit of unpleasantness out of my mind, I drove to Peace River, where I found my brother. He was delighted with the huge red and white varieties of potatoes. He invited some of his neighbors to share in the bounty.

Now, with an empty truck, I started home. Then I remembered my list. My son and his family didn't have any of those beautiful potatoes. Neither did my daughter and her family. I would have to make another trip.

Back at Watino, I dug until I thought my lungs would burst from overuse. When the truck was full, I started out for home again on the secondary highway through Girouxville. Once more, when passing that certain street, the Holy Spirit said softly, "Take some potatoes to Cathy."

I was just too exhausted to be firm. "No, please don't make me. I can't do it. She'll make fun of me or throw them back in my face. I just can't."

As this little scene played out in my mind, I felt that somehow I was wrong about something, but I managed to shake it off, and I drove on without stopping.

On the way to Peace River, I decided to bag the potatoes and take them to the Native Friendship Center. A local supermarket gave me some bags, and the center was very appreciative of the gift. As fast as we unloaded the bags, families appeared to take them away. I felt tired but happy for the many people I had been able to help.

It bothered me that the potato field was still only a little more than half cleared, and there was good daylight left. I had to make another trip. I was driven by images of starving people, and I just couldn't let those potatoes go to waste.

Back I went to the potato field, this time too exhausted and sore even to stand. I crawled from hill to hill and dug with my hands, almost crying with fatigue. From the ground I would throw the potatoes into the back of my truck.

Once again, when passing through Girouxville, the still small voice told me, "Take some potatoes to Cathy."

Broken at last, I said yes and prayed that God would protect me from any verbal onslaught. He did better than that. Cathy wasn't home to say anything at all. But, strangely enough, a large empty laundry basket sat on the step waiting to hold something. Potatoes perhaps?

As I placed each big, beautiful potato in the basket, I realized that my resentment toward Cathy was gone. Only love remained. I forgave her that moment, and I prayed that God would forgive me for my own unforgiving spirit.

Perhaps in heaven God will answer my question: If I had done what the Holy Spirit asked the first time that He asked it, would He have let me give just one load of potatoes instead of three?

Now no chastening for the present seemeth to be joyous, but grievous: nevertheless afterward it yieldeth the peaceable fruit of righteousness unto them which are exercised thereby. Hebrews 12:11.

Sylvia Davidson lives in Ascot Beach, Alberta. She is a member of the Onoway, Alberta, Seventh-day Adventist Church.

You have a stewardship testimony you need to share and we need to read. See page 224 for details.

The TENTH MEETING

Come and hear, all ye that fear God, and I will declare what he hath done for my soul.

Psalm 66:16

Christine Ewing

Josh Sink

John G. DePalma

Sylvia A. Germany

Lorin Wentland

Andy Moore

Margarita Jones

Donald W. Maddy

Stephen L. McPherson

Lorna Baker

A TEXTBOOK CASE

By Christine Ewing

IT HAS been a very exciting time to be a member of the Traverse City Seventh-day Adventist Church. For more than a year we have been raising funds for a building program to erect a new church that can accommodate our growing community. We have been amazed to watch the Lord work in magnificent ways to turn our meager efforts into milestones.

Throughout this process I had been questioning my part in this divine adventure. How could I, a struggling college student, help? In December 1999 we had our Covenant of the Heart Sabbath to lay our faith on the table, so to speak. Knowing that I would be going off to school soon, I made a pledge of $360. A dollar a day wasn't much but I wanted to give back to my Lord who has brought me so far.

Soon however, I learned that the pledge wasn't for a year; it was needed in four months. If the ground breaking was going to take place in the spring, the money had to be in by April. Prior to that special Sabbath of committing ourselves, as a church, to God's work in Traverse City, I had made a personal commitment of $140 to the building fund. I now had a $500 commitment and felt unsure of how it would be fulfilled in just a little over a month before I headed back to school. I prayed that the Lord would help me to keep my pledge. I had made it with a sincere passion for the work going on in Traverse City.

After my bills were paid I set aside everything I earned for the building fund. When it was time to leave for college I was excited to have fulfilled my pledge and even have $20 in my pocket. My delight soon turned to consternation. I had forgotten about buying my college textbooks. Where was I going to get the money? I prayed again, asking God to help me to get the books I needed. I knew that it was up to God.

The morning came to leave for college. The car was packed and my mother and I were just about to walk out the door when the phone rang. It was my uncle asking if we had time before we left town to stop by his house. When we arrived I found that my aunt and uncle had prepared a "boodle box" for me, full of food and other things that become luxuries to a college student. We visited for only a short time and as I was putting on my coat to leave, my uncle handed me an envelope. He said, "This is just a little something to help you out. I know sometimes it would be nice to buy a pizza or do something fun." I took the envelope and hugged them both with gratitude.

As my mother and I drove out of town I looked at the envelope lying on my lap. I felt full of the love with which it had been given me. I turned it over and opened it up. Inside were five one hundred-dollar bills. My eyes filled with tears as my heart filled with the love of my Heavenly Father who had, through my aunt and uncle, given back *everything* I had given in faith to Him. But He gave me much more than money. He gave me a real, experiential demonstration of His unfailing love and concern for me. He had been working out a plan for me before I even knew I had a need. On April 2, 2000 the ground-breaking ceremony for our new church was held. I am thankful for this personal illustration that I will always remember, a time when I was poignantly reminded of Who is in charge of my life and to Whom my money truly belongs.

Give, and it will be given to you. A good measure, pressed down, shaken together and running over, will be poured into your lap. For with the measure you use, it will be measured to you. Luke 6:38, NIV.

Christine Ewing is a junior at Oakland University in Rochester, Michigan. She is a member of the Traverse City, Michigan, Seventh-day Adventist Church.

....

GOD IS NOT MY CO-PILOT
By Josh Sink

FLYING has been my passion from a very early age. While children typically change occupational choices a dozen times, I was settled from the moment I could walk that someday I would be an airline pilot. Not only did I want to fly above the clouds, but I wanted to take other people there, too.

Upon reaching adulthood I realized that very few Adventists are in the airline industry. People have often talked about how hard it would be to get Sabbaths off, so that alone scared them away from trying.

I see the airline industry as a wide-open field, and I believe that God wants witnesses for Him among those who work in the air as well as on the ground.

A popular bumper sticker reads, "God is my copilot." I don't really agree with that level of self-sufficiency. In effect, it is saying, "God, when I can't handle the control panel anymore, I'll let You take over!" I think God wants a little bigger role than that. He has to be my pilot, and *I'll* do whatever *He* asks.

One thing He has asked me to do is keep His seventh-day Sabbath holy, and the following story is an example of how God made it possible to do that, even when it seemed impossible.

I planned to complete my training at a well-known airline company in the summer of 1998 after receiving assurances that there wouldn't be any classes or instruction on Saturdays. I dived into my training full speed ahead.

That all came to an abrupt halt one Monday afternoon. The director of the training program announced that a very important class was to be held the following Saturday, and we were required to attend. In the airline industry, if a student misses any classes, he's out. If I missed this class, my dreams of becoming an airline pilot would be virtually thrown out.

"God," I prayed, "You have led me to this very point, and I can't believe I'm supposed to turn around and go back home!" I reflected on my progress so far. I had gotten my private pilot's license before I got my driver's license, when I was seventeen. After graduating from high school, I moved to Andrews University to attend the flight school. A few weeks after graduation I married a beautiful woman, also a pilot, whom I met while being a student missionary in Guam. A short time later I was accepted into the training program for a regional airline company. And now it seemed, after all that, I was staring at exit doors.

I must admit that I wrestled with the idea that this training was just as important on Sabbath as any other day. Since God had obviously led me to this point in my life, surely He wouldn't mind my attending this class, because these circumstances were beyond my control.

God had other ideas. He has magnificent powers beyond all human comprehension.

The week dragged by slowly. Sabbath was looming, and still it seemed that I had no escape from attending that class.

Friday morning our director announced the impossible. There would be no class the next day. The teacher's pregnant wife had gone into premature labor two months before her due date. Of course, I wasn't sure whether I should be happy or sad about this. This was good news for me, because I didn't have to worry about attending the class on Sabbath. But what about that mother and baby? Soon enough, the director announced that they had come through their ordeal safely. But the class still had to be postponed until the middle of the following week.

I am now happily employed with this airline company, and I have had numerous chances to tell many pilots about God. The Lord has rescued me many times from having to work on Sabbath, because He has promised that if He commands me to obey Him, He will make it possible.

God is my pilot. If I had ever let Him be just my "copilot," who knows where I'd be today?

But they that wait upon the Lord shall renew their strength; they shall mount up with wings as eagles; they shall run, and not be weary; and they shall walk, and not faint. Isaiah 40:31.

Josh Sink is an airline pilot in West Palm Beach, Florida. He is a member of the Communities West Seventh-day Adventist Church in Boca Raton, Florida.

GOD FINDS THE WAY
By John G. DePalma

WHEN I WAS baptized and joined the Adventist Church, I was working as finance director for the city of Portland, Maine.

Baptism, though a freeing experience, brought a host of financial challenges. With a new home to pay for and four children to educate in Adventist schools, I found it difficult to make ends meet. To make matters worse, my wife, a teacher, was not employed at the time. We agreed for her to stay at home with our children. As a result, I became the sole breadwinner for our family.

I realized the devil was not happy with me and was doing all he could to discourage me. And he almost succeeded. I struggled briefly with reducing my tithe and offerings to meet my expenses. But then I remembered the promise that if I was faithful, God would take care of my needs. I claimed that promise, even though I had no clear picture of the way out of my difficulties. But God had a plan already in place.

In addition to my responsibilities as finance director, I was also city treasurer and tax collector. By virtue of these positions I became very active in the Treasurers and Tax Collectors Association in the State of Maine. This gave me some recognition among my colleagues and opened the door for God to work His plan.

The University of Maine Governmental Resources Office contacted me and asked me to author a book on fiscal management. This I did and entitled it *Cash Management for Smaller Municipalities*. Shortly after its publication I was again contacted by the university to perform an evaluation of treasury and tax collectors' management procedures in a number of municipalities.

These towns asked me to help them improve their financial systems. For this I received a stipend and expense monies. Every time after that when the end of the month found me short, I was called by the university to teach workshops on municipal finance. All of our needs, and even some of our wants, were met. "Praise God, from whom all blessings flow!"

The Lord is my shepherd; I shall not want. Psalm 23:1.

John G. DePalma is secretary-treasurer of the Northern New England Conference of Seventh-day Adventists in Portland, Maine. He is a member of the James White Memorial Seventh-day Adventist Church in Portland.

A NEW WAY OF LIVING
By Sylvia A. Germany

GOOD food often costs more than bad food. I couldn't see how our family budget could be stretched to afford this new way of living. But we knew we needed to make this change.

Our family had spent a few days at a lifestyle center. Just making the decision to go had been a blessing itself, for it prompted us to start better eating habits even before we got there. Usually when our family traveled, we would eat snack food along the way. This time we left the snacks at home. We decided that during our stay at the center we would eat only what we were served in the regular program.

All the good things we learned at the center made me worry about our grocery bill. We would have to dispense with cheaper, less healthy food and "invest" in better food. In the previous year our family had experienced major illness and a loss of income. According to my calculations, our resolve to start eating right would be a financial challenge. But with faith that we were doing what God was calling us to do, we moved ahead.

We started this new way of living, knowing we would see a difference in our health. And even though we are not yet where we need to be, we are not where we used to be. Not only are we experiencing the primary blessing of better health, but we are also seeing the rewards of our good stewardship in other areas. Many times we have been surprised to see how the Lord seems to honor our commitment by stretching our income to cover our increased grocery bill. What we thought would be too expensive for us now seems to fit right into our budget.

So, with faith in God, we press forward in our efforts, with His blessing, to be healthy and fit to do His work. Praise Him!

Beloved, I wish above all things that thou mayest prosper and be in health, even as thy soul prospereth. 3 John 2.

Sylvia A. Germany is interim director of human resources at Oakwood College in Huntsville, Alabama. She is a member of the Mt. Calvary Seventh-day Adventist Church in Huntsville.

A DREAM TO SERVE
By Lorin Wentland

MY WIFE and I attended a regional Adventist Laymen's Services and Industries convention at Sun Valley, Idaho. We were inspired as we heard a prominent Adventist businessman whom I had long admired tell of how God had blessed his business. Clearly God was using him as a channel through which His blessing could flow on to others. As I heard this man tell of his involvement in building mission churches in many Third World countries, I was moved to do the same.

I had a dream not only of participating in building a church with Maranatha Volunteers International but funding a church entirely as well. My family caught the vision, and we figured how much we would need to fully fund a church and pay the transportation cost for our family of six. Our business had never before seen that much profit in one year. We knew that God is pleased when we expect great things from Him, and we asked the Lord to bless as we began to set money aside for this dream. The account grew steadily, and we eagerly awaited the Maranatha newsletter to see what projects might be available.

In August we saw in the newsletter that Maranatha was making plans to build fifteen churches in Belize, some of them during the Christmas holiday. I called the Maranatha office and shared my dream with the staff. I learned that they didn't have the funding in place yet, but they were going forward in faith with these projects. I told them that, Lord willing, we would like to take one of the churches on as a project, to which they agreed. Now we were committed. However, we actually had only 60 percent of the money in hand and only two months to come up with the rest.

I knew that with God's help we could do it. In seven months we had been able to set aside 60 percent of the money, and I had made no change in the management of my business. If God wanted us to build a church in Belize, He would find a way to come up with the balance by October.

We eagerly watched our financial statement to see how much money we could set aside. Early in October God worked it out. The money was in hand.

But we also needed a minimum of 25 people to build the church. We were sure that our relatives and friends at church would readily participate. We made up some flyers on our color printer, complete with pictures and maps. Many people were interested, but only a few made a commitment to go.

The deadline was fast approaching for finalizing our project with Maranatha. We had been praying earnestly that God would direct us to people who would like to share in our project. We had only a few more days, and we had only ten people committed and about twelve or thirteen "maybes." Even if they all decided to go, we still didn't have the 25 people necessary for the building project. And none of the "maybes" were skilled builders.

The deadline arrived. Greatly discouraged, I called the Maranatha office and told the staff that even though we had the money in hand, we were going to have to cancel because we didn't have enough people, either skilled or unskilled.

Late that afternoon I received a return call from the Maranatha office. They told me there was a group from Canada who also was planning to go to Belize

141

during the Christmas holiday. They, too, were recruiting people but were also short of the necessary 25. We were put in contact with each other and decided to join our two groups. This turned out to be a double blessing, because several of their group were professional builders as well as some having the other skills that we needed.

As the work on that little church went forward over that Christmas season, I marveled at how the Lord had brought these people together. We had among us an engineer, a mason, a welder, builders, an administrator, a doctor, a dentist, a nurse, a cook, a VBS leader, a bus driver, and plenty of young and willing workers for all the general labor of building the church.

As we worked, played, and prayed together, we experienced the joy of being *together* in the service of our Lord.

It was he who gave some to be apostles, some to be prophets, some to be evangelists, and some to be pastors and teachers, to prepare God's people for works of service, so that the body of Christ may be built up. Ephesians 4:11, 12, NIV.

Lorin Wentland is the owner and general manager of Wentland Diesel Service, Inc., in Milton-Freewater, Oregon. He is a member of the Milton Seventh-day Adventist Church.

THE GUARANTEE
By Andy Moore

IN THE spring of 1970 I was a research mechanic for Lockheed Aircraft Corporation and also in a baptismal class, preparing to become an Adventist.

At Sabbath school one day, the lesson study was about stewardship. It was taught by a very seasoned colporteur from India. As a relatively new Christian, I was uncertain about the idea that "all we have belongs to God."

The teacher gave us a challenge: "Don't take my word for it," he said. "Put your trust in God. Take the biggest, not the smallest, bill in your wallet and put it in the church offering. I guarantee you that before the week is over, it will return to you tenfold!" In retrospect, I'm not sure everyone would agree with the teacher's guarantee, but I was a new Christian and had no reason to question his certainty.

At the time, my wife and son were out of town visiting relatives. I had only one twenty-dollar bill in my wallet. It was all I had for gas and food for the next week until payday. I was driving a 1965 Dodge Charger that got about eight miles to the gallon of gas. I was 30 miles from home with a whole week ahead to drive to work on one tank of gas.

When the time came to give my offering, I was sweating profusely! I took my twenty-dollar bill and put it into God's hands. I have never felt so relieved and at peace as I was just then.

When I got home, I found a letter in the mail from Boeing Aircraft Company, where I previously worked. I was stunned to find a check for a savings investment in the amount of $257. Immediately I called my wife and told her what had happened. She knew God and rejoiced with me.

Monday morning at work I received a ten-percent incentive pay raise, unusual in aviation. The next Friday I received a seven-percent cost-of-living pay increase.

No surprise that now I trust God with everything.

For every beast of the forest is mine, and the cattle upon a thousand hills. Psalm 50:10.

***

Andy Moore is a retired maintenance safety inspector for the Federal Aviation Administration. He lives in Buena Vista, Colorado, and is a member of the Salida, Colorado, Seventh-day Adventist Church.

MY MOTHER'S LEGACY
By Margarita Jones

I GREW UP with a great example of generosity. My mother would bring home struggling families she encountered on the street, sharing with them from her limited income, giving them food, water, or clothing. She didn't belong to any church; she did these things because she cared, not calculating the amount of her kindness to strangers, family, and friends.

I remember her saying that after paying rent, utilities, and groceries, there was always more money left than she expected. Her example has stayed with me since.

I found Jesus as Lord and Savior twelve years ago, and giving to others and returning tithe to the Lord have become a part of my life, built on my mother's legacy.

When our home needed a new roof a few years ago, I found myself studying with the two Hispanic young men who were tearing off the old roof. "Here are two candidates for heaven," I told myself.

A job that normally takes one day or two this time took a month. Bad weather (and the grace of God) made it possible for me to get to know these young men, give them Bible lessons, and take them to church. The Lord even allowed me to pay their salaries from the contractor's amount when he unreasonably withheld their pay.

In time both were baptized into our church! They eventually returned to their home countries, taking with them the seed of the gospel.

God's kindnesses to us continues to flow. During the last week of December 1998, the Lord saw to it that my husband, after an emergency quadruple bypass, also found a new spiritual heart–and celebrated his 67th birthday.

What a great God we serve!

Verily I say unto you, Inasmuch as ye have done it unto one of the least of these my brethren, ye have done it unto me. Matthew 25:40.

Margarita Jones is an attendance clerk for the Waco, Texas, Independent School District. She is a member of the Waco Seventh-day Adventist Church.

TURNAROUND IN ARIZONA
By Donald W. Maddy

WHEN I was released from the U.S. Navy in 1956, I decided to leave my parents' home in Ohio and live with my sister and her husband in Scottsdale, Arizona, hoping to find a job there. Traveling with me by car were my mother and my sister, Marge. They planned to visit family there for a few weeks and then return by train.

Marge was the first Adventist from our family of twelve children, and she was conscientious about caring for God's money. The day before she and Mother were to board the train to return to Ohio, she received $100 with which to buy her $87 one-way ticket. She faithfully set aside her tithe from the $100 and then stopped by a store to pick up a few necessities for the journey. Paying for these items took more than she had to spare, however, and left her with less than enough to purchase her $87 ticket.

Instead of asking to borrow from Mother or me, she decided to claim the promise in Malachi that God would open the windows of heaven. Only she and God knew her plight.

In the meantime, I was dealing with a dilemma of my own. My sister and family in Scottsdale suddenly had decided to move back to Ohio in about a month. Another brother had invited me to join him in California, where he had a job and housing for me, but I didn't feel right about that option.

The next day, as we were loading Mother's and Marge's luggage to go to the station, I felt impressed to return home. After all, most of my loved ones were in Ohio or returning there. I pondered all these things and made up my mind. Surely God could help me find a job at home.

While I helped my sister carry the last of the luggage to the car, I said, "If you will help me pack my things, I'll drive you and Mom back in my car." Her heart nearly stopped!

144

As the three of us drove those many miles back to Ohio, I kept saying repeatedly, "I don't understand why I am doing this!" Then Marge told me her story, with all the details, leading up to that last trip to the car. She was over-whelmed at how God was answering her prayer.

I was impressed also, and after my Scottsdale sister moved back to Ohio, I accepted Bible studies from her husband and was ultimately baptized in 1961. I immediately established the habit of returning tithe, of course!

The costs for that trip back to Ohio came to nearly $40 (remember, this was 1956!), which my mother and Marge shared, bringing her total travel expense to $20. Once again, God delighted to bless a faithful steward and those who put their trust in Him.

O taste and see that the Lord is good. Psalm 34:8.

Donald W. Maddy is a semiretired electrician in Wahkiacus, Washington. He is a member of the Wahkiacus Seventh-day Adventist Church.

DIFFICULT, WORTHWHILE, AND BLESSED
By Stephen L. McPherson

ONE hundred thousand dollars seemed like a lot of money to my wife and me. That's how much we guessed it was going to cost to educate our three sons in the Adventist school system. With me on denominational income and with my wife employed part-time, we knew we faced a big challenge. It seemed we were about to climb a huge mountain—with no sight of the top.

We faithfully resolved to continue our practice of returning tithe and offerings, to manage everything that was left as carefully as we could, and to keep our school account current.

Things went well through the elementary and academy years. Then came the last hurdle—college. During the ten years our children were in college (six of those years we had two attending at the same time), the whole family worked very hard. The boys worked each summer and during the school year.

Could we manage without educational loans? During that ten-year period we received many loan offers. However, we had decided to continue on a pay–as–you–go basis. So we lived in a rental home, drove older-model cars, and watched every dollar carefully.

Three college degrees and $100,000 later all three children had received the benefit of an Adventist education from elementary school through college.

However, the most amazing part of the story is that during the college years, due to God's blessing, our family's net worth increased in direct proportion to the amount spent on education.

We have been immeasurably blessed to see how God honors faithfulness in worthwhile, though difficult, endeavors.

Trust in the Lord, and do good; so shalt thou dwell in the land, and verily thou shalt be fed. . . . Commit thy way to the Lord; trust also in him and he shall bring it to pass. Psalm 37:3-5.

Stephen L. McPherson is president of the Idaho Conference of Seventh-day Adventists in Boise, Idaho. He is a member of the Nampa, Idaho, Seventh-day Adventist Church.

A FULL TRUNK AND
A FULL HEART
By Lorna Baker

FOR SEVERAL months after my marriage failed, my five children and I lived on a small disability pension. The monthly routine when the pension check arrived was always the same: return the tithe, pay the rent, go to the food bank.

Waiting in the bank that Friday afternoon to deposit my check, I began to think about how good it would feel not have to rely on the food bank that month. I longed to be able to visit the grocery store and make purchases, as other families did. As I approached the window, the struggle felt like all-out war. I was bombarded by so many feelings that I had to force myself to put the right amount of money into a tithe envelope I always carried with me.

By the time I reached the food bank, it was closed, and again the struggle began. "Use the money," a voice inside whispered. "God won't punish you this one time." Needless to say, by this time I was crying, feeling very sorry for myself and my children. Not paying attention to where I was going, I made an illegal left turn right in front of a police car. Real, genuine tears flowed down my cheeks at my double predicament, but the officer was unmoved by my story. He wrote the ticket for $48 and then wished me a good day.

As I drove slowly away, the voice kept saying, "Use the tithe money. It won't hurt."

At sundown worship that night my heart was heavy. At bedtime the thought returned: "Use the money. No one will know." On Sabbath morning the struggle continued. I prayed, and God helped me honor my vow to Him.

146

During the worship service one of my sisters in Christ mysteriously asked for the key to my car. When the service ended, she returned the key but told me not to open the trunk until we got home. Curiosity, however, got the better of us. As soon as we left church, we opened the trunk, expecting to find lunch. What we found instead was more food than the tithe would have purchased plus $100.

I don't have to tell you how happy I was that the Lord helped me honor my vow. He knew that my faith needed support, and He made sure I got it.

I have been young, and now am old; yet have I not seen the righteous forsaken, nor his seed begging bread. He is ever merciful and lendeth; and his seed is blessed. Psalm 37:25, 26.

Lorna Baker is a registered nurse at a community health center in Toronto, Ontario. She is a member of the Willowdale, Ontario, Seventh-day Adventist Church.

You have a stewardship testimony you need to share and we need to read. See page 224 for details.

The
ELEVENTH
MEETING

*Come and hear,
all ye that fear
God, and I will
declare what
he hath done for
my soul.*

Psalm 66:16

Jill McCann

William D. Fisher

Tamie J. Faw

Margaret Roelke McNitt

Eckhard Hubin

Beth Davis Nelson

Ernest Dunning

Mike Mamoulelis

George N. Walker

Bryan A. Richardson

WONDERFUL WINDOWS
By Jill McCann

WHEN WE purchased our home, we knew that the windows were in poor shape. Winter arrived, and we realized that replacing them would have to be sooner rather than later. We started calling for estimates. All the contractors said it would take two days to do the job. We selected a contractor and waited to hear when the installation would be scheduled.

My husband, Mark, called me at work one day to let me know the dates selected. When I checked the calendar, I nearly choked. The dates were a Friday and Sabbath.

"Mark, can we switch the dates?"

"Jill, if we don't do it then, we'll have to wait several more weeks; it also fits with when I can be home to supervise their work."

"Can't they start Friday, with your supervising? Then I'll get off work on Monday, and they can complete it then."

Mark wasn't so sure about that solution. After all, what did I know about window installation? Mark also knew that my Sabbath was important to me, but being of another faith, he did not share the same conviction.

"I'm sorry, Honey. This is what works best."

Not to be deterred, I told him that I was going to pray for rain, so the crew couldn't work on that Saturday.

I started checking the weather reports on Monday. There were no predictions of rain. Nothing changed throughout the week. On Friday morning I offered up one last prayer before I left the house.

"Lord, you know I don't want the new windows installed on Sabbath. You also know that I've been praying for rain, so that the workers won't be able to finish tomorrow. I've seen no forecast showing rain is on the way. This problem is bigger than me. I need for You to work it out. Thank You. Amen."

About 2:30 that afternoon Mark called. "Honey, I've got some good news and some bad news."

"Okay. Give me the bad news first."

"Well," he said, "the bad news is that they won't be able to work on the windows tomorrow."

I could barely contain my "yippee."

"The good news is that they'll have the windows finished today."

By then I shouted, "Hallelujah!" Of course, I asked how this could be.

"I don't understand it either," Mark answered. "But when the project manager arrived this morning, he said, 'I don't know why they told you it would take two days to do this. Would it be okay if we did it all today?' So I said, 'Yes. You'll make my wife's day.'"

Sabbath arrived, and I basked in the light of those new windows, and in the light of a God Who beamed through them the evidence of His care.

"Thanks for answering, and without the rain."

Commit thy way unto the Lord; trust also in him; and he shall bring it to pass. Psalm 37:5.

Jill McCann is an administrative secretary in Newport Beach, California. She is a member of the Westminster, California, Good Samaritan Seventh-day Adventist Church.

BAD DEBTS AND GOD'S GOODNESS
By William D. Fisher

I AM A family physician, and my wife is a registered nurse. When we married in 1965, we determined that we would be a team in the service of the Lord. We also pledged that we would double-tithe our income.

Soon after completing our medical educations we were very busy with the many things it takes to run an office and to raise a growing family of three boys. Financially we were still struggling under the weight of our medical educational expense and the costs for starting up a medical practice. It took every penny just to live, but we were faithful to our pledge in our tithe and offerings. God had blessed so often in the past that we had no complaints. We trusted our Great Benefactor to provide for us.

In 1977 our local church wrestled with an unusually large financial burden to keep the church school operating. The board decided to ask members for pledges to meet the crisis. My wife and I prayed about the problem. Then we pledged $2,500, having no idea where we would get the money. Our simple motto was "The Lord will provide." Each day we laid the matter before the Lord.

In our medical practice we had long ago determined that we would do the Lord's work, and He would take care of the finances. It was our long-standing practice never to deny anyone medical care for financial reasons. Not surprisingly, we accumulated many bad debts and outstanding accounts owed us, dating back as far as the day we opened the office doors.

Ten days after we had made our $2,500 pledge for the church school, our secretary excitedly reported to us that over the past few days she had collected $2,500 in past-due accounts. Among other examples, she told of one woman we had not seen in our office for four years. The woman came in to pay off her account and said she had awakened that morning with a feeling that "I must go pay the doctor." She tried to ignore the impression, but it persisted, so there she was in our office, paying off her four-year-old account.

Ten days after we had made our pledge to the Lord for the church school, He had provided enough to meet it! To this day He has never failed us. Praise and glory to His name!

And my God will meet all your needs according to his glorious riches in Christ Jesus. To our God and Father be glory for ever and ever. Amen. Philippians 4:19, 20, NIV.

William D. Fisher is a physician in Richmond, Indiana. He is a member of the Richmond Seventh-day Adventist Church.

A PLACE TO SERVE
By Tamie J. Faw

WHEN I first began attending the Seventh-day Adventist Church, I was impressed with how smoothly everything seemed to be run in my local congregation. All the offices and positions were filled and operating so efficiently that I wondered if there would be a place for me to serve the Lord in any capacity. This naturally became a regular topic in prayer—for the Lord to use me in every way and any way He saw fit and to involve me in the activities of the church.

The faith to which I previously belonged didn't employ the talents of women whatsoever. Women were not placed in any office or leadership role or consulted on any matters. However, I could see that the Adventist Church most definitely utilized the talents of women and believed that this was, above all, according to the Scriptures and God's purposes.

Right at this time one of the spiritual elders in the church fell and broke her arm. After her surgery the hospital recommended that someone spend the night with Herta, giving her assistance, since she was somewhat unsteady on her feet due to the accident. I was elated when Herta called to inquire if I could help her. This was a wonderful opportunity for me to show love for God by ministering to His family.

When I was baptized the next Sabbath, Herta presented me with a hard-bound set of The Conflict of the Ages series by Ellen G. White. How could she have known that I had been praying for that set of books? I cherish those books not only for their spiritual insight and knowledge, but because they were a gift from a dear friend and a direct answer to prayer!

I've continued praying for the Lord to use me more and more in His service, and I've been blessed over and over again with the joys and privileges of serving Him. Since my baptism I have had the honor of being a deaconess in my church, the personal ministries leader, director of the Discover Bible School, a prayer warrior leader, a greeter, and a hostess, plus being able to serve on numerous committees and assisting in various activities. Serving my church is a joy, an honor, and a great privilege.

The Lord has answered my prayer. I continue to pray for Him to use me now and always as He knows best.

And this is the confidence which we have before Him, that, if we ask anything according to His will, He hears us. 1 John 5:14, NASB.

Tamie J. Faw is a health-care giver and homemaker in Billings, Montana. She is a member of the Billings Seventh-day Adventist Church.

THE MAN IN THE IRON LUNG
By Margaret Roelke McNitt

MY PARENTS regularly took my sister, my brother, and me to Sunday school and church. But of the scores of sermons that I heard as a child, only a sermon on tithing remains indelibly imprinted in my memory.

Our church members did not believe in or practice tithing; I never had even heard of it. But during that sermon the Holy Spirit convicted me that this was God's plan. Others in my family weren't similarly convicted. I knew that my father did not tithe. I regularly saw him fill his offering envelopes with only quarters on Sunday mornings. This concerned me, but the Holy Spirit stored these memories away, awaiting another day.

Years later a Seventh-day Adventist nurse with whom I worked stayed up all night to share an overview of the whole Adventist message with me. I was thrilled to hear many Bible truths of which I had been totally ignorant. But when my friend began to read from Malachi 3:10, "Bring ye all the tithes into the store-house," I was suddenly a small child again in a church pew in Maryland, listening to those same words, words that I had forgotten for many years. I was overjoyed to discover that Seventh-day Adventists tithe.

Even before I was baptized as an Adventist, I was convinced that God wanted me to return tithe for the year that I had already worked. Of course I didn't have the cash on hand to do that. I still had a bank account from childhood and knew that it had enough money in it to pay the year's tithe, but this account also required my father's co-signature.

I wrote to my parents, explaining that I wanted to return tithe for my first year of work, but my mother wrote back with a refusal. My father had worked hard for that money, she said, and they would not let me use it foolishly. They even threatened to disinherit me if I became a Seventh-day Adventist.

I tearfully took this problem to my pastor. "Margaret," he said, "God knows that you want to honor Him by returning your back tithe. Just ask Him to help you save, and return it as you can." This seemed logical, and I rejoiced that I could implement his suggestion. But God had an even better plan.

I was one of several nurses caring for a man in an iron lung. Shortly after my talk with the pastor, the patient in the iron lung, who required round-the-clock care, told me that his night nurse was leaving. He asked if I could work both the night shift and the morning shift. So now I would have two jobs and could sleep for most of one of them. My income would be doubled.

The double job lasted just long enough for me to earn what I needed to return tithe on my first year's earnings and to begin giving offerings. By working through the needs of the man in the iron lung, God provided what I needed to keep my commitment to Him. That was, and always is, enough.

Cause me to hear Your lovingkindness in the morning, for in You do I trust; cause me to know the way in which I should walk, for I lift up my soul to You. Psalm 143:8, NKJV.

Margaret Roelke McNitt is a retired nurse midwife in Mt. Pleasant, South Carolina. She is a member of the Mt. Pleasant Seventh-day Adventist Church.

THE CARREL OR THE CHAPEL
By Eckhard Hubin

MAKING it through seminary at Andrews University was a personal and financial challenge. I was married; had three children, all under the age of eight; and I wasn't sponsored to attend by any church organization. So I had many responsibilities and pressures besides the usual academic ones.

I spent most of my time studying at my carrel in the library and working part time. This left little time for my family. It was a real struggle, and I had to make choices. All seminary students were required to attend chapel services on Wednesday morning, but the pressures were so great that many students often skipped chapel to spend the time studying. I myself did this once or twice.

One quarter the seminary administration announced that it was reviving the lapsed practice of holding a Week of Prayer especially for the seminary. Two services would be held each day—one at 10 a.m., with attendance required of all students, and an optional service at 7:30 p.m. The speaker for the week was George Brown, then president of the Inter-American Division.

Elder Brown had a powerful message on Monday morning to start the Week of Prayer. Unfortunately, many students decided they couldn't take time from their studies to attend the services. Monday evening I was in the library studying for an upcoming test. At 6:30 I remembered that the optional evening meeting would begin in one hour. I debated long and hard about what to do. It was easy to argue that I couldn't take that hour away from my studies. The test was looming, and I needed to prepare. But the Holy Spirit was urging me to understand that I couldn't afford to miss meeting with God that evening. Five minutes before the meeting started, I surrendered and hurried over to the chapel.

I received such a blessing from that meeting that I couldn't keep away from the others. I attended every one. That week was probably the personal and spiritual high point of my entire seminary experience.

What academic liability had I incurred by going to those meetings? It's hard to tell, because that quarter I received the highest grades of my time at the seminary.

God's promises are still true. Make God first, and He will add everything else we might need according to His plan.

Let us not give up meeting together, as some are in the habit of doing, but let us encourage one another—and all the more as you see the Day approaching. Hebrews 10:25, NIV.

Eckhard Hubin is associate director of planned giving and trust services at Andrews University in Berrien Springs, Michigan. He is a member of Pioneer Memorial Church in Berrien Springs.

....

A TIME FOR EVERYTHING
By Beth Davis Nelson

WHEN our conference constituency voted to construct a new cafeteria at our academy, I wanted to make a significant contribution. I had graduated from Wisconsin Academy many years earlier and had fond memories of my four years there.

The conference officials set a date for commitment Sabbath, and asked members to make pledges on that Sabbath for the building project, payable over a two-year period. Since our income varies greatly, I hesitated to make a monthly pledge. My husband felt we could not help at all, since our daughter was just starting academy and we were unsure we would even have the funds to pay her monthly bill. We struggled to reach a decision.

The week before the commitment Sabbath our local church elder made the final appeal. I again prayed for guidance, wondering how far to stretch my faith. Suddenly a thought popped into my mind, and immediately I knew this was the answer. Yes! I had all but forgotten my savings bonds that had been in a bank safe-deposit box for more than 30 years.

Ironically this was money that should have gone to Wisconsin Academy years before to pay my student bill. After my father's death when I was seven years of age, my sister and I received a small supplemental pension each month, but the government would not allow our mother to use it for academy bills. She saved the checks, as the government requested. Every time the amount reached $75, she would purchase a $100 savings bond. Even though she wasn't able to use that money, the Lord blessed her hard work and faithfulness in returning tithe, because our academy bills were always paid.

When the bonds began to mature seven years later, I cashed in some of them for college expenses. Feeling that these bonds were almost sacred, I kept the rest tucked away in my safe-deposit box and more or less forgot about them. Just a few years before the cafeteria project was launched, I took the bonds to a bank teller to see what they were worth. She did some calculations and told me they were worth about $300 each. I returned them to the deposit box, planning to cash them only if I clearly felt impressed to use the funds for a very special project.

After I made the decision to donate the bonds to the cafeteria project, I assumed they were still worth about $300 each. Imagine my shock when the cashier added up the total. Each savings bond was worth between $600 and $700! I cried for joy. The Lord had provided a way for me to make a significant donation without taking out-of-pocket money.

The following month I had full-time work as a substitute teacher, and the wages went up $20 per day! I know that the Lord will provide the funds to pay my daughter's academy bill, even as He did for mine, if we are faithful in tithe and offerings. And I am honored to own even a small piece of that new cafeteria.

To every thing there is a season, and a time to every purpose under the heaven. Ecclesiastes 3:1.

Beth Davis Nelson is a substitute teacher in public schools in Clear Lake, Wisconsin. She is a member of the Clear Lake Seventh-day Adventist Church.

....

WORK LESS, RECEIVE MORE
By Ernest Dunning

THE night before I was to leave for a training session that would teach me how to conduct Revelation Seminars, I learned that the person I was scheduled to travel with couldn't take me. It was a 1,000-mile trip, and I didn't have the money to go on my own. I got on my knees and explained to God that I didn't have the money but was willing to go if He provided a way to get there.

The next morning another phone call came. A voice on the other end said, "I feel impressed to pay your way on the plane if you want to go." I went.

When I arrived home after the session, I ordered 5,000 brochures and secured a site for the Revelation Seminar. It was an act of faith. I'm an auto-body shop operator, and business was slow at that time. When I started the seminar, I was $2,000 in the red at the bank. It was also tax time, and I owed another $2,200 in income taxes. The seminar ran three nights a week, and on those days, I quit work at 3 p.m. so that I would have time to study and pray and also to be sure to arrive at the meeting early. As the seminar progressed, I also had to take time to visit the homes of students.

Twenty-seven people arrived the first night, and we had a wonderful time throughout. In the end, twenty people graduated, and four were baptized.

Did God honor my faith? Despite the time commitment to run the seminar, I was able to pay the income tax and the overdrafts, and also have an extra $2,000 in my bank account.

More seminars followed, and in 1993 I received a call from the British Columbia Conference to pastor a small church on a volunteer basis. In one month's time God helped me wrap up all my business details, sell $40,000 worth of cars, and rent my shop. Soon we began pastoring the Powell River Company.

Seven years later, still as a volunteer, we continue to pastor the church while living on a small stipend, some rental income, and a small pension. God has given us enough for our needs and some to help others. And God has blessed the church with twelve baptisms, a five-day-a-week soup kitchen, a clothing ministry, a wonderful church family, and a large addition to the church building. Most of all, He has blessed us with peace of mind, knowing we are where God wants us to be.

Therefore do not worry, saying, 'What shall we eat?' or 'What shall we drink?' or 'What shall we wear?'. . . For your heavenly Father knows that you need all these things. But seek first the kingdom of God and His righteousness, and all these things shall be added to you. Matthew 6:31-33, NKJV.

Ernest Dunning is the pastor of the Powell River Seventh-day Adventist Church in British Columbia.

 # EMPTY CUPBOARDS AND A MOTHER'S PRAYER
By Mike Mamoulelis

MY FATHER died quite young and left my mother with seven children, ages two to seventeen. We were living in Athens, Greece, at that time. My mother worked hard to support the family.

Through a lady she met on the bus, my mother started attending an Adventist church and was baptized a short time later. She freely claimed the Bible promises of God and relied on Him to provide for all our daily needs. She believed in the Sabbath very much and kept it faithfully.

Because she would not work on the Sabbath, she often would lose her job at the end of the week and would start looking for a new job the following Monday. Whenever she earned any money, she set aside the tithe and offerings first. Whatever was left over, she would use to provide for our family needs.

Sometimes she could not find any work for days. On one of those occasions the kitchen cupboards were empty, but her faith would not waver. She told us that the Lord would provide for our needs. She gathered all of us together to pray and to claim God's promises.

The next day the postman arrived with a letter from the United States. We had no idea whom it could be from. It turned out to be from the mother-in-law of a missionary in Greece at that time. The letter was very brief, and in essence it said: "Sister Vivian Mamoulelis, I felt impressed by the Lord to send you $20." In Greece, 45 years ago, $20 was a lot of money.

We all knelt and praised God for providing for us during that difficult time.

Blessed is the man that trusteth in the Lord, and whose hope the Lord is. Jeremiah 17:7.

Mike Mamoulelis is a physical therapist in Lodi, California. He is a member of the English Oaks Seventh-day Adventist Church in Lodi.

A MESSAGE AT CALVING TIME
By George N. Walker

A FEW years ago when I was a young Christian, I was trying to figure what it meant to tithe. Being a rancher by trade, I wondered how it would be possible to give ten percent of my gross income. Very few farmers or ranchers have that kind of profit margin. A margin of one percent or less is a realistic figure. I talked to my pastor and pointed out that if I were to use my IRS Form 1040 to decide my increase, the church would owe me money.

During this time I was between being a ranch laborer and being a self-supporting rancher. I also had a job in town, as a mechanic. The job I had on a ranch allowed me to have a few cows for my own. My father had died, and I was taking over the operation of the home ranch. To make this transition, I was increasing the size of my herd. Soon it grew to 40 cows. As I thought about the idea of ten percent of that increase, I could not see how I could meet my financial commitments. What should I do?

It was not difficult to figure my tithe from the paycheck of my town job. The Bible says that the Israelites gave a tithe of the firstfruits. I knew this concept from the Bible. My problem was a lack of faith. Did I really trust God enough to give Him ten percent of my gross income from my cattle?

This was when I feel God stepped in to give me a message about how to solve this problem. It was calving time. I had 40 cows that would be having calves. The first four calves were born dead. I got the message. The Lord was telling me I did not need the increase from this first ten percent of the calf crop. I could make it without it.

Since then I have been tithing on all I receive when I sell any livestock. God has blessed me by increasing my cow herd to the point where I no longer have to work in town and have become self-supporting.

However, a first-born among animals, which as a first-born belongs to the Lord, no man may consecrate it; whether ox or sheep, it is the Lord's. Leviticus 27:26, NASB.

George N. Walker is a rancher in Hogeland, Montana. He is a member of the Havre, Montana, Seventh-day Adventist Church.

GIVING AND RECEIVING
By Bryan A. Richardson

EVER SINCE our marriage in July 1983 my wife and I have tested God's promises, and He has never failed us. These tests have often been acts of faith in moments of extremity. In the beginning we had to decide whether to tithe on our gross or net income. We chose the former. It wasn't easy.

We lived in New York. My wife and I, both college premed graduates, were working substandard jobs, barely making ends meet. We took the bus fifteen miles to church each Sabbath. Money was so short that we spent considerable time scouring the ground at bus stops, looking for valid transfers. Or we would pay a partial fare and plead our case with the driver. The choice was honest tithing of my gross wages or a comfortable ride to church and maybe funds left over to pay bills.

We marveled at God's response to our growth from initial tithing in our net income to tithing on our gross, so we added an additional commitment of five percent of our gross for offering. God's blessings followed so quickly that in our second year of marriage we increased our giving to a double tithe.

Within months we had a new address, new jobs, stronger financial security, a brand-new Acura Integra, and funds to help a few mothers in Israel provide Christian education for their children. After six months the car was paid for in full and a college loan was retired.

Our tithing practice continued through medical school, and blessings poured down, but the best was yet to come!

In September 1995, after my wife and I completed our respective medical residency training, we reluctantly accepted jobs in our specialties in Chattanooga, Tennessee. Like Jonah, we didn't want to go, but we felt that was where God was leading us.

Within 24 hours of our arrival in Chattanooga, we were arrested and interrogated for being on the wrong side of town and at the wrong bank, attempting to open joint savings and checking accounts. We were accused of credit-card fraud.

Needless to say, nothing was wrong with our credit histories. So now we were forced to prove our good name and to ask the bank and police department to retract their accusations and issue letters of apologies. When they demurred, we felt it necessary to protect our good name with a suit in federal court, but we remained open toward a settlement. The case received enough publicity that our adversaries felt the pressure. We came to an agreement and received a large financial settlement.

Through this difficult ordeal we had been blessed to help with five soul-winning efforts in Chattanooga. Now we had to decide what to do with the legal settlement. According to our practice, we double-tithed on the gross amount (including legal expenses). We sent $1,000 as a gift to a dear saint. And the entire remainder we turned over to God's treasury to purchase a new church for more than 280 new members who were the result of a Revelation Seminar.

By the time we left Chattanooga three years later, it was very clear to us that God wanted us to play strategic roles in the establishment of this new congregation. And when that was accomplished, He showed us it was time to relocate.

Even though I am a physician, I have always loathed working on Sabbaths except for emergencies. Through the years this has been a burden on my heart and the focus of some trials. My original medical residency program was at a prestigious university in Washington, D.C., but Sabbath conflicts forced me to transfer to one in New York City that gave me Sabbaths off. After I had completed my residency, it was difficult to find a medical practice that allowed me to honor my convictions.

I joined an anesthesiology practice in Michigan, serving a local hospital. The practice was managed by one of the universities in the Chicago area. The schedule was heavy, but it didn't require Sabbath work except for on-call emergencies.

A short time after I joined, the university sold the practice to new owners. My options were not pleasant. I could remain with the university, serving as a faculty member in the medical school at significantly less pay than I was receiving at the practice. This would require daily commutes to Chicago, giving me very little time with my family. Or I could remain with the local practice, with higher pay but where the new arrangements would require Sabbath work.

I simply couldn't accept the idea of the Sabbath work. So I reluctantly chose the lower-pay option that also required the long commutes to the medical school in Chicago.

My wife and I, now responsible for an infant daughter, put the matter before the Lord. We knew that God wants families to be together, so the long days of commuting weren't ideal. And we knew that He expects us to honor the Sabbath. Our experience with double tithing had taught us that the more we trust to God, the more He can do for us. So, even though we were facing a significant pay reduction with the Chicago option, and even though we still faced huge loans from medical school, we decided to begin triple tithing.

Very soon after we made this commitment, my department chair astounded me with a new offer. He arranged a new employment package that gave me a significant increase in pay and required that I travel to Chicago only two days a week instead of five. So now I have time for family, I work less, and get paid much more.

Yes, Caesar gets his 40 percent of our gross, God gets 30 percent of our gross, and with the remaining 30 percent we have since retired all credit cards and five academic loans. And, with frugality, we are able to help some mothers in Israel as they struggle to provide Christian education for their children.

My testimony is that the first ten percent is already God's and is just the beginning of our stewardship relationship with Him. Our experience is that the blessings really come with what we do with the remainder. For us it may well be a barometer of our Christian maturity. The more we give, the more we see the wonders of God's mathematics come alive and turn impossible dreams into reality.

"Bring all the tithes into the storehouse, that there may be food in My house, and prove Me now in this," says the Lord of hosts, "if I will not open for you the windows of heaven and pour out for you such blessing that there will not be room enough to receive it." Malachi 3:10, NKJV.

Bryan A. Richardson teaches anesthesiology in Chicago, Illinois. He is a member of the New Life Seventh-day Adventist Church in Chattanooga, Tennessee.

You have a stewardship testimony you need to share and we need to read. See page 224 for details.

The TWELFTH MEETING

Evelyn J. Lewis

Robert Thompson

Fernando Munilla, Sr.

Josephine Varley

James Kincaid

Larry R. Evans

Ruth Ericson

K. Jollimore

Conrad L. Neft

Elsworth A. Hetke

JUST IN CASE
By Evelyn J. Lewis

WHEN I was elected Community Service leader for our church, I promised God and the church that I would faithfully open the Community Service Center every Wednesday afternoon from two o'clock to four o'clock.

Each time a family came to the center for help, I was sure that I had been more blessed to help them than they were to be helped. When I was a child, my family had been very poor, and there were no Community Service Centers. Many nights I went to bed hungry. I had only one outfit to wear to school. As an adult, I thanked God to be able to share His love with others.

As the year went on, to my dismay, there were many weeks when no one showed up for assistance. As other areas of my life got busier and the weather got colder, I grew weary in welldoing. Each week I tried to talk myself out of going to the center, because it seemed unlikely anyone would show up. But the thought of someone in need going to the center and my not being there kept me going. I had to be there just in case.

One Wednesday everything about my day that could go wrong went wrong. So I convinced myself that I was not going to the center that day. It was too cold; snow was on the ground; I was sure it would be a waste of time. But at the last minute conviction seized me, and I rushed out of the house to get to the center "just in case."

On the way to the center I thought about the frustrations of my regular job at the department store. It was hurting my spiritual life and not helping much financially. I was spending my check on items at the store before receiving it. It was like an alcoholic working in a liquor store. I prayed to God that He would help me find a different job and rescue me from my plight.

At the center I huddled at the desk, still in my coat and feeling sorry for myself, with a little electric heater at my feet. I stared blankly out the door, wondering why I was there. No one would come out in the snow. Just then a well-dressed couple came up the walk and tapped on the door. They didn't look as if they were coming for assistance. I put on a pretense smile, as if life were just wonderful and I didn't have a problem in the world.

The man explained that he was a recruiter for an insurance company and was out visiting churches in the community. They wanted to employ a Christian because the company found Christians were honest and could easily pass the background check and drug testing that his company required. He had a flyer he wanted to post. The lady cleared her throat to get his attention. The man smiled and said, "Ma'am, I have admired your professional demeanor, and I would like to offer this job to you."

I smiled politely and said that I was flattered but had no experience in the insurance business. He said they had on-the-job training. He offered me a guaranteed salary plus commission. I told him I would pray about it and let him know.

Four years later I am still in the insurance business. The first year God and I broke every record the office had set. He let me win several awards, monetary gifts, prizes, and trips, including an all-expense-paid Bahamas cruise for my husband and me. After my first year I was promoted to district manager, the first female and African-American in that office. My salary has almost tripled. I also have the freedom to set my own work schedule, so for the rest of my year as community service leader, you can be sure I kept my promise to open the center every Wednesday—just in case.

Our God is an awesome God. I praise Him for allowing me to be faithful in my commitment to Him and for answering prayer all at the same time.

And therefore will the Lord wait, that he may be gracious unto you, and therefore will he be exalted, that he may have mercy upon you: for the Lord is a God of judgment: blessed are all they that wait for him. Isaiah 30:18.

Evelyn J. Lewis is an insurance agent in Wichita, Kansas. She is a member of the Grove Heights Seventh-day Adventist Church in Wichita.

CHEERING UP THE GIVER
By Robert Thompson

WHEN we bought our first house, the closing costs totaled $2,000 more than we had been told to expect. This left us short for paying off one of our cars. And that meant we had nine months of payments of $375 each before we could meet budget again! We paid our bills, juggling, weaving, and bobbing to accomplish the task.

During this time I was faithful with my tithe, but my offerings had dramatically dropped from ten percent to two percent, and I felt ashamed. I wanted to give more, but I felt powerless to do anything about it. I knew that the Lord loves a cheerful giver, and the emphasis is on the spirit rather than the amount, but I wasn't even feeling cheerful. The only thing that would make me cheerful was giving an offering out of faith, an offering based, not on the hard numbers, but on God's tender mercies. I made up my mind that I would trust the Lord with my next paycheck and not lose faith as I had before.

As I was going over bills the next Friday, I saw that I was two months behind on a couple of obligations and another was due. Since I wanted electricity, gas, and telephone service over the weekend, I went out for a day of bill-paying. I owed the electric company about $275. I was about to write the check at the window when the clerk told me that I should be on a fixed-rate plan. She set it up for me right there, and my amount due was only $80. I was excited, to say the least. I rushed over to the telephone company to pay them and was told that there was a credit on my account from the last bill, and I owed only $74. I couldn't wait to find out what would happen at the gas company. The line was long, and it was about two hours away from sunset and the beginning of Sabbath. Closer examination of the bill led me to discover it was not due for another week.

Not until I was in church the next morning did I realize God had blessed me *when I made the commitment* to increase my offerings, not after they were received.

Before they call, I will answer; and while they are still speaking, I will hear. Isaiah 65:24.

Robert Thompson is director of pastoral services at Walton Rehabilitation Hospital in Augusta, Georgia. He is a member of the Augusta First Seventh-day Adventist Church.

ARE YOU HEARING ME?
By Fernando Munilla, Sr.

IN 1980 I was a successful general contractor. I had accepted the Lord and had become an avid Bible student. It seemed to me that if everything had been so good without Him, now that I was following the King of kings, the sky was the limit. Or so I thought.

Then the economy slumped. My business partner took some liberties with my signature. Overnight it seemed I was without a partner, with more than my share of debts, and with limited financial liquidity. Soon after, I had to lay off my office staff. I relocated the offices to the double garage of my house.

What's happening, Lord? Are You hearing me? No reply. In the meantime, I sold my wife's Cadillac, exchanged my new Nissan 200SX for a four-year-old pickup truck, and canceled my membership at a private club. We couldn't pay the $1,600 per month mortgage on our home, so I contracted with a realtor to sell it. I quit hunting, sold my guns, reduced our going out, and quit going to movies. Through all of this my wife sometimes questioned my sanity, but she was right beside me all the time. Where, on the other hand, was my Lord?

Meanwhile, I was still going to my church. But I began to notice certain flaws in its doctrines. After much prayer my wife and I decided to visit other denominations. The next was just as bad. And the next was worse. Are we so close to the end of time that every church is flawed? Isn't there a remnant? We quit attending a church and began to meet at home. At first it was just us; then a few friends joined us.

166

Through all of this, our house still had not sold. A listing with a second realtor came and went. We had no choice but to sell our TVs and our oil paintings. We gave up drinking, smoking, and some unnecessary foods. Eventually we sold all our jewelry in order to survive.

Then a flier came in the mail, advertising a series of lectures. In bold letters the flier proclaimed: "The Bible and Bible only." *Oh Lord, let it be!*

Our house-church group didn't want to try it, but my wife and I had to. Just about every doctrine we had found at home was confirmed in the lectures. And we learned about one we had never noticed (although it is in neon signs all over the Scriptures): *The seventh day is the Sabbath of the Lord your God.* His greatest emphasis was my greatest need!

The lectures ended, and five from our small group were baptized. When I got home from church that first Sabbath, I turned the "FOR SALE" sign (which was now "by owner") facedown on the grass. I would not attempt to sell my house on such a glorious day. As my wife and the others prepared the meal, I wrote a note and taped it on my front door. It said: "Today is the Sabbath of the Lord our God. We are going to celebrate by resting in Him. If you want to join in, just knock. If not, please come tomorrow."

As the Sabbath closed, I received a call from one of our small-group members. "Brother," he said, "as I was leaving your house this afternoon, a man gave me his card and asked me to tell you to call him."

When I called, the man told me he liked the neighborhood, he liked the house, and didn't mind the price. By Monday noon we had a contract for the full amount and a handsome deposit for a complete remodeling job. The buyer also allowed us to live in the house rent-free for four months.

My God is awesome! At the right time, even without a sign, He sold my house. And through all that time of trouble, was He hearing me? Of course He was! He was drawing me to Himself.

Commit your way to the Lord, trust also in Him, and He shall bring it to pass. Psalm 37:5, NKJV.

Fernando Munilla, Sr., is an engineer and general contractor in Miami, Florida. He is a member of the Miami Temple Seventh-day Adventist Church.

REFINANCING ON FAITH
By Josephine Varley

FIVE YEARS into our newly purchased house we learned that the county had not assessed property in more than ten years. We were concerned over continuing increases in property taxes, and decided to take advantage of decreasing mortgage rates and refinance our loan.

The loan agent told us that our total cost, after bank fees and taxes, would be $14,000. We were stunned. We had expected some closing costs but nothing like this. The agent told us the bank would review our application and look for another way to process our loan.

Payday came, and according to our custom, we wrote out our tithe and offering check. But this upcoming mysterious closing cost was on our minds. We didn't know what to do. Without talking about the matter, we left the tithe check in the checkbook that Sabbath.

In the days and weeks that followed, we called the bank regularly to get a closing figure. Eventually we were told it would be at least $1,000, but that wasn't final because they didn't have all the information yet. Of course, that was more reasonable than $14,000, but it was still higher than we wanted.

A third payday arrived, and we realized we must do something about those tithe and offering checks in the checkbook. My husband thought and prayed and made a decision. He pounded the table and said, "I don't care if we can't get that loan. God must come first." We turned in the checks to the church.

We went forward with the loan, expecting that our closing costs would be more than $1,000. When closing day arrived, I called the bank early in the morning to get the final cost. "It will be about $85," the agent said. I asked her to repeat what she had just said. "Yes," she said, "You heard right, about $85 to close."

We were skeptical because of our earlier experience. We knelt and prayed for help and assurance, trusting that God would work His will.

At the closing table the agent told us that they had made a mistake. Right then our hearts must have stopped beating, expecting the worst. "What mistake?" we asked in unison. She said, "It's not going to cost you a cent." Instead we would get back $300 that they could not carry over from our previous mortgage agreement, and an additional $1,300 from our escrow account.

When we put our trust in God by being faithful with Him, He gave us our new loan and an extra $1,600.

But my God shall supply all your need according to his riches in glory by Christ Jesus. Philippians 4:19.

Josephine Varley is a literature evangelist in Allentown, Pennsylvania, serving the Lehigh Valley area. She is a member of the Bethlehem, Pennsylvania, Seventh-day Adventist Church.

AN UNLIKELY CANDIDATE
By James Kincaid

OUR Wednesday-night Bible study at the church included a time when all were invited to share their hearts' joys and sorrows. A recent convert told of a teamster friend and fellow fur trapper who was hospitalized with terminal cancer. She noted with despair that the man was very bitter, resentful, and without hope. He had grown up in a Christian church but had not attended for years. He had practically run off any pastors who came to call in his hospital room.

As a pastor, my heart went out to the family, the friends, and the hopeless man himself. On one hand, I didn't relish the prospect of going to visit where I hadn't been invited and being treated rudely when I could easily avoid it. But on the other hand, what were the risks? Would it really hurt me to be cursed at for the cause of Christ? Maybe there was still time for God to work.

Still I hesitated. All through that meeting I debated whether I should visit the man—this difficult case. The Holy Spirit won out. After the meeting I went to the hospital, located the room, and found the patient by himself. I introduced myself as a friend of his friends, the fur trappers, and a fellow airplane owner and pilot. He smiled through his pain as we talked briefly about our common acquaintances and interests. I told him that I was their pastor and that when I heard he was sick, I wanted to visit him. He told me that he appreciated my visit. He promised that when he got better and out of the hospital, he would give me a ride in his airplane. I offered to pray for him, and he agreed without a moment's hesitation. I prayed that God would heal him according to His will and that he would be ready when Jesus comes. As I squeezed his hand, I noted a small tear rolling down his cheek.

During the next week I visited that room two or three times and always found a warm welcome from the emaciated figure in the bed. We shared a prayer each time. He rallied, his family gained hope, and then suddenly he died.

A week later I officiated in a unique memorial service, at a park behind the Teamsters Building. I was called the only preacher that "Del" ever was friends with. The park benches and folding chairs were taken by teamsters of every description; bearded fur trappers stood along the back fence. What a privilege to speak of a God who is no respecter of persons, who will save to the uttermost anyone who will come to Him, no matter if it is late!

What a humbling experience it was to be an instrument for God to use as He wills!

My brothers and sisters, if anyone among you wanders from the truth and is brought back by another, you should know that whoever brings back a sinner from wandering will save the sinner's soul from death. James 5:19, 20, NRSV.

James Kincaid is secretary of the Alaska Conference of Seventh-day Adventists in Anchorage, Alaska. He is a member of the Midtown Christian Fellowship Seventh-day Adventist Company in Anchorage.

THE GOD WHO SURPRISES
by Larry R. Evans

WHAT was supposed to be just another pastoral/administrative assignment turned out to be a life-changing experience for me. It not only changed my vision for the church, but it also changed my conventional understanding of God. This came about because of one family's desire to be open to God's unconventional leading. In this case I ended up being the beneficiary of their faithfulness.

When I was a district pastor, the conference president where I was serving decided it was time to reevaluate the role of the laity. He formed a small task force to explore the issue and to bring back a report to the constituency. A layperson who was a friend of mine was named chairperson, and he invited me to be part of the task force.

Eventually our group proposed some unconventional but pragmatic approaches and structures for providing resources to local congregations. These new methods were common in the business world but uncommon in the world of religion, or so we thought. We knew we would need to send someone for a training program, but we knew of no specific training program that would meet our need.

Several months later I found a brochure advertising a training program for the very kind of program our task force was recommending. My excitement quickly turned to disappointment when I noted the cost. It was far too expensive. I dared not ask the conference for assistance to attend. Nevertheless, it was good news to know that such a training program did exist!

With the dream still alive, I wrote to the chairperson to let him know of my discovery. I explained that our dreams for the church weren't so wild after all. Others were already doing it and were even holding training seminars. While we might not be able to send anyone for training for a few years, at least we could have confidence that we were on the right track. My letter carried my enthusiasm for how our dream as a task force was indeed a practical possibility.

Uncharacteristically, I didn't get around to mailing the letter for several days after I had written it. Was this an oversight? I don't think so.

What I didn't know was that my friend—the chairperson—and his wife had recently covenanted with God to set aside a certain percentage of their business income above their regular tithe and offerings to assist with some special project.

They set two conditions. The Lord would have to make very plain to them exactly what that project should be, and the project would need to be brought to their attention within a specific period of time when they would make their decision. All of this they made a matter of special prayer.

As only God could arrange it, my letter about the training program arrived on the first day of their set time period. The timing of my letter and their careful follow-up inquiry led them to believe that this project was indeed God's plan. They told me of their plan to help with the cost of training, but they were uncertain of the actual amount, since it would be determined as a percentage of income from their business.

Soon enough, their business prospered far beyond their expectations. The income percentage they had reserved for the special project was more than enough to cover the actual cost of the training program. The family was blessed, and so was I. The insights and skills that I learned from that training program have been invaluable to my ministry and a blessing to many congregations.

All of this was made possible by the faithfulness of a single family who dared to dream about what the church could become and by the intervention of a God who sees possibilities where we may not!

Scripture is replete with similar stories. Peter exclaimed to the onlookers after the healing of a crippled man: "Men of Israel, why does this surprise you? . . . Why do you stare at us as if by our own power or godliness we had made this man walk?" (Acts 3:12, NIV.)

Perhaps we are too astounded by miracles. After all, we have a God who not only cares but One who also surprises.

And God is able to provide you with every blessing in abundance, so that you may always have enough of everything and may provide in abundance for every good work. 2 Corinthians 9:8, RSV.

Larry R. Evans is president of the Georgia-Cumberland Conference of Seventh-day Adventists in Calhoun, Georgia. He is a member of the Georgia-Cumberland Academy Seventh-day Adventist Church.

....

TWICE BLESSED
By Ruth Ericson

WHEN our congregation in the 1960s undertook to finance both a church-building project and a new school in concert with two other congregations, it was quite a strain. Though we had no builders in our congregation, our new pastor knew a Christian man whom I'll call Mr. K. He had skills as a builder, painter, and plumber. Ostracized from his family because of his faith, he came to help us build our new church.

But Mr. K needed a place to live. An elderly church member volunteered to let him stay in her home but said she didn't feel she was able to feed him. Though we didn't have a spare room in our house, we did have enough food. I saw this as an opportunity to hasten the building of our church.

For several months Mr. K came every morning for a hearty breakfast. I also packed a big lunch for him to eat on the job. In the evening he was back for supper with our family. We all enjoyed his company. He ate heartily and restricted himself to only the best of fare.

During that time my husband's paycheck came every other Friday. Usually, by the second Monday, the food money was long gone. But after feeding our boarder for two weeks, I was surprised to find that I had money left over. At first I couldn't understand this, because I was buying extra food. This blessing continued the entire time Mr. K remained with us. It was obvious to us that the Lord was stretching our funds, making it possible for us to increase our building-fund giving.

Mr. K worked on our church until it was completed. He not only used his expertise but also organized volunteer workers as they came to help.

His hard work—and the meals he ate—made it possible for there to be a "beacon on the hill" on the corner of Barber and Evergreen Avenues in Woodbury, New Jersey.

Do not neglect doing good and sharing; for with such sacrifices God is pleased. Hebrews 13:16, NASB.

Ruth Ericson is a retired accounting clerk in Fletcher, North Carolina. She is a member of the Upward Seventh-day Adventist Church in Flat Rock, North Carolina.

THE WORST FOR THE BEST
By K. Jollimore

HOW CAN we afford to put two kids in a Christian school?"

We pondered this many times as my husband and I started our Christian experience. We were relatively new to the church and trying to survive on his income as a literature evangelist. Christian education wasn't the priority for us that it was for others in the church who were encouraging us to enroll the boys in the local church school.

Our two sons, ages sixteen and thirteen, attended public school and were not eager to make a change. However, they were beginning to feel out of place in the public school system as they became more involved in the church. Their circle of friends slowly grew to include their new church friends, and their social activities became less related to their old acquaintances.

Shortly after Halloween of the year that our youngest son was in seventh grade, he came home from school one day quite upset. The events he related became the deciding factor in our stepping out in faith and allowing God to provide the means for their education in a Christian school.

In late October, the students in his public school decorated their classrooms for Halloween and then voted on which room was the best decorated. When our youngest son entered one of the ninth grade rooms, he was shocked to see certain phrases written on the chalkboard. Three in particular stuck out in his mind: "Satan Rules," "666," and "Kill your parents for Satan." He asked the teacher why he allowed "that garbage" on his board. The teacher replied, "What's the matter? Is it too scary for you little Grade Seven's?"

I contacted the school the next day and was surprised and shocked to learn that not only did they freely admit that the whole incident had in fact occurred, but they saw nothing seriously wrong with the message they were conveying to their students. Of course, I know this is an extreme case, and many—if not most—public schools would not condone or defend such activity. However, as unfortunate as this incident was, especially where young, impressionable minds are concerned, it became the catalyst for a good thing in our family. It prodded us to put our boys in church school sooner than we otherwise would have. If we hadn't done it then, our oldest probably would have missed out entirely, as he was already in the tenth grade.

With the love and support of our church we were able to send our sons to a better school. To our amazement, we not only had enough money, but from that time on our financial situation has improved dramatically. We now have a very successful painting contracting business and I am employed as a computer instructor.

God can use the worst for the best.

And all thy children shall be taught of the Lord; and great shall be the peace of thy children. Isaiah 54:13.

K. Jollimore is a computer instructor at a private trade school in Halifax, Nova Scotia. She is a member of the Tantallon, Nova Scotia, Seventh-day Adventist Church.

TESTING THE LORD
By Conrad L. Neft

IN 1977 I was working in a factory, assembling various items for sale to other factories. I was baptized into the Adventist Church, and I felt that the Lord wanted me to test His Word in the area of the Sabbath and all His commandments, as well as on the matter of tithe. The Lord had already given me the victory over cigarettes and alcohol.

I told my wife that the tithe would have to come out of the monthly budget. I owed about $2,000 in miscellaneous bills. I decided, as a way of a test, that any overtime should go to paying off those bills. At the time, I was making $5 an hour, which was a decent wage for the work I was doing.

I told my employer I would no longer be working on the Sabbath. Our section consisted of eight people, so having the Sabbath off could create a problem. Our work came in blocks with deadlines, so overtime was required. We worked 40-hour, five-day weeks.

The Lord worked quickly on my boss, for shortly he changed our schedule to a 40-hour, four-day week, with Friday as an overtime day. So within six months I had all my bills paid (out of the overtime income) and had started putting money into the bank. My Sabbaths were free, and with ten hours of overtime available instead of eight, I realized an immediate increase in my pay.

When I joined the church, I had quit drinking alcohol. About the same time, I finished an electronics course. These two self-improvement efforts earned me a wage scale upgrade of two steps.

As my merit pay increased, I divided my raises three ways: one third for offerings, one third for taxes, and one third for retirement investment. Over the next few years my giving rate rose from ten percent to nineteen percent of my total income, minus the amount set aside for my retirement. Now that I am retired, the Lord still enables me to maintain a sixteen-percent giving ratio. I'm glad I tested the Lord.

And now, Israel, what does the Lord your God require of you, but to fear the Lord your God, to walk in all His ways and to love Him, to serve the Lord your God with all your heart and with all your soul, and to keep the commandments of the Lord and His statutes which I command you today for your good? Indeed heaven and the highest heavens belong to the Lord your God, also the earth with all that is in it. Deuteronomy 10:12-14, NKJV.

Conrad Neft, M.Sgt., USAF retired, is a member of the Madison, Wisconsin, Seventh-day Adventist Church.

A HERITAGE OF FAITHFULNESS
By Elsworth A. Hetke

BEFORE I was born, my homesteading, immigrant, Lutheran parents became interested in the Adventist faith by reading the German *Signs of the Times*. One afternoon they were working at the kitchen table, processing a whole pig they had purchased from the general store owned by a Jewish man.

My father had just removed the animal's head when two visitors arrived. One, a distant neighbor, was a lay leader in the local Adventist church; the second, a stranger, was an Adventist pastor. The pastor kept a noticeable distance from the pig. The neighbor helped my father remove the dead animal from the house while mother washed and scoured the table. The four sat down at 2 p.m. for a Bible study. By 2 a.m. my parents were Seventh-day Adventists.

During that Bible study the pastor thoroughly indoctrinated my parents on at least three points: Sabbath observance, stewardship, and clean and unclean meat. This last point was somewhat perplexing to my parents, who were struggling with a depression-era family economy. They had made a large investment in the hog, at five cents per pound, intending that it keep them in meat for the winter. After a short night's sleep and considerable time spent in prayer, my father took the carcass back to Wittenberg's store. He explained that he had become a Seventh-day Adventist overnight and could no longer eat pork. Would Mr. Wittenberg buy back the hog? He would. Then my father told him that he had already cut off the head. "Good," Mr. Wittenberg said. "I will now give you six cents a pound."

Thus began a lifelong journey in trusting God. Sabbath and stewardship went hand in hand. My early memories include riding to church on a one-horse sleigh, never arriving late. Each time the offering plate passed by, my father put something in. I remember sitting on his lap in church, rubbing my face against his, and getting a whisker rub. Father did not shave on Sabbath. The pastor had taught him that shaving was unnecessary work. And it probably was, since the only means of shaving was a straight razor.

As we children grew, so did our father's desire for us to have a Christian education. He sold the farm, and we moved west to a fruit-growing area. This move also took us from a German-speaking community to one where English was the predominant language. Even before my father bought an orchard, he made sure we children were enrolled in a church school.

He spoke five languages, but English was not one of them. We children were conscripted to do all the check- and letter-writing, as well as envelope-addressing. That was how I became aware of my father's faithfulness in tithing his income. Even after he learned to speak and read English, spelling remained a constant battle, so the children continued with the scribe assignment.

OVER AND OVER AGAIN!

The orchard usually provided a comfortable living for a family of six, but when crops failed, it was belt-tightening time. The single event fruit farmers feared most in late summer or early autumn was a hailstorm.

Very few such storms hit our beautiful valley, but one particular late August day the weather forecasters predicted hail. My father was concerned, but he did not panic. He called his family around the kitchen table. The well-worn German Bible produced cherished texts, including Malachi 3:11. Then he prayed. It was a fervent prayer of a righteous man. He reminded God that he had tried to follow His will and to be faithful. Then he asked for protection for his farm.

I went outdoors just as the heavens opened. What a rainstorm! There was no hail, and the storm quickly passed. Soon the next-door neighbor paid us a visit. He had already surveyed his orchard and vineyard. They were devastated by hail.

We went out to look at our orchard. There was no damage. Other neighbors who had received hail damage heard of our "good luck" and wondered why we were so fortunate. My father said simply, "I asked God to protect my orchard, and He did!"

Forty years ago, when my wife and I set up our own home, we agreed that returning to the Lord His own would be a habit with us. It still is!

I will rebuke the devourer for your sakes, and he shall not destroy the fruits of your ground. Malachi 3:11.

Elsworth A. Hetke is director of human resources at Southern Adventist University in Collegedale, Tennessee. He is a member of the Collegedale Seventh-day Adventist Church.

You have a stewardship testimony you need to share and we need to read. See page 224 for details.

The THIRTEENTH MEETING

Come and hear, all ye that fear God, and I will declare what he hath done for my soul.

Psalm 66:16

Glenda-mae Greene

Emma Van Komen

April McNeil

Virginia Casey

Donald W. Murray

Gary S. Force

Suzanne Waters Street

Frances Johnson

Clinton Jones, Sr.

Carol and David Tasker

STUFFED STRAWBERRIES AND A FULL HEART
By Glenda-mae Greene

ACOLLEAGUE asked me to host a small group of students at my home on a Friday evening for vespers. I swallowed hard, caught on the edge of a personal dilemma. I wanted to entertain the young scholars, but I had no more than $7 of disposable cash until the next paycheck.

"It'll be only about ten of them," my friend continued. I accepted willingly. It simply entailed providing light refreshments, and my cupboards were not exactly empty.

But I really wanted the students to experience a very special Sabbath welcome. Rummaging through my purse, I searched for any money I might have overlooked. I discovered instead the check for last week's tithe and offerings that had been missing ever since that church service. I paused for a nanosecond. I would not consider using it. Nor would I use my credit card.

Driving along the country roads that afternoon, I spotted a roadside fruit stand where huge red strawberries were on sale. Moments later, with the luscious berries in one hand and $2 in the other, I walked triumphantly to the car. Stuffed strawberries, I decided, would be Friday evening's specialty.

As I stuffed the fruit with a delicately flavored cream filling, I used the time to commune with God. As music floated from my stereo, I prayed for a blessing on our vesper program and for the students who would be my guests.

Just before the sun set that Friday, laughing students spilled from their cars. Clearly I was about to host more than 30 students. Could they all fit in my modest bungalow? Would I have enough food?

I left the details of the programming to the Father.

We had a lively songfest. Then the young adults broke up into small discussion groups to talk about God's love. They spread all through the house. Some prayed in the bedrooms, others chatted in the dining room, and yet others moved to the kitchen. Some even knelt by the dryer in the laundry room. My house seemed to expand. I could feel God's blessings upon us.

After we formed a circle of prayer around the table, we sat down to eat. The food seemed to take on the dynamics of those five barley loaves 2,000 years ago. It was enough, and it was good.

That ending was only the beginning. Three days later I felt a gentle tap on my shoulder. "Your tire has gone flat," one of my Friday-evening guests reported sadly. "But I have an open period right now. I'll help you change it."

As he put away the jack, he said, "I'm glad I got to know you."

I was the happy one. It had finally occurred to me that although the strawberries, with their creamy centers, were to be the focal point of the Friday-evening celebration, God had a different agenda. He intended to open my eyes to the blessings—both spiritual and material—that He had been stuffing into my life all along. And I will never have enough room to hold them all!

O Lord, how manifold are your works! . . . When you open your hand, they are filled with good things. Psalm 104:24-28, NRSV.

Glenda-mae Greene is assistant vice-president for student services at Andrews University in Berrien Springs, Michigan. She is a member of Pioneer Memorial Church in Berrien Springs.

CRAZY ED, A LITTLE CHURCH AND 21,000 RUSSIAN BIBLES
By Emma Van Komen

IN THE early 1990s, when Russia opened its doors to Christian evangelism, our little church learned through *The Carter Report* of the need for Russian Bibles. Each Bible could touch the lives of an estimated five to eight people. We felt a call to help these people, so starved for Christ, by providing them with Bibles printed in their own language. Each Bible could be bought for a dollar.

We had approximately five months to raise money for these Bibles, and we set a goal of $13,000. To most of us, this seemed an impossible amount for our small congregation of about 75 active members, but my son-in-law Ed assured us that this was nothing for the Creator of the universe. We rewarded his enthusiasm by calling him Crazy Ed.

We all set to work. The church-school children gave up ice-cream cones and candy and gave the money for these things to the Bible fund. One girl sold candy at her public school. She told everyone that the money was for Russian Bibles. It impressed the teachers and students so much that they started giving Shauna a lot of business.

We ran several garage sales, with members donating doors, lawn mowers, and other miscellaneous items. Each sale raised more than $700. Many members' families and friends outside of our church community heard of our efforts and began donating.

That Christmas my family decided not to buy presents for each other, but instead to give that money to the Bible fund. We all later agreed it was the best Christmas we ever had!

Money poured in. Crazy Ed challenged us many times with his confidence that we could not only reach the $13,000 goal, but exceed it. With many prayers

179

the money continued to pour in. God was blessing our efforts of stewardship and giving.

Through God's great love for His Russian people, our little church was able to raise $21,000 for Russian Bibles. That is 21,000 Russian Bibles that might not have been in that country except for the blessing of God's stirring up the Fallon, Nevada, Seventh-day Adventist Church. As many as 100,000 people might be affected for eternity by those Bibles.

All of us, from the youngest to the oldest, felt blessed by this project. We saw firsthand that God really does work in remarkable ways through His people to spread the good news of salvation.

For where your treasure is, there will your heart be also. Matthew 6:21.

Emma Van Komen is a self-employed bookkeeper in Fallon, Nevada. She is a member of the Fallon Seventh-day Adventist Church.

A PECULIAR MINISTRY
By April McNeil

ONE DAY last spring, my husband mentioned that some women were hoping I would consider teaching their children and themselves karate. He knew I had decided several years ago to leave that behind me. I had no intention of changing my mind.

As we discussed their interest in classes, he mentioned that since I had stopped practicing martial arts, I had lost some of my muscle tone. He wasn't being unkind; it was just one of those innocent observations husbands can make, which, I noticed, happened to be true.

I had recently reached an age milestone and hoped the next 50 years would be at least as good as the first. In the interest of maintaining my health, I thought I should at least consider the teaching request. So I decided to pray about it.

I had no problem with the idea of teaching self-defense. But I was uncomfortable with some of the Eastern traditions that had been part of my own training. My instructor was a Christian and had, in part, been responsible for my becoming a Christian. But his methods were laced with subtle Eastern practices that made me uncomfortable. I needed to settle this conflict, or I would not teach.

As I lifted the matter to God, I was shown just what to do. I changed a number of things, and I have been teaching again this past year. Respect, self-control, self-discipline, and focus are the keys to all that I teach.

I always prayed that each class would be an honor to God and a blessing to every student. I prayed for my students and their families and specific needs I could see. I gave those classes to God, and He gave me this rather peculiar ministry.

My class was made up of a wonderful group of students from six years old through adults, many of whom were Christian. They knew I loved them and prayed for them. They also knew I'm a Seventh-day Adventist. Some have even visited our church.

I continually saw God's hand at work. Amazing transformations occurred. An uncontrollable hyperactive child, struggling in school, now became a calm, focused student, earning all A's and B's. An obnoxiously difficult child became an agreeable, happy, helpful son. One adult student noted the "peaceful spirit" in my teaching. That's not generally something one would notice in a karate class. I let her know it was the Lord.

When my husband and I were asked to pastor in a different district, I grieved over the thought of leaving my students and this ministry. Some adult students and some parents wept. So did I. It was truly a test of faith and submission. Once I understood and submitted, the weight of my grief lifted. Now I eagerly await God's next adventure, knowing He will use me wherever I am if I am willing.

For we are His workmanship, created in Christ Jesus for good works, which God prepared beforehand, that we should walk in them. Ephesians 2:10, NASB.

April McNeil is a martial arts instructor and pastor's wife in Wray, Colorado. She is a member of the Wray Seventh-day Adventist Church.

....

NO NEED FOR SUBTERFUGE
By Virginia Casey

WHEN I became a born-again Christian and joined the Seventh-day Adventist Church, I was faced with a dilemma: How was I going to be faithful in returning tithe without my husband's knowledge?

Not having belonged to a Bible-based church before, I found the matter of tithing difficult and strange. For the previous 62 years of my life, I had belonged to a Sunday-keeping church in which tithing was almost never mentioned. Our "collection," as it was called, consisted of whatever loose change we had in our possession at the time, or in recent years, the occasional dollar or two. When a "special collection" was taken up and we parted with real paper money, we thought of it as a generous and sacrificial act.

I knew that my husband would "flip his lid" upon discovering the amount of my tithe, not to mention what I gave in offerings. I dared not write a check for fear of the repercussions that would surely follow when my husband scrutinized the bank statements. Returning tithe with cash wasn't a good option either as we kept very little cash on hand. Our monthly checks were deposited directly into our bank account.

One day we received our brand new "Cash-Stop" debit cards. I'll never forget the first time I used mine to make a purchase and how surprised and delighted I was when those five magical words stared me right in the eye—"DO YOU WANT CASH BACK?" What a stupid question! Yes, yes, of course I wanted cash back!

Returning my tithe with "extra" cash from ATM purchases worked very well until tax return time when my tithe and offering receipts from the church arrived in the mail. Needless to say, my deed was discovered, and I was found out. I had no choice but to give my husband an explanation. I bravely quoted to him exactly what the Bible says about tithing. He wasn't charmed with my quotation. In fact, he was very upset. Thankfully, however, the irritation was short-lived.

As a result of this unpleasant experience and my husband's more accepting attitude I decided to write checks for my tithe. When the bank statement comes now he never refers to the matter.

I should have trusted the Lord long before I did and saved myself a lot of unnecessary worry and stress. I tried to work out the problem all by myself instead of consulting the One who could really help.

I'm learning the hard way, but with His help, I *am* learning to grow in His love and grace.

Trust in the Lord with all your heart, and lean not on your own understanding; in all your ways acknowledge Him, and He shall direct your paths. Proverbs 3:5, 6, NKJV.

Virginia Casey is a retired municipal government employee for the city of St. John's, Newfoundland. She is a member of the Conception Bay South Seventh-day Adventist Church in Upper Gullies, Newfoundland.

THIS IS YOUR SCHOOL
By Donald W. Murray

THIS is your school! Someday you will be a student here!" When my mother spoke with such conviction, I usually believed her, but this was different. She was referring to Walla Walla College and my future enrollment there. That worthy goal seemed well beyond the grasp of a family like ours.

My parents had joined the Adventist Church in the 1940s, and the implications of that decision meant that a poverty-level subsistence became the reality in our home. Dad had worked in the hard rock mines of northern Idaho as a young man, and then for 25 years he had been a meat cutter.

Saturday was the prime shopping day in the meat market. When he became a Seventh-day Adventist, he turned away from his Depression-era generation's obsession with financial security to follow Jesus. His decision meant that he would never again hold a steady job.

But being faithful to God and the teachings of their new church was a commitment my parents made with a firm resolve. In their view, that commitment included providing an education in Adventist schools for my sister and me right through college. So when I was still a boy, they took us regularly to visit Walla Walla College, to attend programs there. And my mother's familiar refrain was "This is your school. Someday you will be a student here!"

Dad worked hard, and he knew how to find jobs; but in his fifties, with limited skills and education, and faithful to his understanding of the Sabbath, finding work that lasted more than a few months was difficult. Many times the focus of our family prayers was asking the Lord to lead Dad to a job so the bills could be paid. My parents' dreams for my sister and me to be educated in Adventist schools must have seemed foolish at times. But they continued to arrange visits to those campuses.

In 1953 my mother found work as a receptionist for a Pasco, Washington, physician. Our attendance at an Adventist academy was now within reach, but college at Walla Walla still seemed a far stretch. But my mother, in her quiet way, kept the dream before us. "This is your school. Someday . . ."

During the Depression, Dad had invested in a few shares of stock in the silver mines of northern Idaho. The price of ore was very low, and the shares had provided no source of income for our family. But for some reason Dad had wanted to keep those stocks.

In the late 1950s, almost overnight, a boom hit the mining industries. Stocks split, and then split again. What had been purchased for pennies was now worth more than a hundred times that—and then still a hundred times more. Faithfulness, long taught in our family as its own reward, was now rewarded with the blessings of heaven.

The mining boom didn't last very long—just long enough for me to complete my educational goals and to be well launched in life; and just long enough for my parents to move into a more comfortable home. While their lifestyle remained basically unchanged in retirement, they enjoyed a measure of financial security they had never known before. Dad used his extra money to assist in worthwhile projects and to invest in people.

Both Mom and Dad are now deceased. In their will they gave a substantial gift to Walla Walla College. Since 1989 this memorial scholarship fund has provided tuition assistance for up to four students per year.

God rewarded my parents' simple faithfulness to His truth in ways that blessed me and now bless others. Mom's dream is still being realized for others: "This is your school . . . ."

"Well done, thou good and faithful servant: thou hast been faithful over a few things, I will make thee ruler over many things: enter thou into the joy of thy Lord." Matthew 25:21.

Donald W. Murray is the dean of men at Andrews University in Berrien Springs, Michigan. He is a member of Pioneer Memorial Church in Berrien Springs.

GIVE AND IT SHALL BE GIVEN
By Gary S. Force

IF YOU DON'T have a need, you don't need a miracle.

Self-supporting ministries are often in need of miracles; that is why we call them faith ventures. Our school was going through a need. We were experiencing some financial difficulty. Tuition payments were slow coming in, and the staff members were waiting for their stipend. This was a common problem for some of us. However, the longer we waited, the more our faith was tested.

During our daily prayer time we asked the staff to pray for God's intervention and blessing. We were reminded of the principle of sacrifice as originally stated in Luke 6:38 that we learned at the Institute of Basic Life Principles: If you need a blessing, pray to find how God wants to use you to be a blessing to someone else. So we did just that.

"God," we prayed, "is there someone to whom You want us to be a blessing?" God answered by making us aware of several families with needs. We discussed these needs at the weekly family council meeting of the students and staff and soon decided to help a family who had no housing because the father had lost his job. They needed first and last months' rent.

We took up a collection among the students and the staff. This was a real test for us. It took a special measure of faith to give to a family in need, even though our own families had not received any income. We mailed the check to the needy family on a Thursday.

That very next Sabbath morning, before receiving the check we had sent, the father in that needy family told his wife, "We have enough money to pay the rent or to return tithe but not enough to do both. What do you think we should do?"

They discussed their options and decided to return their tithe first and leave the rent to God. They wrote out their check for tithe and placed it in the morning offering. They both sighed with relief, knowing they had done the right thing.

Later that day when they got their mail, they found the letter from our school. They opened it, not knowing what to expect, and found our letter of explanation and our check that would cover the expense of the rent owed. This time they didn't sigh with relief. They jumped for joy!

God led us to send a check, knowing exactly what day they needed to receive it for their faith to be rewarded. It had taken three days for the mail service to deliver our check to them. It took five days for the mail service to deliver their thank-you note to us. God not only can work miracles of the heart to give gifts; He can also work miracles with the U.S. Postal Service.

As for our staff stipends, we got them soon enough. God touched the heart of a very generous person to give us an unexpected donation. God had rewarded the faithfulness of His people. With God all things are possible!

Give to others, and God will give to you. Indeed you will receive a full measure, a generous helping, poured into your hands—all that you can hold. The measure you use for others is the one God will use for you. Luke 6:38, TEV.

Gary S. Force is president and principal of DayStar Adventist Academy in Castle Valley, Utah. He is a member of the Castle Valley Seventh-day Adventist Church.

....

A TEST OF TIME
By Suzanne Waters Street

MY STOMACH turned as I considered my dilemma. I had to work, and I had a major exam to take in the middle of my workday. Was I prepared for the exam? No!

I could quickly recount the many hours I had spent in church and in church work. In fact, I had attended a weekend meeting, prepared an extensive financial report, attended a prayer meeting, and finally, had attended a special board meeting. As a result, the evening before my exam I had fallen asleep with my textbook and notes in my hands.

"To keep the Sabbath holy is one thing, but all of this other stuff I'm doing is just too much," I fumed. I was so angry that I couldn't even ask for my Father's help. I felt strongly that in spending so much time on church activities, I had not used my time wisely. It was an easy matter, after the fact, to see how I could have maneuvered work, school, church responsibilities, and home so that I could have been prepared for that exam.

Overwhelmed with fear, self-pity, and anger, I decided I was fed up with being pulled in so many different directions all of the time. I had always worn many hats, but I had begun to feel that I was just one step ahead of self-destruction.

When I had started college in 1997, I was convicted that I must continue to serve God in my small home church. I had already promised to tithe my time in support of God's work, no matter what my life circumstances were. But many times I found myself tormented and struggling to keep that promise.

Now, through the burning tears of anger and pain, I opened my prayer journal to record my plea. I simply wrote, "Dear Father, I am tired physically and mentally, and I am grossly unprepared for my exam. Would you bring what I have read and written back to my mind so that I can do well? Please guide my hand."

I left the office that day and rushed over to my class. I sat down and whispered yet another prayer as my anger melted into helplessness. I was fearful of just flat-out bombing on the test.

After a little delay the professor stepped into the room and stood before the class. In a state of unbelief I listened as he apologized for somehow losing the exam while attempting to print it from his computer just before class. Needless to say, the dreaded exam that had shaken my soul was canceled until the next class meeting.

At that moment I was forced to see that God had never forsaken me but had continuously rewarded me for giving my time to His work. I saw a God of love, who is concerned with all that concerns us and who constantly works to cause all things to work together for the good of those who faithfully give of their time.

We know that all things work together for good to those who love God, to those who are the called according to His purpose. Romans 8:28, NJKV.

Suzanne Waters Street is an administrative secretary at the University of Maryland, Eastern Shore, in Princess Anne, Maryland. She is a member of the Pocomoke City, Maryland, Seventh-day Adventist Church.

FROM HOUSEBOUND TO HOMEWARD BOUND
By Frances Johnson

MY HUSBAND was a dedicated Christian who worked as a typesetter for a newspaper. I had a job as a secretary and bookkeeper. I worried constantly about our financial security, fearing that we might end up losing our home. I asked my husband, "How can we continue giving tithe to the Lord with one of our daughters in nursing school and the other one in high school?" My husband calmly told me of his confidence in God's faithfulness. He also continued returning tithe and offerings. I worried so much that I had a nervous breakdown.

For two full years I didn't leave our home even to go to church. In desperation I finally reached out to the Lord and asked Him to heal me. I promised Him that in thankfulness I would begin to work for Him.

God heard my plea and healed me. I was able to go to work again and do a job I truly enjoyed. God and I have been in partnership ever since. I can truthfully attest that God is faithful, and I desire to remain faithful to Him not only in tithing but in every area of my life.

It is of the Lord's mercies that we are not consumed, because his compassions fail not. They are new every morning: great is thy faithfulness. Lamentations 3:22, 23.

Frances Johnson is now retired. She is a member of the Washington, New Hampshire, Seventh-day Adventist Church.

THE WORDS OF DAVID
By Clinton Jones, Sr.

I HADN'T missed a single day of work in ten years. I took pride in my job as a route salesman for a major bakery and was considered an exemplary employee. Reliability was an essential in my job because the bakery products were time-dated, and freshness was the company priority.

While my work life had been very consistent for a decade, things were changing in my personal life. I had discovered the Sabbath truth. The conviction to follow God all the way had already pierced my heart, and I took a stand for Jesus. I felt that was the least I could do, now that I understood how He had taken a stand for me.

The same day I was baptized (I was still damp from the service), I went to see my work supervisor. I took a deep breath and said, "I'm sorry, but I can no longer work on Saturday."

"What? That can't be allowed! You're a route salesman. Saturday is part of the job!"

I was prepared for the worst, but I was comforted by the promise in Psalm 37:25.

The strangest thing happened that evening of my baptism. A still small voice whispered to me as I lay in bed, saying: "Don't worry about the stand you have taken for My Sabbath. In three months something will happen, but you will be able to hold on."

On several occasions at prayer meeting in the weeks ahead, I shared my testimony about hearing that still small voice, though I didn't fully understand it myself. Soon enough, however, God intervened on my behalf. The supervisor assigned others to work on Saturday while I was given a Sunday route. And three months after my baptism, the company was closed.

Now I knew that the voice had been from heaven. I had no job, but I had peace in my soul. My wife was very loving and supportive during this difficult time. Again the words of David rang in my heart. I did not know what the future held, but my peace came from knowing who held the future.

The next six months were surreal. I started work as a literature evangelist. I had many experiences through which God revealed His power to me during this great work. Once I was working in Greenwood, South Carolina. My pouch was full of books, and my pockets were empty. I asked many people to purchase the blessings in the volumes of books that I had. They all said no. Desperate, I uttered a very simple prayer to God: "Lord, You know my needs today, and I have faith that You will meet them." Miraculously, the very same people who said no earlier all came to me and with a sense of urgency bought my books—*all of them.* Again the words of the psalmist rang in my heart.

After six months of working as a literature evangelist, I began receiving an unemployment check. Those payments would last for only six months. On the last day of receiving payment I was hired as a route salesman for another major bakery. The Lord has blessed me to work there for 25 years. I have been confronted and threatened many times by Satan because of the Sabbath—even briefly fired and rehired. Through all that, God's wonderful Sabbath has remained undefiled.

I have been young, and now am old; yet have I not seen the righteous forsaken, nor his seed begging bread. Psalm 37:25.

Clinton Jones, Sr., is a route salesman for Dolly Madison Bakery in Augusta, Georgia. He is a member of the Ebenezer Seventh-day Adventist Church in Augusta.

....

GOD'S DIFFERENT TIMETABLE
By Carol and David Tasker

WE HAD planned our wedding for two years, but we were poor college students. Our best efforts to save money for starting our life together resulted only in the cash purchase of a fifteen-year-old EK Holden (the Australian General Motors equivalent of a Chevrolet) for $300. On our wedding day (four days after Carol's graduation) we had just $50 in cash to pay for the honeymoon and the first two weeks' groceries.

Before our marriage we had set up a budget plan. It seemed that we were bankrupt before we even started, and David had one more year of college studies. In spite of these dim prospects, we resolved to continue our practice of tithing and to add a second tithe. We also decided to return offerings equivalent to half of the tithe amount; making a total of 25 percent of our income returned to the Lord.

We also wrote down a list of four "luxury" items that we hoped to acquire in the years ahead: a piano, a sewing machine, a radio-cassette-turntable music system, and a freezer. We guessed it would take us at least 20 years of careful saving to purchase those items.

God had a shorter timetable. Before our first wedding anniversary He had arranged for us to own all four items, and He had fascinating ways of doing it.

Not long after our wedding we heard that the Primary Sabbath school department was disposing of its piano. A letter to the church board and a $30 check made us the proud owners of an older, out-of-tune but serviceable, piano, and we were glad to have it. Four years later in New Zealand another family was delighted to pay us $200 for that piano, rejoicing in their bargain, while we were able to upgrade to a very nice instrument.

During that same first year a recently remarried widower realized he didn't need two sewing machines in the house. We bought one of his—an older but adequately functioning, machine—for $20. Three years later that machine became a $100 trade-in toward a brand-new machine.

Both of us had come from families who saved money by canning and freezing, so a freezer seemed to us to be a good investment. A number of relatives unable to attend our wedding sent gifts of money. We decided that a freezer would be the ideal purchase with that gift money. However, we wanted to return the first and second tithe and give offerings on the cash *value* of all our wedding presents, not just the cash; it seemed to us that those gifts of household goods should be counted as "increase" to us.

We used the cash gifts to return the tithe and offerings on all the gifts, and thus we had to wait on the freezer. A few months after our wedding we had saved up an amount of money equivalent to what we had returned to God for the wedding gifts.

The timing was right. The appliance store offered an $80 discount on their freezers, so were able to purchase a bigger and better freezer than we could have purchased immediately after our wedding.

And the music system? Carol's sister, on mission service at the time, asked us if we would mind looking after hers.

In all, we had paid only $50 of our own money toward these four luxury items, and we were using them less than six months after we had begun our new partnership with God.

We discovered a further benefit. Until recently we had never shared this story with anyone, even our children. We thought that it might be seen as some sort of personal ego trip. However, this story is clearly one of *God's* greatness and goodness, not ours, and when we pass on these precious personal stories of God's blessing to our children, it builds their confidence and faith in God.

Recently we shared our story with our sons. We should have done it years ago. As Nathan thought of our story, it made him think of how God had blessed him in his finances as he has returned tithe. He commented, "I'm convinced that it's impossible to get poorer by giving to God."

Humanly speaking, this just doesn't make sense at all, but God invites us to take a risk so that He can impress us with how much He can be trusted. Having God as our senior partner in our financial affairs is the wisest, most exciting, and most rewarding thing we can do for ourselves and our families. We highly recommend it.

Blessed be the Lord, who daily loadeth us with benefits, even the God of our salvation. Psalm 68:19.

Carol and David Tasker are completing doctoral studies at Andrews University in Berrien Springs, Michigan. They are members of Pioneer Memorial Church in Berrien Springs.

You have a stewardship testimony you need to share and we need to read. See page 224 for details.

The FOURTEENTH MEETING

Come and hear, all ye that fear God, and I will declare what he hath done for my soul.

Psalm 66:16

Elizabeth R. Buck

Joan Waterman

Robert L. Thorpe

Dagmar Cepica

Martha Walwyn

Bill Strong

Bryce Newell

Larry E. Stapleton

Beverly Moody

Esther Ramharacksingh Knott

A BIBLE AND A BUS
Elizabeth R. Buck

IT'S NOT A BOAST, but a fact. My favorite book in college was my Bible. The Bible I read was my textbook, my devotional, my study guide. In it I wrote sermon notes, jotted down special insights and answers to prayer. It went everywhere I did.

Time, however, took its toll on my favorite book. My beloved Bible began to get ragged, and finally it literally began to fall apart. I wanted a nice new one with all its pages intact, but I couldn't afford one.

As Thanksgiving approached during that fall term, I longed to be home in Indiana with my family. But knowing my finances, I pushed the idea away.

One day during my special time alone with God I felt a strong and unusual urge to balance my checkbook. Puzzled, I went over my checkbook ledger later in the day and discovered to my amazement a mathematical error that gave me enough money for a round-trip bus ticket to Indiana.

Arriving in Chicago I put my ticket in my bag for safekeeping. But when time came to load the bus, the ticket was nowhere to be found. I spread my things out on the curb beside the bus and laid my Bible on top of everything while I searched.

The bus driver was kind, but he explained that he had a schedule to keep. I knew his situation, but I also sent up a quick prayer as the bus started to leave: "Lord, this is the last bus that can get me home in time for Thanksgiving. You found the money for me. You didn't bring me this far to leave me stranded in Chicago. Help me get on this bus." And then the bus stopped.

The driver climbed down the steps to tell me that someone had promised to pay for my ticket if I couldn't find mine. We quickly loaded everything back on the bus, and I was on my way home.

At the next stop my seatmate got off. I upended my bag into the seat and turned it inside out. There was my ticket hidden in the folds at the bottom. When I presented my ticket to the driver, he pointed out the gentleman who had guaranteed my travel.

I went to thank my benefactor, only to discover that he was an evangelist. "When I saw your Bible, how worn it was," he told me, "God told me I couldn't leave the station without your being on the bus too."

God showed me that time spent with Him and His Word, however well-worn His Word may be, always pays, often in ways we never could have imagined.

And I will walk at liberty, for I seek Your precepts. I will speak of Your testimonies also before kings, and will not be ashamed. Psalm 119:45, 46, NKJV.

Elizabeth R. Buck is an oven operator at Wen Products in Akron, Indiana. She is a member of the Rochester, Indiana, Seventh-day Adventist Church.

THE PIE LADY
By Joan Waterman

I WORKED at a factory on the night shift for 20 years. The workers had the custom of often bringing in snack treats for each other. My specialty was fresh berry pie. Some of my friends began asking me to sell them pies, so the Lord opened the way for me to make some money for ADRA (Adventist Development and Relief Agency). With each pie I sold I included a card with an ADRA child on it and a thank-you note stating that all the money went to feed hungry children around the world.

The Lord blessed the project right away. He sent me people who wanted my berry pies. At times I would have six pies to carry to work at night.

On my way home in the morning I would pray, "Lord, you know how many berries I need for the new pie orders. Please help me to find them in the berry patch."

Other times I had plenty of berries and no orders for pies. On faith, I made pies and asked the Lord to help me sell them. Sometimes I'd be in the parking lot, ready to go home, when people would ask me if I had any pies left. Never once in all the time I worked did the Lord leave me with unsold pies.

One night a woman asked me if I was "the pie lady." She wanted two pies the next day. I told her that the berries were almost done for the season and I was not sure I could find enough, but I would look.

On the way home the next morning, I asked the Lord to give me enough berries, since the money was for ADRA. Then I remembered a friend whose husband had cancer. So I asked the Lord to please give me enough berries for three pies so I could surprise her with a pie.

When I got home, I went to the berry patch. My heart sank. There were almost no berries. But I knew that the Jordan did not part until the children of Israel put their feet in the water. So by faith, I stepped into the patch. I wish I could say that berries suddenly appeared all over the place. That didn't happen. I still didn't see any berries. However, the Lord gave me peace and as I began to lift each branch I found a few berries here and there. When I had picked over the whole patch and looked into my bucket, I saw enough berries for two pies, but not enough for three.

I went into the house and set out two pie shells, and started to get the berries ready. Then I said to myself, "O ye of little faith! If God can grow the berries,

He can supply enough in the pail for three pies." So by faith I set out a third pie shell and began filling the shells with the berries. I must tell you that God multiplied those berries in the pail so that I had enough for three pies. I thanked Jesus for giving me the faith to trust Him. He will answer our prayers when we are faithful stewards in helping others.

Ask, and it shall be given you; seek, and ye shall find; knock, and it shall be opened unto you. Luke 11:9.

Joan Waterman is a retired factory worker in Freeport, Illinois. She is a member of the Freeport Seventh-day Adventist Church.

AND THEN MY RED SEA OPENED
By Robert L. Thorpe

I WAS NOW a registered, certified diagnostic radiographer with a new baccalaureate degree in business administration. The Lord had blessed my wife and me tremendously, and we were ready for new ventures. I was hired by a large banking institution into a promotion-qualification program. We had a new baby girl, a new degree, a new career in banking, and a new salary—substantially more than we had ever seen. Surely nothing could go wrong with this picture.

At the bank I decided to start on the credit side as a commercial credit analyst. I was placed in a department with MBA graduates from the top schools of business in the country. I soon understood that the road to the top went through the credit department. Surely I was in the right place at the right time, and nothing could go wrong with this picture.

After six months of leading the entire credit department, even the MBAs, in securing and analyzing new commercial loan applications, I received a call for an appointment with the executive vice president of the prestigious department known as the "National Division."

Upon hearing of the appointment, my assistant supervisor asked me what had I done wrong. I could think of no errors. But I began to wonder if one of my analyses had caused the bank to make questionable loans or if the bank had lost a large sum of money due to my recommendations.

As I entered the waiting area of the executive vice president's office, I was visibly shaking with fear. It was all I could do to keep my knees from knocking together. He came out to greet me and to invite me into his ostentatious office. "Tell me something about yourself," he said.

"I am Robert L. Thorpe, a 1971 graduate of the . . ."

"No," he interrupted. "Tell me about your upbringing and where you are from."

After hearing my short story, he remarked that he was a young man about my age when he started his banking career. We exchanged pleasant conversation for a few additional minutes, and then he asked if I had any questions.

"Sir, have I done anything wrong? Have my analyses caused any trouble for the bank?" He quickly assured me that my work had been excellent. Furthermore, because I had done so well in such a short period of time, I would be "tapped" in about six months for a higher position.

Within six months I got an invitation to head my own branch bank. I would be fully in charge of all banking operations. Only one "minor" thing came to my mind amidst all of the excitement. The sun sets earlier than the bank's closing hour of 6 p.m. during the months of November and December.

Perhaps I could leave just a little earlier on Fridays during this time of the year, and I could have my assistant close up for me. Surely the Lord would cause them to understand.

To my utter surprise I received no accommodation. The executive vice president stated empathetically that I could not leave the bank on any Friday evening before closing time. He advised me to talk to my rabbi, priest, or minister for Sabbath clearance. He gave me two weeks to make a decision.

I prayed that the Lord would open my "Red Sea," as he had done for Moses.

Two weeks later I was summoned to his office to give my decision. My mouth told him I would not take the new position because of Sabbath observance. However, my heart could not believe that the Lord did not open the "Red Sea," nor did He change the banking hours to accommodate the Sabbath.

After hearing my final decision, the executive vice president told me I now had two strikes against me. I asked to know the first strike. Without hesitation he said it was that I was black, but by my superior work had overcome this initial factor. The second strike, of course, was being a Seventh-day Adventist and my unwillingness to compromise even in the face of great personal opportunity for my family. He said the company had great plans for me in future managerial positions. However, they could not trust me to make important banking decisions if such decisions conflicted with my religion. Therefore, he told me, I had no future in top administrative positions.

Although I had said "no," my heart desperately wanted the new opportunities. For all of the month of December I questioned and pleaded with the Lord for some type of response. I received nothing. I became deeply disappointed and troubled with my sudden rise to the top and the equally sudden fall to the bottom. Why did the Lord bless us and then take all the blessings away? Why, why, why, Lord? No response.

The first working day of the new year, in my small office, I bowed my head in prayer and said, "Lord, I said no to the position of opportunity a month ago with my lips. I now, today, say 'no' to the position with all of my heart. Please forgive me for my initial response to You. I thank You for all that You have done for me and for all that You will do in the future. I am back, and I want to be the very best commercial credit analyst again. In Jesus' name, I pray. Amen."

At that very moment, before I could open my eyes, I felt complete peace, restoration, and calm. I felt as if a very heavy burden had been lifted off of me and I was at peace with my Lord. My entire office became very bright, and I heard, as clear as day, a voice that said, "Go back to Chapel Hill, North Carolina."

I opened my eyes to see who was in the office talking to me, and no one was there. In my ears rang the words, "Go back to Chapel Hill." It was now 1972. I had not been to Chapel Hill since graduation in 1967.

I hurried into my supervisor's office and apologized for my unproductive conduct over the past month. I assured him I would once again lead the department in all indices of productivity. I made one request to go to Chapel Hill the next day. Without hesitation he granted my request, and he handed me an envelope. It contained a salary-increase notice on the inside. He had held the salary increase because he was confident I would leave my job.

I hurried home to apologize to my wife for my moody conduct and to let her know I was going to Chapel Hill, but I did not know why. She offered no opposition or inquiry.

In the next 24 hours, during my visit to Chapel Hill, I had a very successful day of job interviews (organized by my Lord), an opportunity to go to graduate school (with assurance of a full scholarship and a biweekly dependent-spouse income check), and a near-certain academic appointment upon completion of graduate studies. My Lord had opened the "Red Sea" for me after I completely and wholeheartedly yielded to His will. For whatever reason, He opened, not the world of banking, but the world of allied health education and administration instead. Halfway through my graduate studies, I accepted an academic position at the University of North Carolina at Chapel Hill with a salary nearly double what I had been making in banking a year earlier.

He giveth power to the faint; and to them that have no might He increaseth strength. Even the youths shall faint and be weary, and the young men shall utterly fall: But they that wait upon the Lord shall renew their strength; they shall mount up with wings as eagles; they shall run, and not be weary; and they shall walk, and not faint. Isaiah 40:29-31.

Robert L. Thorpe is an associate professor of allied health sciences in the School of Medicine at the University of North Carolina at Chapel Hill. He is a member of the Immanuel Temple Seventh-day Adventist Church in Durham, North Carolina.

A WALK IN THE WOODS
By Dagmar Cepica

I HAD $37 left in my purse. That was all we had, and our bills weren't all paid. Suddenly, I remembered the tithe I owed God from my latest income: $37.

I rationalized: Perhaps God wouldn't mind if I simply delayed returning my tithe. Even as I thought it, I knew it wouldn't be right. I should return the first portion to God.

That Sabbath I put my tithe—the whole $37—in the offering plate. I'll admit I didn't do it with a very cheerful heart, for now I was truly broke!

On Sabbath afternoon my husband and I went for a walk in the woods with our dogs. Alongside the path we glimpsed something that looked out of place. There on the grass lay two 20-dollar bills. I was shocked and pleased—and grateful.

When God supplied my need, He even gave me $3 extra!

Give, and it shall be given unto you; good measure, pressed down, and shaken together, and running over, ... For with the same measure that ye mete withal it shall be measured to you again. Luke 6:38.

Dagmar Cepica is a literature evangelist in Prince Edward Island. She is a member of the Charlottetown, Prince Edward Island, Seventh-day Adventist Church.

FAITH FINDS A PLACE
By Martha Walwyn

A TRUE attitude of stewardship grants a follower of Jesus abundant opportunities to exercise faith and trust. Of course, the degree of this abundance varies from one steward to another. However, "it is required in stewards that one be found faithful" (1 Corinthians 4:2, NKJV).

Some may regard stewardship of wealth or talent as a higher quality of stewardship than the somewhat intangible stewardship of faith. However, 1 Corinthians 12:9 lists faith as a special gift to some in the church.

Gifts are to be managed. Management is stewardship. So it is my responsibility to be a good steward of faith, as with any other gift.

Not long ago I decided to help our small group of Hispanic believers in Madison, Tennessee. Our group had been drawn from area Anglo-American churches, and the organization ceremony was held at one of these churches on a

Sabbath afternoon. However, we hadn't found a place to meet for worship on the following Sabbath.

We discussed several options. The easiest would be to hold our Sabbath services and other meetings at the homes of members, rotating on some schedule. But I thought our church should be a beacon, and that wouldn't happen if we met in someone's house. I decided to put my stewardship of faith to the test. I asked God to provide a suitable place for us to worship the next Sabbath, now just five days away.

The Lord gave me a very clear dream that He wanted us to meet in a picturesque little church that was close by. It belonged to a congregation of Sunday-observing Christians. I had never visited there. I knew no one who attended or had ever visited that church. To go there and ask to rent the church was the last thing I had expected to have to do. But conviction is conviction, so I did my duty.

When I drove onto the church property, apprehensive and confident at the same time, I found the office was closed. I drove around to the back, hoping to find an open door. Just then a man passed by. When I told him what I wanted, he said he knew whom I should contact. He had never been a member or a visitor of that congregation, but he was nevertheless absolutely certain that the sanctuary would *not* be available for rent.

Several phone calls later I finally was able to talk with a man who was a member of that congregation. He confirmed my worst fears. Absolutely and emphatically he asserted, the church was not available for rent. He could not even conceive of it. Period.

"But I had a dream that I should come and ask you."

"Sorry. In any case, it would have to go through the higher organizational authorities in Texas."

"How long would that take?"

"Ma'am, they meet only every few months; it could take months."

"I need to be able to start using the sanctuary for Sabbath school and church this coming Saturday. Do you think you could do anything?"

"Ma'am, today is Tuesday already!"

On Thursday night, I received a phone call, inviting me to come to the church on Friday at 3 p.m. to sign the contract. Only after the call did I realize that we had not discussed the terms.

At the meeting, after nervously greeting the gentleman, my first question was about the cost. I sheepishly said that we were a very small group that could hardly afford typical rent payments. He said they had not yet decided on a price, but assured me it would not be more than we could afford. It was not.

Our little group met in that church the next morning.

I have long felt that the true rewards of stewardship are inherent in the stewardship itself. No extrinsic benefit surpasses the sense of fulfillment derived from being a faith partner with God.

His lord said unto him, Well done, thou good and faithful servant: thou hast been faithful over a few things, I will make thee ruler over many things: enter thou into the joy of thy lord. Matthew 25:21.

Martha Walwyn is a retired teacher in Nashville, Tennessee. She is a member of the Nashville First Hispanic Seventh-day Adventist Church.

THE BLESSING OF THE DOUBLE TEN
By Bill Strong

My FIRST pastoral position after leaving the seminary was as an intern pastor in the Kentucky-Tennessee Conference, where I was assigned to the Memphis First-Whitehaven district. The senior pastor pretty much let me be in charge of the smaller Whitehaven congregation, while he led out at the Memphis First congregation.

The Whitehaven church had experienced a major setback just prior to my arrival. The members had purchased a large house and were renting the living area to my predecessor while remodeling the double garage into a sanctuary. But because of zoning problems they had to stop the remodeling and sell the house at a significant loss. When I arrived, the congregation was renting a Lutheran church and was heavily in debt due to the loss on the sale of the parsonage-sanctuary project.

I was also at a loss to know what to do. The Conference stewardship director came to the church for a series of budget-planning meetings as well as a two-weekend series of sermons on stewardship, with a pledge Sabbath at the conclusion.

In order to pay off the debt in a timely manner, the church would need members to contribute an average of five percent of their incomes to help with the current rent and basic budget needs and another five percent for debt reduction. All this would be above the ten percent of regular tithe. I had heard of the double tithe concept before, but I hadn't practiced it. My wife and I were faithfully tithing and giving a modest amount to the local budget, but this second ten percent would be a major stretch.

Dixie and I talked it over long and hard. We were the leaders, and we needed to set the example of what we hoped the majority of the members would do. And besides, we knew that there was a blessing for us as well. But we were just out of seminary on an intern's pay. Dixie was pregnant, expecting our first child. We had no washer or dryer, not even a kitchen table. Pledging 20 percent in tithe and offerings seemed impossible unless God was truly with us.

On Friday evening we got our pledge card ready and signed it, trusting in God to supply our needs. The next morning at the worship service we turned in that pledge card.

The rest of the story is a testimony to God's goodness and faithfulness. The very next week we got a totally unexpected $100 check in the mail. Also that very week a kitchen table, washer, and dryer were given to us.

We were overwhelmed with God's providence, and we still are.

And my God will meet all your needs according to his glorious riches in Christ Jesus. Philippians 4:19, NIV.

Bill Strong is pastor of the Delaware and Westerville Seventh-day Adventist churches in Ohio.

....

HONESTY AT CUSTOMS, AND CUSTOMARY HONESTY
By Bryce Newell

IN 1954 we received a call to go overseas to Indonesia. I was to be the principal of North Celebes Training School.

During our preparations we were instructed to buy a kerosene cookstove and were advised to light the burners a little bit so that it could be listed as a used stove. Import duties on new equipment amounted to about 100 percent of the original cost.

When our goods arrived in Indonesia, the customs agent asked if the stove was new. I lied and said it was used. True to form, the duty was much less than if it had been new.

But my conscience smote me. I was a missionary to this Muslim country, and I was being dishonest with the government. I had to make this right.

I returned to the port, received a special pass, and went in to see the customs agent I had lied to. Lines were long, but in about an hour I stood before him. I told him I had lied and that I was willing to pay whatever he might impose upon me. He thought for a long minute, then said, "We have put this through as you told us; we are going to leave it as it is."

About four years later I was again going through customs, bringing in more goods. Among other things I had a new washing machine. The customs man wanted to open the carton it was in.

When he took me before the customs chief of the port a little later, the chief slyly asked, "Perhaps this washing machine has been used?"

"No, sir," I said, "it is brand-new."

"Well," he mumbled, "you are very honest."

When it came time to settle the bill, the washing machine and everything I had was brought in duty-free.

Another time I had been on vacation out of the country and was getting back to Djakarta on an Indonesian airliner. The plane was filled with Indonesians coming home from Bangkok. I was eager to get back to my place of duty, so I got as close to the head of the customs line as I could, but the customs agents couldn't seem to see me. I watched as they pulled things from the suitcases of the Indonesians for them to pay duty on. The lines slowly made their way through customs until all of the Indonesians were through.

Suddenly the customs man discovered me and asked, "Are these all your bags?" I said, "Yes." Without so much as opening one of them, he went down the line, put check marks on each one, and told me I could go.

In all the traveling I did in Indonesia, going through customs many times, I was never charged a single dime to pay for any customs duty.

A just balance and scales belong to the Lord; all the weights of the bag are His concern. Proverbs 16:11, NASB.

Bryce Newell is a retired pastor in Pendleton, Oregon. He is a member of the Pendleton Seventh-day Adventist Church.

GARDEN PESTS
By Larry E. Stapleton

I WAS living with six other young men in a school home at a medical missionary training center in the southern part of the United States. The long, hot summer days were readily used up with classes, studying, home duties, meals, and working in the garden.

In the evening we would gather in the living room in front of the large picture window that looked out over the garden and discuss our mutual blessings and problems. Our garden wasn't doing as well as we would like. We had too little rain, too many weeds, and too many bugs.

Someone asked if we were tithing the garden produce. We hadn't thought of that before.

We read the promise that God would rebuke the devourer if we brought all the tithe into the storehouse. Our garden was certainly being devoured, and we needed that promise. While praying and claiming the promise, we heard the most raucous noise coming from the other side of the garden. Everyone jumped up, looked out the window, and saw what appeared to be three dogs having a ferocious fight. We stood there watching, wondering what to do. As the fighting dogs moved closer to us, we could finally see that they were tearing into a groundhog.

We ran outside, grabbed our hoes, and chased the dogs away. We had never seen these dogs before and never saw them again. The dogs left behind a mangled, pregnant groundhog with its two back legs dragging uselessly behind it. Feeling sorry for the poor thing, we put it out of its misery with car exhaust. Not until then did we realize our request to rebuke the devourer was being answered, even before we had finished praying. Imagine what damage a groundhog, especially one about to increase its tribe, could do to our garden.

The next day, while I was pulling up some of the many weeds that had a stranglehold on our broccoli plants, I heard a loud rustling noise coming from the thicket next to the garden. I looked up and saw a rabbit come running out, and right on his tail was a fox. The fox chased the rabbit through the garden and back into the thicket. I never again saw the rabbit or any damage that could be blamed on a rabbit.

I settled back to my work and noticed some green worms munching on the broccoli leaves. I started picking them off. As I reached for a particularly fat one, a large wasp flew by my ear, swooped down on the worm, and carried it away. I knew for sure that tithing the garden produce was the right thing to do.

"I will prevent pests from devouring your crops, and the vines in your fields will not cast their fruit," says the Lord Almighty. Malachi 3:11, NIV.

Larry E. Stapleton is general manager of Mountain Missionary Institute in Harrisville, New Hampshire. He is a member of the Washington, New Hampshire, Seventh-day Adventist Church.

"INASMUCH . . ."
By Beverly Moody

AT CHRISTMASTIME in 1958 my husband and I had been married six months. We were living in a one-room basement apartment in Takoma Park, Maryland, where my husband was attending the Seventh-day Adventist Theological Seminary.

We wanted to share what little we had with someone as we celebrated the birth of our Lord and King. Our own families were too far away to visit, so we decided to adopt a family for the day.

We asked the local Community Service Center staff if they knew of a family we could bring to our home for Christmas Day.

"Yes," the director said, "we have just the family for you—a mother with several children. The father is not with them right now. They live about an hour's drive out of town and have no telephone."

This was just the kind of family for whom we were looking. I told the director I would drive out to see the family.

About a week before Christmas I drove through the rolling hills of the countryside, praying that I would find the place. I found the family crowded into a little house, and I was gratified to realize that I would be able to fit them into our small apartment. The mother was pleased with the invitation and said she would have the family ready by ten o'clock Christmas morning, when I promised to return for them.

As an afterthought she asked, "Do you cut hair? Would you please bring scissors and cut the children's hair before we go to your house?" I agreed.

Preparations for Christmas took on a new meaning for my husband and me as we got gifts for the family and prepared a special holiday dinner. While looking through a magazine for an idea for a special holiday dessert, I was drawn to a picture of a layer cake with white icing and pretty red-and-green trimming on it. I've forgotten the rest of the menu, but that cake turned out to be special.

When I arrived in our VW bus at the family's little house on Christmas morning, armed with scissors and comb, the children greeted me with shouts of "Daddy's home, Daddy's home, and it's his birthday."

What a pleasant surprise! We'd gladly find some way to squeeze one more adult into our little place, and that decked-out layer cake would serve well as a birthday cake, complete with candles left from my husband's recent birthday. I finished the hair-cutting and hurried the family back to the dinner awaiting us.

Needless to say, the time sped quickly by as the children opened their gifts and devoured their dinner. Eyes sparkled as I brought out the birthday cake, shining with candles. We sang, "Happy birthday, dear Daddy" and "Happy birthday, dear Jesus," since He was the real reason for the celebration.

By the time we were ready to take the family home, it was dark outside. However, our hearts were full of light, joy, and happiness. We headed out into the hills with my husband driving and leading out in singing. We were pleased to hear our guests joining us. The parents could harmonize, and the time passed quickly while we had fun singing all the way to their home. To this day I am often reminded of this experience when I sing, "Do, Lord." It was a Christmas I shall never forget.

Inasmuch as ye have done it unto one of the least of these my brethren, ye have done it unto me. Matthew 25:40.

Beverly Moody works at Moody's Marina in Aleknagik, Alaska. She is a member of the Aleknagik Seventh-day Adventist Church.

CATCHING UP
By Esther Ramharacksingh Knott

EVERY time the phone rang, I was afraid to answer it. Lately the calls had been from creditors: the credit card companies and the utility companies. The mortgage company said I was two months behind, and I shouldn't pretend the problem didn't exist; it wouldn't go away.

Things hadn't worked out as planned. When the house was purchased, the basement was to be fixed up as a rental apartment to provide extra income. The realtor assured me that I shouldn't believe the stories about the leaky basement; the current tenant, according to the realtor, just didn't want to move and would say anything to keep the house from selling.

After the house was bought, I discovered that the basement did leak badly, and money spent on a backhoe, sealant, and repairs to the accidentally damaged septic-sewer line didn't make any difference. Instead of now having a rental unit that would help pay the mortgage, I had extra expenses. The basement couldn't be fixed for a rental. Then the township decided to run city water pipes down the street. That increased the taxes by a couple thousand dollars. Debts piled up.

As a child, I had the privilege of putting my father's tithe envelope into the offering plate each week. It had been a great thrill when I earned my first money and was able to put my own envelope into the offering plate.

Now I was an adult, and almost a year had gone by since I had returned to God what was His. I just didn't see how I could. The expense column always totaled much more than the income. The creditors came, asking for their money—by certified mail, by collection agencies, by phone. I felt ashamed. I tried to hold back the tears until the call ended; this didn't always work.

Somehow I had to get ahead. I was desperate. I had to stop the ringing phones and the embarrassment. So I wrote checks for the utilities and the mortgage. I borrowed more money but there was never enough at the end for God. I would take care of that next week, next month or the month after that. Still there was never enough. And it seemed that God never called for it, and no one at church spoke for Him on the subject. I didn't have the benefit of books like *Over & Over Again!* No one reminded me to trust God, to test Him. So I trusted myself, and I failed the test. For two years I reaped the consequences of my choices.

One weekend, after I had moved to a different state for a new job, I attended a stewardship seminar and realized that my sin was one of unbelief in what God says about Himself. I hadn't trusted His promises. And it dawned on me that I had a lot of catching up to do. During that meeting I confessed my sin and asked

God to help me not only to be faithful in my tithe but to find a way for me to give back what I had kept from Him.

At home I listed all my debts and my income. The monthly debts still outweighed my income, but I put eleven percent for tithe at the top of the list. Then I listed my debts and monthly payments from highest to lowest, with the goal to pay off the smallest debt first and then apply that payment to extra payments on the next largest debt. I asked God to bless this plan.

I changed my phone to basic service and economized every way possible. I turned down the heat in my apartment. My friend in the apartment directly below mine reminded me that heat rises so she figured she was helping to heat my apartment. Again I saw God's providence: I had not gotten the ground-floor, walk-out apartment I had requested, but instead had been assigned one that was surrounded by warmth.

For three years I bought no new clothes for myself. On two separate occasions a friend in Pennsylvania sent me two suits that she said had reminded her of me. My mother often sent clothes and kept me stocked with panty hose.

During this time I never had a Sabbath dinner alone. Once a month the church had a potluck, often I was invited to someone's house for lunch, and even on my limited budget I practiced hospitality.

I did travel a lot with my job, and a meal was always provided, with good company. I usually had seconds instead of dessert, because I wanted to get nutritious calories. I'm sure that kept me healthy.

During that time I received an unexpected check for $270. To celebrate I went to the shopping mall, determined to treat myself to something new. After three hours I had found nothing that I needed or wanted. That was a miracle.

For two and a half years I worked the plan—smiling each time I gave God what was His and each time He helped me eliminate another debt.

As I was coming to the end of this journey, God brought a man into my life who shared the same values of committing everything we have to God. We also decided to commit everything we had to each other. However, I didn't want him to have any of my previous debts. One year after our wedding I took my last step to being debt-free; I mailed in my final car payment. And a year and a half later, after giving twelve percent in tithe, plus offerings, I returned to God all that I had owed Him. Now I was truly debt-free, yet happily knowing that I owed God everything.

Do not fear, for I am with you; do not anxiously look about you, for I am your God. I will strengthen you, surely I will help you, surely I will uphold you with My righteous right hand. Isaiah 41:10, NASB.

Esther Ramharacksingh Knott is associate pastor of Pioneer Memorial Church in Berrien Springs, Michigan.

The FIFTEENTH MEETING

Come and hear, all ye that fear God, and I will declare what he hath done for my soul.

Psalm 66:16

Dan Trafford

Donna M. Dunbar

Donald R. Halenz

Sara McGuire

Carl Irby

Art and Elsie Hiebert

Rosa M. Ferreras

Bonnie Conklin-Mayer

Helen L. Self

R. Patricia Anderson

GOD PAVES THE WAY!
By Dan Trafford

I WAS an editor on the sports desk of the *Edmonton Journal* in Alberta. Unknown to my colleagues, dramatic changes had been taking place in my life. For months I had been studying the Bible late at night after work. For the first time I was praying for good things in my life and for my friends, loved ones, and even those I considered my enemies.

Seeking more spiritual food, I began attending the Central Seventh-day Adventist Church in Edmonton, where I had been taking my mother on Saturdays whenever she visited from eastern Canada.

The more I studied, the more clearly God spoke to me. Before long the conviction grew that I wanted to follow the pattern Christ had set for my life. As I pored over the Biblical counsel, several things became clear: Working on Sabbaths was not in my best interests, returning tithe and offerings was something I wanted to do, and breaking free of caffeine addiction and a meat diet were important steps in my spiritual journey.

Becoming a good steward of my life in these ways was going to be a challenge. For starters, I ran the coffee fund for the sports desk, and the fund was making money for the first time. Even more troublesome, the newspaper had just gone to a seven-day-a-week operation, and absolutely no one was exempt from the work rotation. My wife, Rose, wanted to quit work because we had two preschool children, and she wasn't even faintly interested in the church or in a vegetarian diet. At every turn the obstacles were intimidating.

Yet the Lord spoke to me insistently: "Come unto me, all ye that labour and are heavy laden, and I will give you rest." My tortured conscience trembled, but I wanted that rest at any price. I told the pastor I wanted to be baptized, and I set the date. I called the managing editor of the paper on a Monday and told him of my decision to be baptized. I explained I wouldn't be available for work that Friday night. I quit the coffee fund, to the shock of all. My wife resigned herself to a new, strange life, and we pored over our finances to find answers.

I felt real joy at my baptism. I knew it was what the Lord wanted me to do. And miraculously my wife and I were able to reorganize our finances in a way we never thought possible. She was able to quit work.

The editor accommodated my request for Sabbaths off, and the sports-desk wit promptly dubbed me "Bible breath."

We ate mushroom patties for what seemed a year until we became more adventuresome with vegetarian dishes.

Rose was soon baptized. The rest the Lord had promised was mine.

During this time I had been so quiet about my newfound convictions that I didn't realize how many other Christians worked at the paper. One of them came up to me after the rumor mill had properly dispensed the news of my conversion and informed me that everyone was surprised I still had a job. He said other Christians had taken the same stand about Sunday when the paper went seven days a week. Management told them to be at work or else. The Lord, in His providence, had kept that news from me.

Not much later I read a letter in *Liberty* magazine from someone expressing appreciation for the excellence of its editorial content and for its championing of religious liberty. It was signed by the editor of the *Edmonton Journal*, the very man responsible for allowing me to be free from work every Sabbath.

The Lord had long before paved over the ruts on the road He called me to travel!

Before they call I will answer; while they are still speaking I will hear. Isaiah 65:24, NIV.

Dan Trafford owns a small construction company in Lombardy, Ontario. He is a member of the Smiths Falls, Ontario, Seventh-day Adventist Church.

GOD NEVER GIVES UP
By Donna M. Dunbar

EVERY time I went through another divorce, I left the church. And each time I left, I not only stopped returning my tithe and giving offerings but also began violating all the standards of the church, as if to say, "There, God, how does it feel to be rejected?"

God was very patient with me. Each time I left, He went out on the mountainside to bring His little lamb back. He knew that my relationship with the church was built on rules and regulations instead of a relationship with Jesus Christ.

In August of 1992 I went through my third divorce, and I decided it was time I changed my approach. God allows us to go through the same trial until we learn from it the necessary lessons. This time I determined I would always put God first instead of putting my husband before God.

In November of that same year I met Clarence and started going back to church. Clarence began watching the videos by Kenneth Cox and was convicted that the Adventist message is correct. We both determined to put God first in our relationship.

In June 1993 God again called me to be faithful in returning His tithe. I vowed to do this the following Sabbath. After I had made this commitment, however, I learned that one of my jobs was ending. My boss had decided to sever all ties with a company we worked for because of their questionable practices. I couldn't see how I could make ends meet with only one job.

Even though I was very conscious of my previous failures, the next week I dropped my tithe into the collection plate and went forward in faith. The same week Clarence determined to quit his job and open a business of his own, under conviction that God wanted him to do this. Though he was planning on giving a two-week notice and counting on that income to help start his new business, his boss told him to leave that very day.

He went immediately to the telephone company and placed an ad in the phone book for his new business. "You sure are lucky you came today," he was told. "Today is the deadline for advertising. Otherwise you would have had to wait another year."

The business grew nicely in that first month, and God has blessed it ever since the two of us made the decision to put Him first.

Recently we determined to increase our giving by another percentage point. We went forward in faith that God would supply all our needs, for He has called us to get out of debt so we can use more of our finances to support God's work. A week later Clarence landed an account that will net us far more than the percentage we gave—and allow us to get out of debt sooner!

If you walk in My statutes and keep My commandments so as to carry them out, then I shall give you rains in their season, so that the land will yield its produce. . . . You will thus eat your food to the full and live securely in your land. Leviticus 26:3-5, NASB.

Donna M. Dunbar is a registered dietitian at G. Pierce Wood Memorial Hospital in Arcadia, Florida. She is a member of the Port Charlotte, Florida, Seventh-day Adventist Church.

....

A NEW TEACHER'S DILEMMA
By Donald R. Halenz

MY WIFE and I were enjoying the relative security of my first full-time teaching job after spending four years in graduate school right out of college. Still, our finances were tight in those early years, and we were starting a family. With a one-year-old child and another one expected soon, we decided to get along on my salary alone, which started at $95 per week.

After about a year of renting, it seemed prudent to purchase an older, inexpensive home to begin to build up some equity. At that time the policy of the college where I was teaching was to give an allowance for homeowners who purchased a home instead of renting from the college at a subsidized rate. The allowance was most appreciated, but it didn't cover our obligations to the bank.

About the same time, our college church started a capital stewardship campaign for a church sanctuary, since there was no college church building at that time. My wife and I were apprehensive about taking on an additional financial obligation, but after some consideration, prayer, and much faith, we decided to make a commitment to the church.

A short time later the college made a dramatic change in its homeowners' allowance policy. Up to that time the allowance had been based on the value of the home. Since ours was one of the older homes, we had been receiving a relatively small subsidy. Other faculty with new, expensive homes had been receiving much more. The new policy now granted housing allowances that were nearly the same for all. This change meant that we received a sizeable increase in allowance, enough to cover most of our mortgage payments and our commitment to the church building campaign. For us, the Lord's timing was perfect, and we were blessed to see Him honor our faith.

Trust in the Lord, and do good; so you will dwell in the land, and enjoy security. Take delight in the Lord, and he will give you the desires of your heart. Psalm 37:3, 4, NRSV.

Donald R. Halenz is associate academic dean at Pacific Union College in Angwin, California. He is a member of the Pacific Union College Seventh-day Adventist Church.

....

HIS PROTECTION, MY WITNESS
By Sara McGuire

I HAD a work-related meeting to attend near Madison, Wisconsin, a six-hour drive from my home on a January day. Before starting out I dropped by a friend's house, and we prayed together. We asked God to protect us and to allow us to be His witnesses that day, as we went our separate ways.

An hour and a half and many miles later I stopped at a small, busy sub shop for lunch. Silently I prayed and waited for a chance to witness for God, but the opportunity seemed to slip by. As soon as the clerk counted my change and handed me my sandwich, she turned to the customer behind me.

Several hours and many miles later I pulled off the highway at a large gas station. While waiting to pay for my purchase I prayed silently for those around me. Everyone was in a hurry. The clerk didn't have time to even make eye contact as she counted my change. "Thanks," I mumbled as I turned to leave.

Tiny, icy flakes of snow blew across the windshield as I continued the long trip. As I drove, I thought about the witnessing part of the prayer. I'd heard descriptions of good witnessing for God. Often they concluded with the comment that "actions speak louder than words." I remembered many times when my actions had fallen far short. I prayed that God would forgive me, that His mercy would cover my miserable shortcomings, and that He would give me strength to be a better Christian.

I recalled powerful stories about people who prayed to be good witnesses and then spontaneously shared the gospel with strangers in public places. Did God reserve that type of witnessing for extroverts with strong handshakes?

When I finally pulled off the main highway toward my motel, a black ice covered the road beneath the snow, and heavy flakes swirled in the beam of my car's headlights. Amazed, I watched other cars successfully clear the way as my car slid out of control through a red light at an icy, busy intersection.

God is so good! I thought as I checked into the motel and unloaded my suitcase. Exhausted and hungry, I forgot about witnessing. I was happy just to be *alive*. I went to dinner at a restaurant across from the motel. After a waitress took my order, a second waitress approached me.

"Do you ever get migraine headaches?" she asked me quietly.

I was startled. Had the long trip left me in such rough condition that I looked like a chronic migraine sufferer?

"No," I said finally, "do you?"

"Yes," she said softly. The young woman then described her life as a single parent. She explained the challenge of balancing work and child care. She explained how her legs and arms ached after a long workday, and how she worried about her children's future. Migraine headaches plagued her with increasing frequency.

"So I was wondering," she asked, "do you know anything about migraine headaches?"

For a moment, I was speechless. Then I prayed silently that the Holy Spirit would give me words. As I talked about healthy lifestyles, prayer, Jesus' love, and peace, the young woman grew increasingly interested and excited.

"Where can I learn more about this?" she demanded. "Do you have any books or pamphlets about these things?"

The following afternoon, as I dropped off some books and a music tape at the restaurant, I prayed that the Holy Spirit would help and comfort the young woman and her family. I thanked God for the amazing ways He shows His love. God is so good!

God be merciful unto us, and bless us; . . . that thy way may be known upon earth, thy saving health among all nations. Psalm 67:1, 2.

Sara McGuire is a teacher/principal at the Ashland Seventh-day Adventist School in Ashland, Wisconsin. She is a member of the Ashland Seventh-day Adventist Church.

SACRIFICE AND THE IRS
By Carl Irby

"EQUAL SACRIFICE, Not Equal Giving." That was the slogan we adopted. We understood that everyone couldn't give the same amount. But each member and family could make an equivalent level of sacrifice.

Our church had started a building program for a new sanctuary to better accommodate our current membership and allow for growth. A wide spectrum of income levels was represented in our congregation, ranging from families on public assistance and retirees to skilled professionals. We believed there was great spiritual value in encouraging every member to be an integral part of our fundraising project. The "Equal Sacrifice, Not Equal Giving" approach seemed best suited to our need.

We encouraged each other to ask God's guidance and then to pledge a sum of money, payable weekly or monthly over a three-year period, that would require genuine sacrifice. As most members, I pledged a sacrificial amount and depended on God's provision to make up the lack I anticipated.

I soon saw evidence of God's blessing in many ways, and I never once missed my designated contribution. Partway through the project a fellow member and I discussed how God was abundantly blessing us. Both of us soon realized that our designated amounts were no longer "sacrificial." My conscience pricked me. I felt out of harmony with the stewardship pledge I had made. So I increased my monthly amount by 50 percent. Now I was sacrificing again.

Some two years after our stewardship program began, I became engaged to marry. As I planned for the expenses of the wedding and the purchase of a home, I calculated that I would finish my original church pledge with my next month's contribution. Praise God for the perfect timing, for I would be able to start saving for the wedding.

During this time, in fact for five years, I had carelessly neglected to file income-tax returns. Despite my indolence, someone generously offered to help me complete that unpleasant task. Largely due to my "sacrificial" contributions to the church stewardship project, my charitable contributions deducted from my taxes enabled me to receive a $10,000 refund. This made it easy to cover the wedding expenses and pay for the honeymoon and the down payment on our new home.

God knew what I didn't—that by my faithfulness I was laying up stores for an unanticipated need. His faithfulness is beyond measure. Honor your vows to Him always, for He honors His vows to you.

213

Now to Him who is able to do exceedingly abundantly above all that we ask or think, according to the power that works in us, to Him be glory in the church by Christ Jesus throughout all ages, world without end. Amen. Ephesians 3:20, 21, NKJV.

Carl Irby is a health educator for the San Bernadino, California, Department of Public Health. He is a member of the Banning, California, Seventh-day Adventist Church.

GOD'S MORTGAGE
By Elsie and Art Hiebert

WE MOVED to Winnipeg, Canada, in the winter of 1977 to make certain that three of our children could attend church school. Christian education was an urgent priority for us, especially as we saw the influences surrounding our children.

We looked for a place to live, where the children could have a way to get to school and still be within a reasonable distance of the church in which I would serve as pastor. A few months later we moved into our first brand-new house. We felt quite pleased about the way the Lord had blessed.

But life always has its turns in the road. Our mortgage was written for five years–the standard term at that time. After two years of living in our new home, we realized the mortgage would come up for renewal in three years, when rates were predicted to be seventeen to twenty percent. At those rates we would be in no position to send our children to academy. For one child this might be difficult; for three it would be impossible.

We asked the Lord to help us as we considered various options. Should we look for an older, smaller house? Should we rent? Finally we asked the Lord to help us take on what seemed an impossible task—pay off the $45,000 we owed on the house. For three years we would work a careful plan of setting aside funds, restricting spending, and giving God room to work. Tithe and offerings would have first priority. Church-school expenses also would have to be met. At the very least, we would minimize the mortgage we would have to renew.

Carefully and prayerfully we moved forward to confront the problem. About a year before the renewal date Canada Savings Bonds offered nineteen percent interest. We moved quickly to invest what funds we had available for these bonds. We still find it hard to believe just how it all came together, but as our mortgage came due, the pieces fell into place. With a small personal loan, the immediate future was secured, and the house paid for.

The Lord kept His promise. Our children could continue their education, and it strengthened our faith.

A few years later it was college for our three. Would it be possible? Again we thanked the Lord as arrangements worked out. All three were enrolled at Union College.

The Lord helped us find a way. His mercies and blessings are "new every morning."

And all thy children shall be taught of the Lord; and great shall be the peace of thy children. Isaiah 54:13.

Elsie Hiebert is a registered nurse in Grand Forks, North Dakota. Art Hiebert is the pastor of the Grand Forks Seventh-day Adventist Church.

THE BEST INSURANCE
By Rosa M. Ferreras

AFTER A YEAR and a half of many different blood tests, orthopedic consultations, and neurological exams, the neurologist confirmed the diagnosis. I had multiple sclerosis.

Having worked in the medical field for eighteen years, I knew exactly what the doctor was telling me. I had a chronic and incurable disease. So my first question to him was "What are we going to do next?"

"There is no cure for multiple sclerosis," he said. "But a new medication has just been approved by the FDA; it slows down the process. But there is a problem. It is very expensive. We will have to see if your insurance will cover at least a percentage of the cost."

My audible response was "Okay!" But in my mind I said, "I have a millionaire Father!" Of course, I didn't say this out loud, for I was afraid the doctor would not attempt to get the authorization from the insurance company and instead would tell me to ask my "Father" to pay for it.

I walked out of his office to my car, and I prayed. I said, "Lord, I have been faithful. I have returned to You the tithe of every single penny I have received up to this point as well as a faithful offering. I know in which bank I have made my deposits. I need to draw some funds now from that account. I do not consider it my account, for what I have done is to return to You a tiny percentage of what You have blessed me with. I need You to pay for this medication. I leave it in Your faithful hands."

The insurance company approved the request for full coverage within a week. All I had to do was call the pharmacy to have it ready for me. On my first visit to the pharmacy I was handed a box with enough injections to last me a month. I had to pay nothing for it, and as I write this testimony, that is the way it has been for 20 months. One month the pharmacy left the price tag on one of the boxes: $852!

Every week, after injecting myself, I sing a song that talks about God's faithfulness, for He has been faithful to me.

Lay not up for yourselves treasures upon earth, where moth and rust doth corrupt, and where thieves break through and steal: But lay up for yourselves treasures in heaven, where neither moth nor rust doth corrupt, and where thieves do not break through nor steal. Matthew 6:19, 20.

Until her disability, Rosa M. Ferreras was a medical-records abstractor in Orange, California. She is a member of the Santa Ana, California, Spanish Seventh-day Adventist Church.

LETTING GO TO GROW
By Bonnie Conklin-Mayer

IN 1990 my husband and I purchased a new home closer to my work. Instead of a four-hour round trip commute, it now took only two hours. In March 1991 I was fired from that job as marketing director after filing a complaint against a vice president for sexual harassment.

Our income went down almost two thirds, and we frantically rebudgeted and paid off as many bills as possible. I decided to do consulting work, since I was fed up with the politics of the business world. During this time of readjustment, my husband was laid off from his job. Steady work prospects began to look grim for both of us.

In January 1992 we put the house up for sale, trusting in the Lord to find a buyer. It isn't easy to sell homes in Minnesota in the dead of winter, but we figured if God wanted us out of this house and somewhere else, who were we to stand in His way?

It was hard to let go. We liked that house. Yet I knew in my heart that the only way God could continue my spiritual growth was for me to stop controlling my life and all the aspects in it. This was going to be a very painful lesson for me.

Within 60 days we had two offers on the house, and we turned down both, since they were less than our mortgage balance. All during this time we managed to meet our monthly mortgage payments, even when we didn't seem to have enough money in the middle of the month to make it to the end of the month. We left our financial situation in God's hands, and He made sure our basic needs were met.

By March I was still struggling to make the consulting business work. In mid-March my husband found work as a CAD designer/drafter for a start-up company, and that week we took the house off the market. Within hours our realtor called back with a new offer, but we declined. It seemed to us the Lord had been testing whether we would let go of our possessions and let Him have control of our life and everything in it. We could only marvel at the way He met our needs and helped us grow during that difficult time, no matter how painful it was.

To this day we tell others of God's leading and ask them to turn their lives and possessions over to Him. They won't regret it.

He has made everything beautiful in its time. He has also set eternity in the hearts of men; yet they cannot fathom what God has done from beginning to end. Ecclesiastes 3:11, NIV.

Bonnie Conklin-Mayer is a landscape designer in Apple Valley, Minnesota. She is a member of the PneuSong Seventh-day Adventist Church in Woodbury, Minnesota.

GOD'S ARITHMETIC
By Helen L. Self

WHEN I was baptized at age 39, I understood the tithe principle, but it wasn't easy to practice under the circumstances.

My husband put up such resistance to my returning tithe that I finally opened a separate checking account, had the tithe portion directly deposited, and rented a post-office box for church-related mail. With trembling and prayer, stepping out in faith, I returned God's tithe faithfully. To my amazement, our financial condition improved!

After a couple of years I was comfortable trusting God with my pocketbook. But God rocked my boat again. The Carolina Conference was encouraging members to adopt the "10+10+" plan. We completed a series of studies at prayer meeting from *Counsels on Stewardship,* which I enjoyed. But still I felt very uncomfortable. Malachi 3:8-12 rang through my mind constantly. It talked about tithe *and offerings.* I had given a dollar here and there in offerings, but the Holy Spirit was convicting me to put God to the test.

I argued with God for six months. We owed thousands of dollars in medical bills for my husband's open-heart surgery, and we needed a new roof, oil for winter heat, major car repairs, and the usual living expenses. I hadn't received a raise in sixteen months. I was scared.

"God, how can You expect more of me?" I argued. But wrestling in prayer only made the conviction stronger. By December of that year I decided to prove God. On the first Sabbath of the new year the Holy Spirit impressed me to give five percent in offerings.

God didn't let me down or have me wait. The next week my boss gave me a raise—for the exact amount of my offerings! Immediately the government also notified my husband of a raise in his small Social Security check; again it was the exact amount!

I continued to increase my offerings by one percent each year until I was participating fully in the "10+10+" plan.

The good news is that God's arithmetic still works! We lacked for nothing. The bills always got paid, and we were able to save small amounts for emergencies. Though I had a very sick husband to support, we never went without the necessities of life. God even gave us some things we wanted, too.

God is faithful and trustworthy. I have learned that He will never let me down if I trust Him enough to be faithful.

And he said unto him, Well, thou good servant: because thou hast been faithful in a very little, have thou authority over ten cities. Luke 19:17.

Helen L. Self, in retirement, works part-time as the church secretary for the Morganton, North Carolina, Seventh-day Adventist Church, where she is a member. This story was first published in He's Alive magazine, Volume 8, No. 1.

A FAMILY, A FARM, AND A FAITH
By R. Patricia Anderson

ABOUT 20 years ago nearly 200 of my relatives from North America celebrated a family reunion. My husband Albin and I were strangers to many people and especially to the children.

A year later I received a phone call from a cousin in Denver, Colorado. "Our daughter Janine spotted you folks at the reunion last year," she said. "Janine would love to spend the summer holidays with you on your farm. She is twelve years old and has never been away from home or even on an airplane, but she is a happy-go-lucky, adventurous youngster, and I'm sure you would enjoy her."

Though I had no idea who Janine was, I agreed to the idea, and within a week we met her at the airport. Janine was a friendly, chatty child who loved the farm and the wide-open spaces. She was especially intrigued with our morning worship and overwhelmed when Albin prayed for her.

On Friday morning, as she helped me prepare the Sabbath meal, she asked, "Aunt Pat, are you going to have a banquet?"

I explained that we would be going to church the next day and that I planned to invite another family with children near her age for dinner.

"But," she blurted out, "tomorrow is Saturday. How come?"

As simply as I could, I told her about the Sabbath.

"That's so different," she said, "but it's okay. I wonder what it will be like."

The pastor shook hands with Janine and warmly invited her to the junior class. She found a group of ten or twelve delightful children happily singing praises, then quietly kneeling in prayer to Jesus. Janine thoroughly enjoyed herself. After dinner with our guests, we all walked down to the coulee to watch the beavers building a dam. As we knelt in prayer that evening, Janine said, "What an awesome day! I'll never forget it." Sabbath became a very special day for Janine that summer.

All too soon, two months passed by, and with hugs and tears we bade farewell to our little friend. Many years passed by, and except for Christmas correspondence with her parents, I lost contact with Janine. Then, about a year ago, I received a phone call from Boston.

"This is Janine. Remember me? Back in 1978, I stayed at your house for the summer? I'll never forget the happy days I spent with you. And I have good news for you. You and Uncle Albin planted the seed many years ago, and though it took 20 years to germinate, today I am a baptized Seventh-day Adventist."

"But," I interrupted, "Janine, it was the Holy Spirit that changed you."

"Let me tell you my story. You see, when I was at college, I fell in with bad company, and after many years of worldly ways, frivolity, and then a divorce, I suddenly decided I was wasting my life. I prayed and asked God to help me.

"I went to several different churches, but the void in my life remained. Then I remembered that wonderful summer. What was the name of that church you folks had acquainted me with? I could remember only 'Seventh-day,' but when I looked in the telephone book, I found several Seventh-day Adventist churches.

"I immediately went to one nearby, and the pastor shook hands and was very friendly. When he asked if I would like Bible studies, I eagerly accepted.

"Within four months I joined the church, and I want to thank you so much. My greatest joy is going with a group of young people to the streets of Boston, singing and praising Jesus for all He has done for me. I love my Jesus, and my cup is running over."

My only regret about this story is that I can't share it with my husband, as he passed away three years ago. But I look forward to that day in the earth made new when Janine will give Albin a big hug and say, "I'm here because of your Christian influence."

Cast thy bread upon the waters: for thou shalt find it after many days. . . . In the morning sow thy seed, and in the evening withhold not thine hand: for thou knowest not whether shall prosper, either this or that, or whether they both shall be alike good. Ecclesiastes 11:1, 6.

R. Patricia Anderson is a retired schoolteacher in Lacombe, Alberta. She is a member of the Lacombe Community Seventh-day Adventist Church.

INDEX OF AUTHORS

INDEX OF AUTHORS

ABOUT THE EDITOR

Ronald Alan Knott is director of Andrews University Press, the scholarly publishing authority of Andrews University in Berrien Springs, Michigan. He is the author of *The Makings of a Philanthropic Fundraiser: The Instructive Example of Milton Murray* (Jossey-Bass, 1992) and executive producer and writer of *The Midnight Cry!: William Miller and the End of the World*, a feature-length film documentary. He edited *College Faith: 150 Adventist Leaders Share Faith Stories From Their College Days* (Pacific Press, 1995); was the editor and publisher of *More College Faith* (Worthy Books, 1997); and has edited the two volumes of *Over and Over Again!* He lives in Berrien Springs, Michigan, with his wife, Esther—a pastor at Pioneer Memorial Church—and their daughter, Olivia.

YOU HAVE A STEWARDSHIP TESTIMONY.
You need to share it.
We need to read it.

The publisher is collecting more personal testimonies about stewardship for possible use in a third volume of *Over and Over Again!* We want to read yours.

Here are the simple guidelines to follow as you prepare your testimony:

1. Share a spiritual lesson rooted in your own faith experience with God in stewardship of time, means, talents/opportunities, health, or other aspects of the Christian life. Make sure the relationship to the concept of stewardship is clear.

2. Write your testimony in no more than 500 words. The shorter, the better.

3. Make sure your testimony is a story. Let the narrative speak for itself. Keep any necessary moral or homily to a minimum.

4. Include a relevant Bible text to be placed at the end of your story.

5. Include the following information about yourself:

   - your name, exactly as you wish it to appear, should your story be published
   - a word or two that describes your occupation (i.e., homemaker, physician, paralegal, bank teller, public high school teacher, pastor, accountant, plumber, college president, etc.)
   - your specific job title at your place of employment
   - the name of your employer
   - the location (city and state) of your place of employment
   - your complete home mailing address
   - your home telephone number
   - a fax number and/or e-mail address (if you have these)
   - the name of the local congregation where you hold your church membership
   - the location (city and state) of your local church

Send your testimony to:

Over and Over Again! ❦ Stewardship Department ❦ North American Division of Seventh-day Adventists ❦ 12501 Old Columbia Pike Silver Spring, Maryland 20904 ❦ Or fax your story to: 301-680-8953

Edited by
RONALD ALAN KNOTT

Over & Over Again! 2

150 Adventists Share
Personal Faith Stories
About Stewardship